UNDERSTANDING DRUG USE AND ABUSE

D0550345

Understanding Drug Use and Abuse

A Global Perspective

Benjamin P. Bowser, Carl O. Word
and Toby Seddon

First published 2014 by
PALGRAVE MACMILLAN

Palgrave Macmillan in the UK is an imprint of Macmillan Publishers Limited, registered in England, company number 785998, of Houndmills, Basingstoke, Hampshire RG21 6XS.

Palgrave Macmillan in the US is a division of St Martin's Press LLC, 175 Fifth Avenue, New York, NY 10010.

Palgrave Macmillan is the global academic imprint of the above companies and has companies and representatives throughout the world.

Palgrave® and Macmillan® are registered trademarks in the United States, the United Kingdom, Europe and other countries

ISBN 978-0-230-30330-0   hardback
ISBN 978-0-230-30331-7   paperback

This book is printed on paper suitable for recycling and made from fully managed and sustained forest sources. Logging, pulping and manufacturing processes are expected to conform to the environmental regulations of the country of origin.

A catalogue record for this book is available from the British Library.

A catalog record for this book is available from the Library of Congress.

To the millions who suffer
addictions to drugs needlessly

Contents

List of Tables, Figures and Boxes

Tables

Figures

Boxes

Introduction

Substance Abuse: A Growing Social Problem

<big>1</big>

Chapter overview

- ■ Introduction to the study of drug abuse
- ■ Perspectives and definitions
- ■ The role of public policy
- ■ The use of science
- ■ Multivariate thinking and orientation
- ■ Book content and organization

The abuse of prescription and illegal drugs is a worldwide problem. Experts were consulted on trends in substance abuse in their countries (UNDCP 1995). The picture that emerged was quite disturbing. Overall we are losing ground worldwide – the number of people seriously addicted to drugs is growing. In the last 30 years the availability of illicit drugs has increased along with awareness of the problem. This growth in availability has been driven by consumption in developed countries, but now drug abuse is becoming a problem in the rest of the world.

When we look at the people behind the problem, they are not anonymous. They are someone's brother, sister, mother, father, friend and relative. Furthermore, their drug use and addiction impacts non-users. The general public pays the cost of drug abuse through government taxes used to pay for social services, medical care and treatment. Taxes also pay for drug-related criminal justice expenses. There are insurance and material replacement costs as well. Substance abuse takes its toll on work and can be measured in terms of days of lost work, income and productivity. These costs are then passed on to consumers in higher prices for goods and services.

Drug abuse is a growing problem because drug dealing is immensely profitable (ibid.). The money made from illicit trafficking in cocaine, heroin and cannabis in 2003 was estimated at $320 billion which was then the equivalent of 2 per cent of the global gross domestic product (GDP) (UNODC 2011a). Considering that it cost only $13 billion to produce all the illicit drugs sold that year, and that it cost $94 billion to buy them wholesale (after costs for trafficking), the production and trafficking of illicit drugs are hugely profitable. These enormous profits make it very attractive for new dealers and entrepreneurs to enter the business.

We need to know as much as possible about all aspects of drug abuse so as more effectively to prevent it, treat subsequent addictions, reduce the profitability of trafficking, lower social service and criminal justice costs, and ultimately reverse the increasing scale of it.

Introduction to the study of drug abuse

Let us start with some basics. What are drugs and how can we abuse them? The answers to these questions are hardly straightforward. Consider the following. Cocaine plants have been used in food and as medicine for ages in the highlands of Peru (Karch 2006). Its psychoactive properties are considered dangerous and its non-medical use is banned worldwide. In contrast, cocoa plants grown in the Côte d'Ivoire provide us with cocoa, a luxury food product and a stimulant similar to cocaine (Dalby 2003). For a time in Europe and the USA, alcoholic beverages were considered dangerous and were banned (Decarie 1990). They are still dangerous but no longer banned. Because of cannabis's psychoactive properties, it too is considered dangerous and is banned; however, it may soon become legal (Room et al. 2010). Then there are betel nuts, ganja and khat. They also have psychoactive properties, but are not universally classified as dangerous or illegal (Gezon 2012). One can get 'high' and form an addiction to all of these drugs. So, why is cocaine dangerous and banned, alcohol dangerous and legal, cocoa not dangerous and not banned, and betel nuts, ganja and khat have no clear classification?

Drug abuse as a social construct

There are no objective and scientific reasons why there are such wide variations in how different psychoactive drugs are classified (Coulson and Caulkins 2012), but there is a way to make sense out of what appear to be arbitrary ascriptions to drugs as 'dangerous', 'legal', 'illegal' and even 'psychoactive': all of these terms can be viewed as 'social constructs'. That is: all knowledge is relative to the person, time, place, language and culture (Gergen 1999). Potentially, any thing and any idea can be described differently and have ascribed to it different meanings. Our actions and habits shape our perceptions, and our perceptions in turn influence our subsequent practices (Gergen 1994). Trace how a substance has been defined and the meanings ascribed to it over time and you will see how we have arrived at such arbitrary views of drugs. If you are looking for absolutes, fixed definitions and unchanging knowledge about drugs, their use and abuse, there are none. From a social constructionist point of view, it is a given that human experiences of drugs and their use differ across time and place (Jordanova 1995).

A social constructionist approach is first of all a perspective that requires taking into account multiple explanations and interpretations of drug use and abuse. It is secondly an analytic tool by which ideological and rhetorical assumptions can be unmasked and by which medical, criminal and scientific concepts can be critically deconstructed (Gergen 1997). By using this approach, we can better understand the phenomenon of drug use and abuse in society and conceive of ways to reduce potentially the personal and social dangers involved. Because it is both a critical perspective and analytic tool, social constructionism is widely used in scientific approaches to health and illness (Lloyd 2000).

Taking the social constructionist approach is not without risks. If all knowledge is socially constructed, then the constructionist position is also a social construct. Nothing is real and empirical and everything is relative when carried to its logical conclusion. Our approach to constructionism is pragmatic. It is our belief that there are underlying realities to drug use and abuse and that many of these realities have yet to be fully discovered and described. Social constructionism pragmatically used can improve our perceptions and also help us to improve our scientific understanding of drug use and abuse.

Perspectives and definitions

There are a series of perspectives and definitions that we need to know in common to appreciate the multi-disciplinary study of drug abuse.

The moral–legal perspective

In the moral–legal perspective, drug abusers are people who have violated moral codes and the law (Greiff 1999): they have done so 'willfully'. It is asserted that everyone recognizes right from wrong, is self-directed and has the willpower to stop any behaviour if they choose to do so. Drugs designated as illegal are so because they are dangerous relative to all other drugs.

The problem with the moral-legal perspective is that it does not take into account the psychology of compulsive drug use. People who are addicted to a substance cannot stop using it even if they really want to (Nakken 1996). Only when their addiction wanes can they stop on their own. Everyone has experienced mild and temporary compulsive behaviour. You are fully aware that you should stop, but you continue anyway – too much dessert, just another biscuit or cookie, driving a little too fast or spending just a few more minutes on one's computer or electronic device. Compulsive drug use is much more extreme than a mild compulsion; and it is not temporary. It is referred to as 'obsessive–compulsive', and as an 'impulse control and substance-related disorder'. The urge to carry out the disorder overwhelms rationality and any sense of self-control (Fontelle et al. 2011). How can a drug do such a thing?

Drugs defined

Consider the following. The food and drink that we consume have in them hundreds of chemicals (Barden 2013); and additional chemicals are created by our bodies, for example, when we exercise (Sklar 2013). By regulating when and what we eat and drink, and how we exercise, we are also regulating our moods and perceptions with drugs derived from external and internal sources. Food cravings and drug craving are very similar and have many physiological parallels (Pelchat 2009). Hormones generated through exercise are also chemicals that we not only crave but cannot do without.

If we suddenly lost access to the food and drink we enjoy and to the exercise we need, we would feel miserable and would experience moods and feelings similar to withdrawal from drugs. Using illicit drugs is no different. Whether a drug is legal or illegal, it works the same way – the underlying mechanics and physiology triggered by food, exercise and drugs are the same (Kalra and Kalra 2004). So, a precise definition of a drug is 'a substance that has psychoactive effects on us'. Whether it is legal or illegal, administered through food, pills or by snorting, is irrelevant. The bottom line is that it can change your mood, percepts and state of mind.

Individual substance abuse as a medical issue

In medical research, drugs are not defined by their legal status but by their psychoactive effects on us. Hence there is a medical alternative to the moral–legal perspective. The two most well used diagnostic tools in the world are the *American Psychiatric Association's Diagnostic and Statistical Manual of Mental Disorders* (DSM) and the World Health Organization's (WHO 2010) *International Statistical Classification of Diseases and Related Health Problems* (ICD).

DSM-5 has adopted the term 'substance use disorder' so as to provide precise clinical descriptive criteria on a continuum from mild to severe symptoms (American Psychiatric Association 2013c). Someone with a mild disorder satisfies two to three criteria; a moderate disorder satisfies four to five; and a severe disorder satisfies six or more. The criteria include a number of earlier descriptions: unable to stop, reduce or control use; preoccupation with use; use that supersedes work, school or home; craving; persistent interpersonal problems; recurrent risk taking to support one's habit; and requiring more and more of the drug (American Psychiatric Association 2013b). This is primarily a physical–behavioural definition that focuses on clinical symptoms rather than legal status.

The ICD uses 'substance dependency', but it goes on also to define substance abuse as 'harmful use' (Charney and Nestler 2009). Based upon reports from European clinicians, the ICD emphasizes the psychological harm to users from any potential substance use along with the physical harm: people can use a substance in a harmful way to themselves and to others and not necessarily be physically dependent on it. These users may be just psychologically dependent. But whether their substance use is driven physiologically or psychologically, the bottom line is not their physical dependency, as emphasized in DSM-5, it is the wider harm they cause.

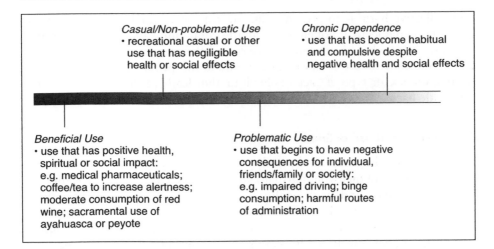

Figure 1.1   Spectrum of psychoactive substance use

Source: www.health.gov.bc.ca/library/publications/year/2004/framework_for_substance_use_and_addiction.pdf.

In DSM and ICD there is nothing inherently wrong with the use of any substance; the real problems are dependency and harm derived from it. Unlike the moral–ethical perspective, a compulsive use disorder is not an either–or dichotomy. As shown in DSM-5, the disorder ranges on a continuum (Kraly 2009). At one end, no symptoms are displayed whatsoever: some individuals are able to hide them completely. They may seem well adjusted and even happy in all other aspects of their life. At the other end of this continuum are those whose addiction is clearly apparent. They make no attempt to hide it and even identify themselves with it. The vast majority of people with addictions to drugs lie somewhere between these two extremes (see Figure 1.1).

Community substance abuse as a public health issue

The DSM-5 and ICD definitions of substance abuse and harmful use are intended for individual diagnosis and therapy. But the misuse of drugs and substances is not just an individual problem. It is social problem in that groups of people can abuse substances (Wickizer 2013). Groups are not simply aggregates of individuals. Groups create rules, have norms, recruit and socialize new members, engage in collective behaviours, can form communities and become whole societies. Groups have influence and take actions far beyond the ability of single individuals. So, drug abuse or any other health risk posed by groups of people becomes a public health concern that must be addressed as such (Institute of Medicine 1991).

So, the public health perspective to substance abuse is that the most effective and cost efficient way to reduce both substance dependency and its individual and collective harm is to prevent it in the first place (ibid.). This is done by focusing on reducing, if not eliminating, the community and social factors that increase the number of substance abusers and the amount of social harm they cause. Substance abuse is viewed as a public health problem, like any communicable disease or type of social behaviour that leads to disease and community-wide harm.

Drug use and abuse defined

We can define 'drug use' as the ability to take a drug once, twice or over a period of time and then voluntarily to stop using it. One's drug use is directed by one's willfulness and intentionality (Greiff 1999). This is consistent with the moral–legal perspective. Drug use becomes 'drug abuse' when a person cannot stop using it despite his or her best efforts (Fontelle et al. 2011). The number and range of people who use drugs and end up abusing specific substances can be increased or decreased by social influences in the community. The personal, social and financial damage of continued use can become self-evident for groups at the community level and has to be addressed as such (American Psychiatric Association 2013a).

The key term that distinguishes drug use from abuse and which is consistent across the medical and public health perspectives is 'compulsion' or 'loss of control'. In addition to being unable to stop, one is preoccupied with getting more of the substance and with using it. One builds one's daily routine around obtaining and using drugs. Everything else, such as job, children, family, friends and even personal hygiene, comes secondary. Another way to describe one's abuse is to say that one is 'addicted'.

The role of public policy

There are three organizational entities involved in addressing the problem of drug abuse – the legal–criminal justice system, medical communities and public health agencies. Now, where do these bodies get their operating budgets? Who determines their priorities? How are they to address the problem? And who gives them the authority to act? Government is the only entity large enough and with sufficient resources and authority to address a large-scale problem such as drug abuse. This is always the case, regardless of a nation's form of government – be it democratic, theocratic, a dictatorship or military rule. Public policies are the laws passed, the budget priorities and the specific actions or inactions taken by government offices and departments to address the problem of drug abuse (Babor 2010). Public policies are also articulated through the missions, goals and recommendations of experts commissioned by government leaders to advise them on how best to address the problem.

The use of science

Besides public policies that regulate courts, the police and public health authorities, many governments use and support scientific efforts to address drug abuse. Whatever is the state of our scientific knowledge of drug abuse, it has to be used by governments to prevent larger numbers of people from becoming substance users and to treat those who already abuse drugs. This means translating scientific findings into effective programmes that will work for specific sub-populations (Flynn and Brown 2011).

Ultimately, prevention and treatment of substance abuse comes down to politicians passing laws, hopefully to support the most effective treatments and prevention practices. This also means providing sufficient funding to have enough clinics, community outreach, treatment programmes, etc. so as to meet the demand. The very best scientific understanding of substance abuse is only as good as its implementation. National governments vary in their willingness to implement prevention and treatment programmes based upon science and our best knowledge. So, there is often a gap between knowledge and implementation. In effect, science only gets us half the way toward solving the problem. It is necessary not only to be scientists to understand substance abuse, it is also necessary to be students of government and policy-making (laws and funding).

Perspectives and definitions tell us what substance use and abuse are. They respond to the 'what' question. However, they do not tell us 'how' and 'why' users begin and sustain their drug use. Nor do the definitions tell us how addictions develop, work and can be treated. Why and how do some people get access to specific psychoactive drugs while others do not? Drug use and addictions are not randomly distributed in the population. It is absolutely necessary to have accurate and real life answers to these questions in order to devise effective interventions to reduce or eliminate substance abuse. There are four leading areas of social and behavioural scientific perspectives of compulsive and non-compulsive use of psychoactive drugs.

The availability–marketing perspective

If one never has access or exposure to a specific psychoactive substance, one cannot very well develop an addiction to it (Tam and Foo 2012). The substance has to be readily available. But availability alone is not sufficient for anyone to begin and continue using a drug. There has to be some incentive and some encouragement as well as ease of access for people to initiate drug use. The drug has to be 'sold' and a 'market' has to be developed and maintained for that drug (Brownstein and Taylor 2007). From the pool of initial users, a sub-population of compulsive users develops. Neither drug trafficking nor addictions can happen automatically and without considerable organization. If somehow availability is reduced and the cost of the drug increases, consumption will decline. There will simply not be enough drugs to maintain the habits of all addicted users. Those who are left out or can no longer afford to use the drug will have to find another drug of choice or go through the dreaded withdrawal. In this case, availability and marketing are important preconditions for substance abuse.

The social and criminal perspectives

Most people who have used drugs, or know others who have, generally think of drug use and abuse as an individual problem. Drug use begins voluntarily, based on free will. Asking users why and how they got started results in endless explanations that can be narrowed down to curiosity, pleasure, recreation or escape. From the moral–legal perspective, a law against the use of the specific drug exists, hence the user is breaking the law. The issue is now a criminal justice matter (Inciardi 1981; Walker 2011).

Another interpretation is that perhaps the individuals who get involved in drugs do so for more social than individual reasons. That is, one's group memberships and social identities select in advance who will be exposed, attracted to or repelled by drugs (Brener et al. 2012). Social identities and influences may also define who will continue to use a drug after the first or second time. Family, friends, community, peers and beliefs about what is normal, acceptable and desirable have tremendous influence in preconditioning an individual's response to the availability of drugs as well as to the first opportunity of use and to ongoing useage.

The psychological perspectives

Two people can have the same social circumstances and influences that give them equally high probabilities of initiating drug use or not. They can be very good friends or siblings and be similar in many ways. Yet one of them may defy all social influences and odds and do just the opposite of what might be anticipated, while the other will do what is expected. The reason for these divergent paths is because there are differences in personality and psychology which dispose each person to respond and perceive the same circumstances and influences in different ways (Walters 1994). There is a very rich tradition of research in social psychology on the fundamental characteristics and properties of individual differences that might explain why individuals respond as they do in social environments. Individuals may be more or less inclined toward, or protected from, addiction based purely on their underlying psychology (Luthar 2003). Therefore, this knowledge of their social psychological influences is vital to understanding the maintenance or loss of control that is characteristic of addiction.

The physiological perspectives

Closely related to underlying psychology are the physiological properties of the human neural system and brain. In the past two decades the major psychiatric problems of manic depression and schizophrenia, which were thought to have purely psychological roots, were found to be triggered by imbalances in brain chemistry (Torrey 1994; Fields 2010). The primary causes of these illnesses are in fact physiological, not psychological. It is possible that there are other human disorders such as addiction that might have similar physiological bases (Kraly 2009). A major breakthrough in this area could result in effective and cost efficient medical treatments for physiologically based addictions.

Multivariate thinking and orientation

In outlining the four major classes of explanation we have not posed an either/or proposition. Any of the four explanations could explain drug abuse. But very few people develop an addiction for purely psychological reasons or just because of availability or simply due to social causes. Usually their addiction is due to some combination of these factors (Scheier 2010). This means that drug abuse is 'multivariate', and when viewed as such it is a closer approximation to reality that can be empirically examined (Berry and Sanders 2000; Meyers et al. 2006). All attempts to explain or reduce any human behaviour to one or even two factors are erroneous, over-simplifications and logical reductionisms. The most compelling scientific contributions to understanding substance abuse and loss of control are multivariate.

Because the study of substance abuse is multi-disciplinary, rapidly moving and has an empirical basis, theories and factors that are thought to explain substance abuse are accepted only until they are disproven or superseded by better explanations. Again, if you are looking for universal truths, unchanging knowledge or ideological beliefs, you will have a hard time with this topic. As suggested by our social constructionist approach, unmasking supposedly true beliefs and getting beyond them is essential to advancing this field and ultimately to fully understanding the issues and being able to intervene effectively.

A note on causation should be made at this point. In the study of substance abuse, we do not yet know enough about any of the current explanations to declare any of them as truly 'casual' (Groff 2008). In the same way that we have to think of substance abuse as multivariate, we have to recognize that none of the current explanations of this phenomenon are *necessary and sufficient* to explain scientifically the loss of control in addiction. What we have are multivariate approximations of cause. There are lots of correlations and probabilistic statements; and this means that the study of substance abuse is not a tour of definitive knowledge as much as it is an exploration of unknowns and of an evolving and exciting interdisciplinary field of study.

Book content and organization

English language textbooks on drug use and abuse are written for students in either the United States or the United Kingdom, and they reflect particular national emphases. In the United States that emphasis is on scientific knowledge, though the application of that knowledge is severely limited by the American public policy focus on the criminalization of drug use (Singer 2008). In the United Kingdom, there is a greater focus on understanding drug use and abuse as ongoing features of modern life (South 1999; Barton 2003), where drug use is not exceptional.

In this text both national perspectives are reflected. But drug use and abuse are certainly not limited to these countries: they are rather global phenomena. Therefore, there are potentially other perspectives which could further characterize drug use and abuse. Until multiple national perspectives are taken into account, we have no way to understand fully drug use and abuse as either fully explored social constructs or as scientific phenomena.

In Chapter 2 we look at the scope of the problem or the prevalence of substance abuse in countries for which we have reliable data. Here we will encounter wide differences in prevalence that need explanation, which we certainly could not understand without a sense of historical background. Hence Chapter 3 is a history of prohibition and war on drugs that have resulted in such wide variations in how psychoactive drugs are regarded. In Chapter 4 we will look at the ways that illegal drugs are trafficked, distributed and made available for consumption.

In Part II we examine in depth the four explanations of substance abuse and addiction. Chapter 5 introduces the central sociological perspectives for substance use. Social structures set up and define the social and even physical contexts in which individuals have varied exposure to drugs, initiate their use, continue to use them or stop using them.

Chapter 6 looks at the criminology perspective. Criminological explanations of substance abuse are closely related to social structural and social psychological explanations. But the in-depth focus of criminologists on the nexus between crime and drug use is a special topic that provides important insights into the motivation for both drug abuse and crime. Chapter 7 then looks at psychological perspectives. There is extensive theoretical knowledge in psychology about addiction. Advances in this knowledge over the past two decades have led to our understanding of the physiological bases of human behaviour and motivation which are the focus of Chapter 8. There is promising evidence that addiction to psychoactive substances may have an underlying physiological basis in brain chemistry and that this basis may be eventually treatable via drug therapies.

Part III focuses on the responses to substance abuse, addiction and scientific knowledge. Chapter 9 outlines criminal justice public policies and reviews their relative effectiveness and social costs. Medical and public health policies and their relative effectiveness are reviewed in Chapter 10. Then in Chapter 11 our focus shifts to prevention. The extent to which a nation responds to substance abuse and addiction as a criminal versus medical problem heavily impacts the ways in which prevention are approached and the effectiveness of whatever approach is taken. The same is true for drug treatments, as covered in Chapter

12, which range in cost and effectiveness and the extent to which they are deployed from one country to another.

A review and exploration such as this will uncover implications and findings about substance abuse and the treatment of dependency. In particular, we will develop a list of things that can be done to improve prevention and treatment worldwide. In Chapter 13, there are a number of suggestions available through various expert and World Health Organization reports. In this chapter we also present our conclusions and an overview.

Review questions

- What is a social construct?
- How are drug use and abuse defined?
- There are several different perspectives on drug abuse. Can you briefly describe each?
- Are the explanations of drug abuse mutually exclusive and are any of them necessary and sufficient as predictors of who may or may not use and abuse drugs?

Further reading

Anderson, P. (2006) 'Global use of alcohol, drugs and tobacco', *Drug and Alcohol Review*, 25(6), 489–502.

Cartwright, D. (2001) *Forces of Habit: Drugs and the Making of the Modern World*, Cambridge, MA: Harvard University Press.

Jordanova, L. (1995) 'The social construction of medical knowledge', *The Social History of Medicine*, 8(3), 361–81.

Singer, M. (2008) *Drugging the Poor: Legal and Illegal Drugs and Social Inequality*, Long Grove, IL.: Waveland Press.

Prevalence of Drug Use and Abuse 2

Since the 1960s the prevalence of illegal drug use has mushroomed. A recent report by the United Nation's World Health Organization estimates 155 to 250 million people aged 15–64 have used an illicit substance at least once in the past year (UNODC 2010). This is almost double the rates of the 1980s. Health care providers and policy-makers are puzzled. What has caused this huge change? In order to understand why this has taken place, we need to examine the changes in drug use, the patterns of use and the differences among countries and groups within societies. We begin with legal substance use, and then move to illegal drugs. The great diversity of use around the world will allow us to examine later a variety of explanations.

Drug use and abuse

When we talk about illegal drug use we need to distinguish between users who may try a drug once, and never try it again, and others whose drug use has devastated their lives. Use may be casual, only in certain circumstances, or for a brief period of time. Large surveys of US adults reveal that nearly one-half (43 per cent) have tried marijuana at least once (SAMHSA 2011). The President of the United States, Barack Obama, admits he used cannabis as a youth. Most people who try an illegal drug do not continue to use it unless they have lost control. Most people who consume alcohol stop using it before continued use threatens or harms their health, their families or their jobs.

If use alone does not induce addiction, what is it that causes some to start using drugs casually and then become addicted? Is illegal drug use the same around the world, or do some countries and cultures handle it differently?

Tobacco

Perhaps no better introduction to drug use and abuse can be provided than by an examination of tobacco smoking. Millions of people around the world have tried smoking tobacco. In the USA, 74 per cent of adults have tried tobacco at some point; while in Europe, 56 per cent of those in the Netherlands and 60 per cent in the Ukraine have tried smoking (UNODC 2010). The majority of regular users smoke every day; and once they do this, they may find it very difficult to give up the habit, even when it begins to affect their health negatively. While legal, tobacco smoking is recognized as currently *the most dangerous substance used in the world.*

It has been estimated that 61 per cent of men and 3 per cent of women in China smoke cigarettes (ibid.). With 350 million smokers, most will die prematurely due to smoking (Zhang et al. 2011). An examination of all 27 European Union states reveals about 26 per cent of those over age 15 smoke every day. The vast majority of those who begin smoking in adolescence become addicted by age 20. Smoking in the USA has declined a great deal in the past 35 years, from 42.4 per cent in 1965 to 19.3 per cent in 2010 (Garrett et al. 2011). What accounts for national differences, and can the success seen in the USA be replicated elsewhere?

Alcohol

Alcohol has been used for thousands of years. There is a rich history from all over the world of its use in religious ceremonies, at celebrations, as medicine, and for every day wine with the family meal. Different cultural and religious traditions govern its use. So, in some cultures it is strictly forbidden, while in others almost everyone, including children, use it regularly. The vast majority of adults report using alcohol in the Americas, Europe, Japan and New Zealand. And in all these cultures, varied proportions of users develop a drinking problem. While users report they drink one, two or three drinks at one occasion, a problem user typically does not stop until he or she is intoxicated.

Scientists have recently defined some cultures as 'wet' and others as 'dry' (Gureje et al. 1996, 1997). In 'wet' cultures, it is normal for people to use alcohol regularly with meals. Yet these cultures disprove of binge drinking. In other cultures, whom scientists call 'dry', regular drinking is frowned upon, but binge drinking, within tightly controlled settings, is allowed (Valencia-Martin et al. 2009). It is not possible to define one of these as 'normal' and the other as 'abnormal'. In order to understand just how some people get into terrible trouble with either legal or illegal drugs, we have to look at patterns from around the world.

Variations in drug use and drug users

Adolescents

Young people aged 12–17 are much more likely to use drugs than older people worldwide. Adolescents also vary in their drug use between countries, and between groups within countries. For example, in the USA 20 per cent of adolescents have tried marijuana by age 15, and 54 per cent have tried it by age 21 (SAMHSA 2011). But in the Netherlands the figures are lower: 7 per cent have used drugs by age 15 and 35 per cent by 21 (Degenhardt et al. 2008). In New Zealand the figures are higher: 27 per cent by 15 and 62 per cent by 21. We use surveys from the USA as an example because American adolescent drug use has been so well studied. A majority of these illicit drug initiates reported that their first drug was marijuana (56.6 per cent). A new development is that nearly one-third began with psychotherapeutics (22.5 per cent with pain relievers, 3.2 per cent with tranquilizers, 3.0 per cent with stimulants and 0.8 per cent with sedatives). Overall, in 2010, of persons 12 or older, 6.9 per cent had used marijuana in the past month (SAMHSA 2011).

Women

In almost every study of drug use worldwide, women are less likely to use both legal and illegal drugs than men, which is a constant across cultures, and groups within countries. This presents a problem for explanations of addiction that rely primarily on genes or the physical effects of chemicals. Or, there is something about the social roles women play in societies that constrains their use of drugs, tobacco and alcohol.

Minority groups

Within almost every country in the world there are divisions within their population based upon some variation of ethnic, religious, racial, linguistic and historic differences. Groups vary in size relative to one another. The same group may also be politically and economically dominant over other numerically smaller or larger groups (Price 1989). Whatever is the case, the extent of drug use and abuse is likely to vary among groups within the country. These variations are generally reflective of the relationships between groups. Many countries do not even collect statistics on their minority groups to get accurate pictures of their drug use or to correct misconceptions about them. For example, in the USA, where extensive statistics on minority groups exist, many assume that racial minorities use more illicit drugs than Americans of European ancestry.

Based upon the National Household Survey on Drug Use and Health, a varied picture emerges. Americans of Asian, Native, Alaskan and Hispanic ancestry have lower rates of drug use than European Americans (SAMHSA 2011).

Overall, African American adults have slightly higher rates of drug use than whites, though surveys have shown that African Americans, while less economically advantaged than other Americans, are less likely to use alcohol or illegal drugs by age 17 (Lee et al. 2010). Drug use for this group does not begin until they are well into their twenties. These variations in drug use and abuse by age, gender and minority status strongly suggest that social positions play very important roles in the incidence and prevalence of drug abuse.

Finally, there are regional differences in drug use within countries that call for explanation. Here again data is very limited. Among those 12 years or older in the USA in 2010, 11.0 per cent used some illegal drug in the West, 9.45 per cent in the Northeast, 8.2 per cent in the Midwest and 7.8 per cent in the South (SAMHSA 2011). There are similar variations in drug use and abuse within Great Britain, between cities and rural areas in Canada, between the western and eastern parts of Australia and China, and between cantons in Switzerland. What is it about these social environments and, perhaps, even physical worlds that lends itself to varied drug use and abuse?

Need for explanations

There is vigorous debate among scientists and politicians about the causes of drug use and abuse. For example, there is evidence linking drug use with psychiatric disorders, especially depression and anxiety (Fenton et al. 2012). This link has prompted some to propose that habitual drug users are self-medicating their ongoing mental health challenges. Some explain differences in use of illicit substances as the result of more stringent legal sanctions. Still others emphasize that drug use typically coincides with youth coming of age, moving away from home and establishing an identity. Still others simply dismiss the search for explanations per se on the grounds that this behaviour is simply a violation of civil and moral codes. Examining drug use and abuse in a variety of cultural settings allows us a unique view; one which is impossible to see from within any one culture.

Variations in use of major illicit drugs

Heroin and cocaine gateways

For many years researchers thought that legal drugs like alcohol or tobacco were a gateway to hard drug use like heroin or cocaine. Recent studies have rejected the assertion that cannabis serves as a 'gateway' to other illegal drugs (Degenhardt et al. 2010; van Leeuwen et al. 2011). The vast majority of those who have used marijuana do not use it as a gateway to stronger, more destructive drugs such as heroin and cocaine. Numerous other studies have found that youths who use alcohol *before most of their peers* are far more likely to develop problems of substance abuse or dependence later in life (Larm et al.

2010). It is not whether or not they use alcohol, it is *when they begin using* psychoactive drugs that is correlated with a high likelihood of later drug abuse (Van Gundy and Rebellon 2010).

Heroin and opiates

When we generally think about drug abuse, we commonly begin by describing opiate use, specifically heroin. Many of those who use heroin lose control and become severely drug dependent. The World Health Organization ranks opiates as the most severe illegal drug problem in the world, especially in Asia and Europe. It was estimated that between 12 and 21 million people used heroin at least once in the past year (UNODC 2010). When we compare opiate use rates for different countries we can get a sense of the magnitude of the challenge posed to different political systems. Variations between countries also challenge assumptions about the causes of drug use and addiction, as is suggested by Figure 2.1.

Scotland has the highest opiate use, followed by the UK as a whole. Why is this? Here we see great differences between countries as closely related as the UK, Canada and Australia. Heroin use in the USA and Mexico shows vast differences. Rates of use in Canada are very similar to the USA despite differences in their political and public health systems. Yet, vastly different countries such as Spain and New Zealand have similar rates. Large differences and similarities in rates of opiate use create problems for explanations of addiction that assume heroin addiction is primarily caused by individual factors such as the quality of parenting or social disadvantage. The countries in Figure 2.1 do not vary that much in parenting practices, yet they are vastly different in heroin use. That is, parents in Mexico are not ten times better than parents in Scotland. Is there something about countries with low opiate use rates that higher rate countries can learn? How can Switzerland with some of the most

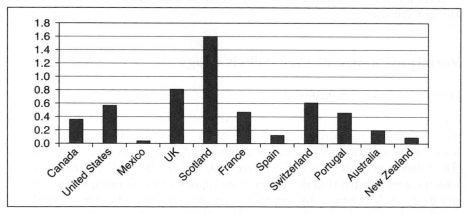

Figure 2.1   Opiate use, age 14–64 (%)
Source: UNODC (2011b).

effective harm-reduction interventions in the world have slightly higher opiate usage than the USA, where criminal sanctions are the most common intervention?

Cocaine

Used by South American Indians for centuries as a stimulant, cocaine is refined from the coca plant. In the 19th century cocaine was a common medicine throughout the USA and Europe before prohibition was enacted. It began to reach large numbers of individuals in the developed world in the 1970s. Before then it was too expensive for mass use and too difficult to obtain. Its use was confined to affluent recreational users. Since the 1970s, cocaine production, traffic and consumption have risen strongly. Recreational use has been increasing for a number of years in the EU, while rates in other parts of the world are declining.

Across the world, between 15 and 19 million people used cocaine in 2010. The World Health Organization estimates that 18 per cent of those users are dependent on the drug. In the USA it is estimated that 16 per cent of adults have tried cocaine in some form at least once (UNODC 2010). In the period 1998–2008 annual cocaine use doubled in the EU from 0.6 to 1.2 per cent of the population. Among countries in the EU, cocaine use varies greatly. Figure 2.2 shows selectively this worldwide diversity.

Spain, England and Wales, Scotland and the USA have the highest rates of cocaine use. France and Portugal have relatively low rates, while the lowest is in Mexico. Several things are striking about Figure 2.2. Mexico is the primary conduit of South American cocaine into the USA, yet its population has the lowest rate of use. France is one of the most affluent countries in the EU and a potential market for extensive cocaine trafficking, yet it has one of the lowest user rates in the EU. Drug use has been decriminalized in Portugal for the last

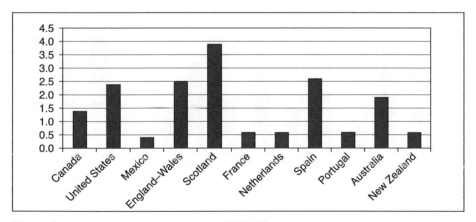

Figure 2.2   Cocaine use, last 12 months, 2011 (%)
Source: UNODC (2011b).

ten years. This means that there are no criminal sanctions or risk in cocaine use, yet the country has lower usage rates than Spain, the USA and England and Wales. In contrast, cocaine use is illegal in the UK, which has four times Portugal's rate. Such findings create major problems for assumptions about whether legal sanctions encourage or discourage illegal drug use. These differences also call for explanations of cocaine use in and between countries.

Cannabis

Globally, cannabis has the largest number of illegal drug users. Millions of primarily young people report using marijuana in the past year. Many cannabis users who begin as adolescents continue using it well into their adult years. Among individuals in the United States over 50 years of age, 4 per cent used cannabis regularly. There are worldwide estimates of between 128 and 190 million cannabis users (UNODC 2010), and this varies greatly across countries, as illustrated in Figure 2.3.

Italy and New Zealand have the highest cannabis usage rates followed by the USA and Canada with roughly equal rates. Mexico, Switzerland and Portugal have the lowest rates. In Europe, Portugal decriminalized cannabis possession ten years ago, but their use rate is much lower than their neighbours in Spain and Italy (Hughes and Stevens 2012). Australia and New Zealand's rates of use are among the highest, as are the rates in Canada and the USA. There is a striking point about cannabis use. There is a greater percentage of young people using it in the USA, as for example in San Francisco where it is illegal, than in the Netherlands where its use has been decriminalized (Reinarman 2009). Such variations again create major problems for assumptions that relaxed legal scrutiny leads to increased drug use.

If we added tables for newer laboratory produced drugs such as amphetamines and ecstasy (MDMA), we would see similar variations in national use.

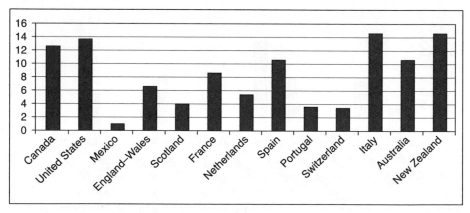

Figure 2.3 Cannabis use, last 12 months, 2011 (%)
Source: UNODC (2011b).

But already, with heroin, cocaine and cannabis, we can begin to see a pattern here. Switzerland has consistently lower rates for each drug reviewed except heroin. Portugal has consistently lower rates despite the decriminalization of illicit drug possession, and Mexico has consistently lower rates despite being a conduit for drugs to the USA. What might explain such variations in drug use? The variations in data all indicate a complex reality: that the factors driving the use of one drug may differ from the factors behind another.

Implications of substance use disorder

If the vast majority of those who have used a legal or illegal drug do not progress to addiction, what about those who do? Which drugs are associated with a more rapid movement from drug use to drug dependence? Studies of alcohol, cannabis, cocaine and opiates reveal that cocaine users, especially crack cocaine, go from use to addiction the fastest (Hser et al. 2008). Amphetamines are next. Opiates follow cocaine. Cannabis is a close third, while alcohol is last. While some observers insist cannabis does not lead to addiction, there is ample evidence that some users become dependent on the drug. It is estimated the one in ten cannabis users becomes drug dependent (Copeland and Swift 2009). This is not to say that addiction to one drug is better than addiction to another. The point is that the use of some substances leads to addiction faster than others.

When we examine trajectories of illicit drug use over a period of time we get a different picture. One study in Australia followed cannabis users for ten years. The vast majority did not become dependent on any substance, though, as pointed out before, those who used cannabis in adolescence were more likely to have some problem with substance use later in life (Degenhardt et al. 2011). Another study followed a largely African American sample of adolescents from age 6 to 42. While the vast majority of those who used cannabis in adolescence did not have a drug problem at age 42, they were at greater risk of developing a 'substance use disorder' (SUD) (Fothergill et al. 2009). While exposure was linked to a risk of later problems, it was *when* an individual *began using* cannabis (earlier or later) that was correlated to problems later in life. Those who began using either legal or illegal drugs earlier than their peers were much more likely to develop an addiction (von Sydow et al. 2002; Baumeister and Tossmann 2005).

Differences among nations

If we look at drug use across legal and illegal drugs, do people in different countries succumb to addiction at the same rates? Here we have to look at rates of drug use disorders comparatively. The World Health Organization conducted a massive study of many countries to determine rates of all mental disorders, as well as related SUDs (UNODC 2010). One should not be sur-

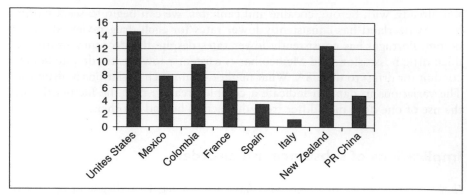

Figure 2.4   Prevalence of substance use disorders (% of population)
Source: UNODC (2011b).

prised to find that rates of SUD vary greatly between countries, as shown in
Figure 2.4.

The USA and New Zealand have the highest SUD rates. Italy and Spain have
the lowest. If using a drug even once *causes* addiction, then individuals in
higher-exposure countries shown in Figures 2.1 to 2.3 should have higher rates
of SUD. The USA and New Zealand do not consistently have the highest rates
of use for each drug reviewed. Nor do Spain and Italy have the lowest. It
appears that the pattern of SUD does not just follow rates of exposure.

If drug disorders were primarily abnormalities in brain chemistry, which has
been proposed by some observers, then we would expect the rates of SUDs
around the world to follow more closely the rates of drug exposure. It cannot
be that only the poor or criminals use drugs, because proportions of those
groups vary tremendously as a percentage of the population between countries.
It cannot be that genetic inheritance is the *primary cause* of addiction, because,
for example, women inherit the same genes as men, but do not develop the
same rates of addiction (Cotto et al. 2010). It cannot be that one's parents'
genes play a major role in drug use and abuse, because the differences between
countries are so much greater than the effects of parental drug use on the drug
use of their offspring.

Social disadvantage cannot be the primary cause of SUD because numerous
surveys in the USA have shown that Mexican Americans are less likely than
European Americans to use both legal and illegal drugs (Breslau 2005). Studies
of the transition from alcohol use to alcohol abuse have shown that African
Americans are less likely to make that transition than other ethnic groups
(Kalaydjian et al. 2009). A re-analysis of US National Household Survey on
Drug Use and Health data reveals that African American adolescents did not
differ from Asians or Pacific Islanders in rates of SUDs (Wu and Blazer 2011).

Finally, it cannot be that legal sanctions play a major role, because such
sanctions vary from country to country in application and severity. Based upon

the above cross-national prevalence data, all of our causal explanations and taken-for-granted assumptions about drug use and abuse are called into question. A different examination is in order.

Emerging drug problems

Abuse of prescription drugs

Problem uses of alcohol and nicotine and of illegal drugs pose already serious and complex challenges. But there is an additional challenge. The past ten years has seen a rapid rise in the use of prescription painkillers for non-medical use. In the USA, an estimated 5.2 million persons aged 12 or over reported using a prescription pain reliever as a recreational drug to get high (CDCP 2011). Among adolescents, one in ten aged 12–17 has used a pain reliever recreationally. It has been estimated that one half of all heroin/cocaine dealers in New York City now also sell prescription opioids as well as heroin. Studies are only now beginning to appear that estimate the extent of prescription drug abuse in other countries.

New drugs

In order to evade laws against existing illegal drugs, a series of new substances has been created. Marketed primarily for youth, these recreational drugs have appeared in the USA, Europe and Australia. While there is a bewildering range of names for these substances, they can be categorized roughly into three groups: amphetamine-like stimulants, synthetic cannabis and hallucinogens.

Mephredrone (4-methylmethcathinone) is a synthetic drug with amphetamine-like effects that is widely available on the internet. Users report effects similar to other stimulants, i.e. increased energy, concentration, talkativeness, an urge to move, insomnia, empathy and increased libido. The drug is said to have high abuse potential with 30 per cent of users in one survey reporting dependence on the drug (Winstock et al. 2011). Adverse side effects include cardiovascular and psychiatric hospitalization.

'Party pills' containing BZP (benzylpiperazine) have been growing in popularity, especially in New Zealand. As with other stimulants, side effects are similar to amphetamine. Synthetic cannabis, called 'K-2', 'Aroma' or 'Spice', is growing in popularity among youth and is sold legally in many parts of the USA, Europe and Oceania. Said to be stronger than naturally grown marijuana, users report symptoms typical for cannabis, but also paranoia, anxiety and short-term memory deficits (McGuinness and Newell 2012). Though recently banned by US drug control authorities, recent surveys of young people find many have tried it (Hu et al. 2011).

These are often naturally occurring substances such as salvia divinorum ('Sally D' in street parlance). Said to produce an experience roughly analogous to LSD, the leaves of this plant are usually smoked. The experience is immediate and short term. Users have reported disorientation and hallucinations. Sellers distribute the substance legally in many states in the USA as authorities have been slow to criminalize it. In another US national survey conducted in 2009, 1.66 per cent of youth aged 12–17 and 5.08 per cent of adults aged 18–34 reported they had tried the drug (Ford et al. 2011).

In the UK many such new substances are marketed online. Most claim to be stimulants, sedatives or hallucinogens. Sellers seldom list ingredients, side effects or contraindications, leaving users at risk to all sorts of unknown complications (Schmidt et al. 2011). While all these 'legal highs' are growing in popularity, it remains to be seen whether one or more of them emerge as a major health problem. In a recent World Health Organization update, many of these legal intoxicants are described, with warnings for users and parents. It all depends on whether or not any of these new drugs become profitable for organized criminal drug dealing networks. So far their use is very limited in most parts of the world, but it is growing, primarily among youth.

Review questions

- Does use of an illegal drug lead to addiction for most persons who try the substance?
- Discuss the evidence that legal sanctions play a large role in illegal drug use.
- Are those who use drugs earlier than their peers at greater risk of addiction?
- Discuss the evidence of marijuana or beer as a 'gateway' to hard drug use.
- Are parenting practices the most important factor in the use of illegal drugs?
- Are rates of drug use increasing, decreasing or staying the same across the world?
- What are the three types of legal intoxicants recently seen in the USA, the EU and Asia?

Further reading

Hart, C. (2013) *A High Price: A Neuroscientist's Journey of Self Discovery that Challenges Everything You Know about Drugs and Society.* New York: Harper.

Merikangas, K.R. and McClair, V.I. (2012) 'Epidemiology of substance use disorders', *Human Genetics*, 131, 779–89.

Sussman, S., Lisha, N. and Griffiths, M. (2011) 'Prevalence of the addictions:

a problem of the majority or the minority?', *Evaluation and Health Professions*, 34, 3–56.

Van Leeuwen, A.P., Verhulst, F.C., Reijneveld, S.A., Vollebergh, W.A., Ormel, J. and Huizink, A.C. (2011) 'Can the gateway hypothesis, the common liability model and/or the route of administration model predict initiation of cannabis use during adolescence? A survival analysis – the TRAILS study', *Journal of Adolescent Health*, 48, 73–8.

Old and New Prohibitions Against Alcohol and Opiates 3

Substances through time

In the ancient world, spices such as cinnamon, cassia, cardamom, ginger, turmeric and black pepper, along with hemp and opium, were traded between the Mediterranean, Africa, the Middle East and China (Czarra 2009). These products were thought to have special properties for curing illnesses, dispelling bad spirits, extending longevity and bringing pleasure. Spices, condiments, teas and cocoa were considered psychoactive, if not because of any intrinsic properties, certainly because of how they were regarded. Substances with beneficial powers that were new, mysterious and restricted were treated then as drugs are now. Ironically, once these spices became widely used, they lost their allure. There is a very fine distinction between consumption for health and nutrition on the one hand and for pleasure on the other (Schivelbusch 1992). With Western colonization after 1600, psychoactive substances were taken out of their historic and local context and given new roles.

Colonies and alcohol

Strong drink became functional and necessary. Survival in the colonies required clearing land, draining swamps, hunting, farming and dealing with natives and aboriginals. There was endless hard work done, mostly on isolated homesteads. A colonist's life was dangerous and dirty. Men and women alike drank heavily and frequently. Fights and accidents were consequences of this excessive drinking. It was not uncommon for wives to have fatal 'accidents' during these binges, and conviction for such murders was rare. As an example, on one occasion, thousands of New Englanders in the USA came to see a man hung for such a crime because it was so rare (Martin 2000). One historian has estimated that the average American by 1850 drank the equivalent of several gallons of ethanol in a single year and that 'this is approximately three times the level of U.S. consumption at the close of the twentieth century' (Dorn 2000, p. 26).

Colonists did not use alcohol just for themselves. It was also used to facilitate colonialism (Bradburd and Jankowiak 2003). In 1785, the Spanish provided Apache Indians, who opposed them, with 'generous amounts of distilled spirits' to make them dependent. At the same time, alcohol made the nomadic Chichimec people in Mexico dependent on the Spanish who then put them to work in gold mines. In Canada's Hudson Bay around 1715 native people were given '2,900 lbs. of Brazilian tobacco … and 950 gals of brandy' (ibid., p. 16). Russian and Yakut traders made the Yukagir people, in what is now Alaska, dependent on their brandy, tobacco, sugar and tea. South African Dutch traders got the Khoikoi people to sell their cattle for tobacco until they were impoverished and had to become labourers and servants for the Dutch.

Rum made from sugar cane has a special history. Because slaves produced it, rum was so inexpensive that by the 1800s it became the English colonialists' liquor of choice. Large plantation owners used it to reward and control slaves (Angrosino 2003). While drinking after work, slaves were distracted from plotting rebellions. If they were addicted to the rum, all the better: they could physically try to run from their owner, but could not escape from rum. In virtually all physical labour performed by slaves, indentured servants and manual labourers prior to 1900, 'drugs were regularly supplied as a means of making difficult, dangerous, and unpleasant work physically and emotionally sustainable' (Bradburd and Jankowiak 2003, p. 22). But alcohol was not the only drug used in colonial state-sponsored social control.

Colonies and opium

After 1773 the British took over the Portuguese trade with China for tea which the Chinese government severely limited to two coastal island trading cities, Hong Kong and Shanghai. To open trade with China, the British East India Company exported one of India's most powerful varieties of opium to China, despite the Chinese government's prohibition against opium smoking (Newman 2007). The Chinese government's attempt to stop this trade led to humiliating defeats in two wars with the British: the first Opium War (1839–42) and the second Opium War (1856–60) (Beeching 1975). By 1900, opium had run its course as a major source of profits for the British but subsequent addictions had become a major problem in China (Derks 2012).

In the early 1900s, the British example was irresistible to other Western nations (Souza 2007). Dutch colonial trade companies brought opium from the British in India and introduced it into their Indonesian colonies to boost profits, reduce rebellions and increase local dependency. The French did the same to undercut restive urban youth and intellectuals who were against their colonial rule in Vietnam. The Japanese inherited an opium problem when they took control of Formosa. While they were deeply opposed to opium smoking, they allowed opium use, though maintained tight controls. Persia and Turkey also benefitted financially from their own opium trade (Poroy 1981).

Toward prohibition

Given the long history that psychoactive substances have had in state sponsored uses, it was inconceivable prior to 1850 that any of these substances would be banned. Besides alcohol, a new use was found for opium. In the American Civil War (1860–65) there were well over 600,000 casualties. A derivative of opium, morphine, was applied directly to wounds after surgery (Zentner 1974). Opium was also used for diarrhoea, dysentery, malaria and for bullet and shrapnel wounds. During the war, the US Army procured over nine million opium pills, over 2,840,000 ounces of opium products and 29,828 ounces of morphine sulphate (Jones 1994). Morphine was used on over one million soldiers and led to serious addictions after the War. US Civil War veterans' addiction to opium was referred to as the 'soldiers' disease'.

For the general public, medical guides such as William Buchan's *Domestic Medicine* first published in England in 1869 and in the USA in 1871 provided directions on how to harvest plants and prepare drugs for medical purposes. There were over 220 different medical guides that went through multiple editions and were found in many English, American and Canadian households. In the first half of the 19th century, 'Native American botanical ingredients then constituted the bulk of recommended remedies in most manuals' (Gevitz 1990, p. 51).

By the second half of the 1800s, medicines in these guides became available in stores, on the streets and by mail order and were called 'patent medicines' (Young 1961). Their content was kept secret by the manufacturer so that competitors could not copy them. These drugs were very popular, were considered effective and were used particularly for 'women's problems'. Opium and alcohol were the main ingredients in all of these products. As a result, middle-aged women were the most common opium addicts by the late 1800s (Cohen 2006). With its 'successful use' in medicines, opium started to be included in food products. Intense competition amongst opium products then led to the addition of cocaine to gain competitive advantage. It is no coincidence that by 1900 Coca-Cola became the most popular drink in the USA: cocaine was its secret ingredient (Cortes 2012). In the same year, 600–1,000 tonnes of coca was imported into the USA annually from eastern Peru, mainly for consumer products (Gootenberg 2003).

Temperance movements

While alcohol was an important tool of colonial expansion and control, its widespread use became a matter of increasing concern. There were people dating back to the British colonial period who protested against drunkenness and its accompanying abuse of women. Initial opposition to drinking came out of religious convictions. So, for example, in 1838, the Irish priest Theobald Mathew got thousands to sign an anti-drinking pledge that established the Teetotal Abstinence Society (Ferriter 1999). The Belfast minister John Edgar poured his whisky out of a window in 1829 in protest against drunkenness. He was soon followed in 1832 by the Temperance Movement started by Joseph Livesey in Preston who opened the first non-alcohol serving hotel (Pearce 1887).

In the USA, Doctor Benjamin Rush believed that excessive use of alcohol injured the health of Connecticut farmers and formed a temperance society to ban distilled whisky. The American Temperance Society by 1833 had 4,000 charters and claimed that 1.5 million people were refraining from alcohol use (Park 2001). By the end of the 1800s, one of the most successful political pressure groups in the USA was the Anti-Saloon League led by Wayne Wheeler (Lamme 2007). The temperance movement in Canada managed to get the passage of the 1864 Canada Temperance Act which allowed counties in upper Canada to forbid the sales of liquor by majority vote (Campbell 2008). By 1878 Canadian municipalities could enact prohibitionist measures by plebiscite. During World War I (1914–18) the Australian and New Zealand temperance movement managed to get all public bars shut by 6 p.m. This produced a rush of after-work customers before closing, which was called the 'six o'clock swill' (Phillips 1980).

All of the national movements to control the availability of alcohol began as protests. Those who were disgusted by the abuses of alcohol mobilized into organizations to advocate reduced consumption – temperance. Complete prohibition was initially out of the question because of virtually universal public support for drinking. Interestingly, temperance advocates focused exclusively on alcohol while opium and cocaine were hidden in patent medicines. Ironically, many tireless advocates of alcohol temperance enjoyed patent medicines and were undoubtedly addicted to the opium and/or cocaine in them. In the USA there was even a patent medicine that specifically targeted prohibitionists, called 'Old Dr. Kaufmann's Great Sulphur Bitters'. It was endorsed by a 'tireless' lifelong prohibitionist, Mrs S. Louise Barton, and viewed by temperance advocates as 'a godsend, enabling them to stay pleasantly (but respectably) tipsy while toiling in the great national crusade to rid America of the demon rum' (Carlson 2008). The only problem is that the bitters contained unspecified other drugs as well as alcohol.

Modern transition in work, society and drugs

After 1900, office work expanded rapidly in the Western world and the demand for thinking and mental skills became paramount (Rumbarger 1989). Alcohol and opiates came to be seen as passé and barriers to this new work. In the new work ethic, inebriation was no longer accepted as normal or necessary. For example, a drunk could be put on his horse and, if he did not fall off, the horse could find its way home. A fall off the horse would only injure the drunk; but it was another thing to drink and drive a car or run dangerous and expensive machinery – others could be killed and injured and costly damage done to the car or machines. If one tried to do accounting while using an elixir with heroin or cocaine in it, the accuracy essential to one's work would disappear.

There was another problem that helped propel temperance into greater prominence. As commerce, industry and manufacturing became concentrated in large metropolitan cities such as London, Manchester, Chicago or New York, the urban working poor rapidly increased in size as well. Drinking and patent drug-taking became associated with the increasingly dangerous lower classes. In contrast to the respectability of the emerging middle class, these people were disrespectable, dirty and lived in rapidly expanding slums where all the old abuses and immoralities associated with public drinking were concentrated. The urban poor were viewed as dangerous and criminally inclined because of the muggings, thefts, rapes, burglaries and street crimes associated with them (Courtwright 1982). Drinking within this class was bad enough, but patent drugs and the outright smuggling of opiates from distant colonies (primarily by seamen) resulted in visible numbers of opiate addicts in the slums. The urban working poor were also dangerous because of their mounting potential for political unrest and rebellion.

Three things happened in this transition. First, coffee and tea became the new drinks of respectable and skilled workers and of the new middle class (Bradburd and Jankowiak 2003). The use of these 'mind-enhancing drinks' increased during the latter 1800s as increasing value was placed on sobriety at work. Second, there was finally a willingness to limit if not outright prohibit alcohol. Third, opiates that had been a source of colonial profits and control up to 1900 became viewed as dangerous with the potential of millions of homeland workers using them.

The prospects of an endless number of opiate or cocaine addicts among the urban lower classes in metropolitan cities as had happened in China was too frightening to even ponder (Wright 1924; Berridge 1978a). Use of these drugs was thought to guarantee not only more crime and moral decline but political revolt as well. Drugs that created such dependency had to be completely prohibited from use in the home country. If this required stopping drug sales and use overseas to keep them from coming to London, New York, Paris, etc., then the international colonial trade in drugs had to be stopped as well. Finally, legislation was enacted to begin limiting if not prohibiting the distribution and use of alcohol and opiates.

Regulation and prohibition

The prospects of the colonial trade in opium coming back to haunt the major industrial nations led to the Shanghai Opium Commission of 1909 (Wright 1909). All of the countries with colonies, including Turkey and Persia, had representatives present. A consensus was formed that the opium trade with China and South East Asia should end. The recommendation was ironically supported by the United Kingdom. Their opium trade in China was declining in profitability and was an increasing political liability (Berridge 1984). The United States was concerned because the use of opium in the Philippines (then a US colony) provided an open door for its flow back into their country (Carter et al. 1905). The Hague Conferences to ban state-sponsored drug trafficking followed the Shanghai Commission and were held in 1911–12, 1913 and 1914.

At these conferences delegates agreed to include bans against cocaine and other opiates in international trade except for medical uses. From these meetings, representatives went home and advocated legislation to enact the various conference consensuses. The results were parallel efforts by world governments to pass domestic laws to regulate and prohibit the availability and use of psychoactive substances. The temperance movements were generally credited for these laws since they were the most visible advocates. Banning alcohol was their most immediate objective. Each country already agreed that they had to bring alcohol use under control. Table 3.1 lists the major laws passed by five national legislations to regulate or prohibit alcohol and other drugs.

Table 3.1 Laws enacted to regulate and prohibit alcohol and drugs

United Kingdom (regulate)	Canada (regulate)	Sweden (regulate)	Finland (prohibit)	United States (prohibit)
1868, Pharmacy Act	1864, Canadian Temperance Act			
	1885, 1902, Royal Commissions on Chinese Immigration	1800s Gothenburg System		1877 San Francisco law against opiates
1908, New Pharmacy Act	1908, Patent Medicine Act; Opium Act			1906, Pure Food and Drug Act
1914, Defence of the Realm Act			1919, alcohol prohibition enacted	1914, Harrison Narcotics Act
1920, Dangerous Drug Bill	1929, Opium and Narcotic Act	1922, prohibition voted down		1920, prohibition took effect
			1932, alcohol prohibition repealed	1933, alcohol prohibition repealed
				1936, Uniform State Narcotic Act
				1937, Marihuana Tax Act

Much has been made of prohibition in certain countries when, in fact, it was part of a much broader world experience. If we look at these attempts to regulate or completely prohibit alcohol, initial transnational lessons in the effective use of government public policies become apparent. The United Kingdom, Canada, Australia, Sweden, France and Germany attempted to regulate the use of alcohol; they did not ban it outright. It was the United States, Russia, Iceland and Finland that attempted prohibition – to ban completely the availability and use of alcoholic beverages.

United Kingdom

Only the hours when alcohol could be served in public were restricted. No other restriction of its availability was imposed. In Table 3.1, the 1868 Pharmacy Act restricted the sales of opium to pharmacies. The 1908 New Pharmacy Act placed morphine, cocaine and their derivatives containing more than 1 per cent morphine under pharmacy control as well (Berridge 1978b). Regulation of these drugs was left to professional pharmacists with minimum state involvement. Then in 1914 amidst World War I, the Defence of the Realm Act was passed and enacted in 1916. It then became a crime for anyone, except doctors and pharmacies, to possess, sell or use cocaine for any reason. The use of cocaine and other opiates among troops during the war prompted this law. The 1920 Dangerous Drugs Bill made permanent war-time restrictions and has been in effect ever since (Berridge 1984).

Canada

The 1864 Canadian Temperance Act was the first legislative attempt anywhere to regulate alcohol's availability and use (Green 1979). Its central provision was that municipalities in upper Canada could vote to restrict alcohol's availability and use it in whatever way they agreed. The first full national prohibitions passed were the 1885 and 1902 Royal Commissions on Chinese Immigration. Both Commissions expressed concerns about opium smoking among Chinese immigrants and increased Chinese workers' entry fees into the country. But in 1908 it came to light that as much opium was sold to white people as Chinese and it was alleged that white women and girls were using the drug. Parliament promptly passed the 1908 Opium Act which outlawed the selling, possession and use of opium except for medical use. Soon afterward, Chinese immigration was stopped completely. The 1908 Patent Medicine Act forbid the putting of opiates in foods and the 1929 Opium and Narcotic Act extended the list of illegal but medically regulated drugs to cocaine and marijuana (ibid.).

Sweden

Sweden like the United Kingdom and Canada also had a very influential temperance movement and the country was well on its way to prohibiting alcohol.

After 1900, prohibition referendums swept the country at the municipal level (Nycander 1998). A government commission strongly recommended prohibition in 1919 and a national referendum was set for 1922. The vote was 51 per cent against and 49 per cent for – prohibition narrowly failed. The failure was due to the work of a prominent Swedish doctor, Ivan Bratt. It was his view that a prohibition against alcohol would be ineffective. A better way to control its use would be to make its retail trade the responsibility of local control boards consisting of citizens with no interest in profiting from alcohol sales. He advocated that private profit due to alcohol sales should also be eliminated in the restaurant and wholesale trade. This system, sometimes called the 'Gothenburg System', was put in place instead of prohibition and remained until 1960 (ibid.). Like the United Kingdom and Canada, Sweden also prohibited the sales of heroin, cocaine and marijuana for non-medical uses.

Finland

Amidst cold and dark winters, Finland had a serious problem with binge drinking and public drunkenness which were first criminalized in 1733 (Hakkarainen et al. 2007). Progressively stronger restrictions made little difference and the problem continued. In response, one of the strongest prohibition movements in Europe developed. After several failed attempts, the movement got a full prohibition of alcohol enacted in 1919. The sales and use of all alcoholic beverages were banned throughout the country.

The United States

As in Canada, there was news of white women patronizing Chinese opium dens in San Francisco and of alleged rapes (Green 1979). This inflamed anti-Chinese sentiment. In 1877 a San Francisco municipal law was passed against opium possession and use (Gardner 1999). Racial fear was a factor in the earliest cocaine use as well. Employers introduced cocaine to African American dock workers in New Orleans to help them work faster at loading and unloading ships on hot humid summer days (Jones 1994; Cohen 2006). These workers' cocaine use was not a problem until some of them began using it in jazz clubs in New Orleans's Storyville; other workers did the same on Atlanta's Decatur Street (Cohen 2006). Rumours surfaced that white women were introduced to cocaine in these clubs, danced with black men and were then raped. By 1903, most Southern state legislatures passed total bans against cocaine sales and its use and possession (ibid.).

In 1900, marijuana use was unknown in the USA. It did not become an issue for drug hysteria until it was associated with Mexican immigrant labourers in the 1920s (Ferraiolo 2007). The script is familiar. Marijuana smoking Mexican American 'zoot-suiters' (a style of dressing) in Los Angeles allegedly gave white women the drug and then allegedly raped them in dance halls during World War I (Pagán 2003). This led to rioting by white service men and to the first city-wide ordinance against the use and possession of marijuana. Other towns and cities in Western USA followed the lead of Los Angeles based upon the same fear. This ordinance was passed, upheld and used to arrest and prosecute Mexican Americans even though it was not clear what marijuana was. It was not until the 1940s that the psychoactive component of cannabis, tetrahydro-cannabinol (THC), was isolated and one could distinguish it from, for example, household 'grass' and 'weed' (Snelders et al. 2006).

European immigrants were also a source of white nativist fear that played into the urgency of alcohol prohibition. The Ku Klux Klan was not a fringe group operating only in the Deep South and only against blacks. They were a major player in advocating alcohol prohibitions in Indiana, Ohio and Illinois and represented mainstream social and political concerns (Moore 1991; Lay 1992). They not only enforced white supremacy, they called for prohibition against alcohol and opiates as necessary to control blacks, Jews and Catholics. The Klan killed several Italians in their enforcement of prohibition against wine making in Denver (Worrall 2004). Then, at the beginning of World War I, the Anti-Saloon League intentionally used American anti-German hysteria to associate all beer production and drinking as anti-American because there were German-American brewers. The General Counsel of the League declared 'kaiserism abroad and booze at home must go' (Carlson 2008). The stage was set to enact full prohibitions against alcohol and opiates in the USA.

In 1906 the Pure Food and Drug Act was passed by Congress. It required manufacturers to label accurately all ingredients and proportions of opiates, alcohol, cocaine and other habit-forming drugs in their products. The main purpose of this Act was to eliminate the abuses of patent drugs. The Act did not ban patent drug makers from selling opiates or cocaine, nor did it restrict the quantity of these drugs that they could put in their products (Speaker 2001). Congress then passed the 1914 Harrison Narcotics Tax Act, the first comprehensive US federal drug control law. This Act nationalized Southern anti-cocaine ordinances and the anti-opium statutes from California and other western states.

It was then noticed that marijuana was not covered in the Harrison Act. By 1930, 48 states passed the Uniform State Narcotic Act that also made marijuana available only by prescription. A successful campaign to prohibit it resulted in the 1937 Marihuana Tax Act (Ferraiolo 2007).

Outcomes of prohibition

The most revealing public policy outcome of alcohol prohibition is that it was repealed in every country that enacted it. No country was able to sustain it. In Finland, smuggling alcohol into the country became a very profitable illegal business, which law enforcement could not match. In some municipalities, public drunkenness actually increased by as much as 500 per cent (Sariola 1954). Because the sales of alcohol were illegal, they were hidden, and this undermined the authority of the state. Crime rates increased dramatically after prohibition was passed and the public turned against the law. As a consequence, temperance and prohibition advocates alike waned in their influence. A national plebiscite showed that 70 per cent of the population was in favour of repeal. Thirteen years after prohibition came into effect, Finland repealed its law in 1932 (ibid.). Other European countries that tried prohibition, such as Iceland and Russia, also repealed their laws for the same reasons.

The prohibition experience in the USA paralleled Finland's. According to American prohibitionists, violence against women, fights and general civil unrest would all disappear with the closing of saloons, bars and liquor stores (Lewis 2008). Poverty and child neglect would also become a thing of the past once men no longer had bars and saloons to lose their wages in and alcohol to distract them from their wives and children (not to mention from work). But what actually happened was a long way from the prohibitionists' promises. The law did not temper alcohol use; alcoholic beverage distillation and drinking did not disappear. As in Finland, it simply went underground. Instead of legal businesses brewing alcoholic beverages, illegal criminal organizations took over the lucrative business of distilling and distributing booze. Then, turf battles between these gangs generated much more shocking violence than before prohibition. It did not help that weapons technology during World War I produced high-power and rapid-fire weapons such as handheld machine guns. Gangs fought pitched battles on downtown city streets where they cut each other down, along with occasional police officers and bystanders with hails of bullets in drive-by shootings (Blumenthal and Colvin 2011). Gang leaders and restaurant patrons alike were machine gunned while dining, and workers at distilleries and rival distribution centres were routinely massacred.

Saloons and bars went underground as well. They became private clubs and speakeasies where one gained entry through passwords and coded knocks. The gambling and prostitution associated with saloons and bars also went underground and intensified. All of this was made possible by liberal payoffs and threats of bodily harm to police and local politicians (Ridings 2010). Despite prohibition, anyone who wanted a drink could get as much as he or she wanted and the cost was not much higher than it was before prohibition. The price of prohibition against alcohol was considerable public violence and far more corruption of public officials than before (Hall 2010). Questions as to whether prohibition was worth it were raised from the beginning.

The collapse of the world economy in 1929 and the subsequent Great Depression caught prohibition supporters by surprise. In the midst of the depression, prohibition became vastly unpopular in all the countries that attempted to ban alcohol. For example, in the USA President Hoover and many prohibition state legislators were swept out of office. Franklin D. Roosevelt became the new president. The outgoing Congress passed a repeal of prohibition in February of 1933 with the Twenty-first Amendment to the Constitution and sent it to the states for ratification. The Amendment was ratified by state conventions even faster than the Eighteenth – which legalized prohibition – in 288 days (Schrad 2007). The prohibition against alcohol had lasted only 13 years in Finland and the USA; its rise and fall left unanswered questions about how and why it happened and what lessons could be gained for modern public policy-making regarding the control of alcohol and other drugs.

Prohibition and regulation compared

The United Kingdom, Canada and Australia chose the middle ground of trying to restrict through regulation the availability and consumption of alcohol. The USA, Finland, Iceland, Norway, Denmark and Russia chose to ban all sales and use of alcohol – prohibition. Which approach was more successful and which was more effective in reducing the abuse of alcohol and opiates?

Alcohol

With regard to alcohol, it appears self-evident that regulation as opposed to prohibition was the more successful public policy measure (Levine and Reinarman 1991). In every case, prohibition had to be repealed and quickly. In contrast, none of the countries that had selected the regulatory route had had to retract their policies. In fact, most of the alcohol regulatory measures established at the turn of the last century remain in effect. Public policies that can be established and then maintained are clearly superior to ones that cannot. Both approaches resulted in some declines in drunkenness and cirrhosis deaths (which is a good measure of public intoxication) (Smart 1974). But neither approach produced more dramatic declines than the other. But when we consider the cost of each approach, it is self-evident that the cost of prohibition was much higher than the cost of regulation. Furthermore, regulatory countries did not see increased crime, violence and corruption directly attributed to regulation.

An irony of prohibition is that, once repealed, regulatory measures then had to be sought as the only alternative. Finland and other prohibition countries made this transition smoothly and pragmatically, based upon the British and Swedish examples. But it was done quite reluctantly in the USA where, ironically, there had been experiments in European type regulations of alcohol before prohibition. As early as the 1890s, the Swedish 'Gothenburg System' had also been tried in Athens, Georgia where it was considered successful and then extended to other towns and counties in North Carolina, Georgia, Alabama and Virginia. The Gothenburg System was an intermediate strategy between the extremes of no regulation at all and of completely banning alcohol. Based on state experiments in the late 1800s, alcohol consumption was regulated through excise tax, production and sales quotas, distribution and sales monopolies, restrictions on advertising and availability, individual rationing and store licensing (Schrad 2007).

All alcoholic beverages were sold through retail outlets controlled by reputable citizens. They served as local trustees who directed all liquor profits into a public fund to promote the general good. The goal of this arrangement was to have disinterested management who removed the profit motive from alcohol sales. There was even a 'Committee of Fifty' – distinguished citizens who researched alternatives to prohibition, starting in 1893. They recommended the Gothenburg System and warned of the violence and corruption that would result from a complete prohibition of alcohol (ibid.).

Opiates

All of the prohibitions against opiates instituted at the turn of the last century are still in place. In this regard the Shanghai Commission and Hague Conference were resounding successes. As an illustration, by 1914 and the passing of the Harrison Act in the USA the number of Americans addicted to opiates had been in rapid decline for over 20 years. The high point of opiate addictions was 1890 (Courtwright 1982). It is estimated that in 1900 the actual number of opiate addicts did not exceed 300,000 (Speaker 2001). Alcohol was far more dangerous and was associated with more ill health, violence and death than all other psychoactive drugs combined. An irony is that by 1914 Americans were less rather than more familiar with opiates and cocaine. The very year the 1914 Harrison Act was passed World War I stopped opiate trafficking worldwide and may have done more to eliminate opiates and cocaine from life in the large cities of Europe and the USA than any regulation or prohibition.

After 1930, opiates, cocaine and marijuana disappeared almost entirely as drugs generally available to the public. In Canada, Australia, the United Kingdom and most of Europe, access and use of opiates were limited to medicine. In the USA morphine was the only opiate permitted in medicine. Once patent drugs were exposed for what they were and doctors turned against their over-the-counter availability, they ceased to be procurable and the large markets for these products that existed in the 1800s disappeared. These drugs became increasingly difficult to find and expensive to buy. What emerged was a small market on the fringes of urban society among artists, musicians, bohemians and professional criminals (Acker 1999; Ferraiolo 2007). Between the 1930s and 1950s opiates could be found in the USA only in some night clubs, at horse races and among some Hollywood personalities.

The new prohibition: war on drugs

World War II (1939–45), like World War I, cut off the supply of illicit drugs from Asia and South America to Europe and the USA. By the end of the war, opiates, cocaine and marijuana were less available than at any time during the century: '1945 presented a clean slate for drugs: a paradise for law enforcement and a personal hell for individuals in search of highs or new drug cultures' (Gootenberg 2003, p. 137).

The USA entered World War II in an economic depression but exited as the most prosperous country in the world. In 1950 it was the only large, potentially profitable market for illicit drugs. Chile and Argentina were distant seconds. The UK, the rest of Europe and most of Asia had been devastated by the War. It would take at least another decade before they could become new markets for illicit drugs from overseas. So, drug traffickers focused primarily on the USA and had no problem getting heroin into the country. In the 1960s, the number of heroin users grew rapidly. By 1970, groups of nodding addicts, high on heroin, became common sights in US cities and record crime rates accompanied them. The 210 ounces of cocaine confiscated in 1949 became an estimated 300 tons by 1997 (Decker and Chapman 2008). Something had to be done.

Demand-side interdiction

The first response of US local, state and federal governments to the heroin epidemic was the vigorous use of the criminal justice system, as was done during the prohibition of alcohol. It was called by President Nixon in 1971 a 'war on drugs'. The first phase of the war was to: enlarge police forces; increase their capacity to conduct undercover drug buys, sting operations and the busting of dealers; and to form special weapons assault teams. Police were armed with more powerful weapons and the number of courts and prisons were increased (Fish 2006; Friesendorf 2007). The object of these efforts and huge expenditures was to arrest, convict and jail anyone and everyone engaged in illegal trafficking, dealing and using.

It was recognized very early on that these efforts poses enormous problems. To up root drug traffickers and dealers effectively would require suspending civil liberties and constitutional rights for many people who had nothing to do with drug trafficking and use (Sweet and Harris 1993). Curfews would have to be imposed; random searches and identity checks would have to be conducted, as are now done in New York and Philadelphia; low-level dealers and community residents alike would have to be coerced into identifying drug suppliers who might be relatives or neighbours.

In the 1960s, the USA had just gone through more than 146 urban race riots, several of which required the regular military to suppress (Kerner 1968). American cities were tinder-boxes of conflict over long-term racial discrimination against African Americans in housing, employment and education. What sparked these riots were incidents of police brutality. An effective fight against drug dealing and use would have required more draconian measures which could spark even more severe rioting. Also, there was not the political will or a public consensus that would have supported the equivalent of martial law in US cities.

Supply-side interdiction

There was an alternative to demand-side policing that may have been more effective and less problematic (Caulkins et al. 2006). This was to stop heroin and cocaine production where they were grown and harvested. This would reduce if not completely eliminate the supply of illicit drugs. The retail cost would increase dramatically and it would become prohibitively expensive to use these drugs. Addicts would be forced into withdrawal and treatment.

The USA did three things related to supply-side prohibition. First, it funded projects to eradicate crops with herbicides in Colombia, Peru and Bolivia (Buxton 2006). Second, it provided military training and equipment to Central and South American governments (Rouse and Arce 2006). Third, the US Coast Guard was deployed with new radar systems to identify and interdict boats and aircraft bringing illegal drugs into the USA. By 1989, supply-side interdictions were thought to be so promising that its budget was 2.6 times larger than demand-side expenditures (Collett 1989).

The effects of the new prohibition

Effects on crime, violence and policing

It is assumed that by increasing the number and visibility of police that drug-related crimes will go down. It turns out that a police presence in high-crime areas does not reduce child abuse, disorderly conduct, rape, shoplifting or vandalism. They do reduce homicide, burglary, assault and robbery, but only where patrols are concentrated (Worrall and Kovandzic 2010). Crime then increases in areas where there is less police coverage. Most importantly, increasing arrests for drugs does not reduce rates of drug dealing or use, neither in the USA (Shepard and Blackley 2005) nor internationally (UNODC 2012b). So, crime does not necessarily go down because of more police, it simply moves; and increasing the number of arrests is not a deterrent.

Furthermore, it is not clear what effect drug use has on criminal behaviour. Addicts who committed violent acts before commencing drug use were found to be more violent than their peers who were not violent before their drug use (Darke and Kaye 2012). It seems that addiction is not a cause of violence for most addicts: other correlated factors are involved, such as being abandoned or physically and sexually abused as a child. After more than 30 years of research, there is no convincing evidence that the massive war on drugs through police services has reduced illegal drug use or addiction to heroin or cocaine; and neither can the current decrease in violence and crime in the USA be directly attributed to it (Miczek et al. 1994; Frampton et al. 2008).

Effects on economy and government

The USA has the highest rate of imprisonment for all categories of crime. Sixty per cent of all prisoners are incarcerated for drug-related offences (Hartney 2006). Government expenditure on the war on drugs for the first six months of 2012 was approximately $26 billion (ONDCP 1997–2012). This is more than the gross national product of half the countries in the world community.

The large number of courts, jails and prisons employ millions. Critics point out that if drugs disappeared and there were no more drug arrests and convictions, many local economies would collapse (Sudbury 2005). Thousands of people are arrested, convicted and jailed each year to keep the system going and to justify its high cost. The average cost to keep a person in prison in 2010 in the USA was $31,286 (Henrichson and Delaney 2012). Critics call this 'the prison industrial complex' (Schlosser 1998).

Effects on race relations and civil rights

The most extensive rioting in US history occurred in 146 cities during the 1960s in predominantly low-income African American communities. Studies of the riots identified rising unemployment and racial discrimination as the main causes and police brutality as the provocation (Kerner 1968). Street-level heroin dealing began in most of these cities shortly after the riots. Soon African American and Latino men were disproportionate in number among all heroin users. The war on drugs centred in these communities and on these men. The results have been devastating. These communities became militarized battle-grounds with residents further alienated from the authorities. Since none of the causes of the riots were sufficiently addressed, unemployment only intensified. Arresting people for drug dealing makes little difference: others simply take their place. Re-arresting and longer sentencing have had little effect (Green and Winik 2010). Civil rights efforts shifted from fighting racial discrimination in employment, housing and education to addressing the heroin and then later the crack epidemics.

Effects on public health

The onset of the human immunodeficiency virus (HIV) which causes acquired immune deficiency syndrome (AIDS) after 1982 posed the most serious public health threat of the last century (World Bank 1997). Heroin injectors were one of the first groups infected because they shared contaminated needles and syringes. They could further spread HIV by continuing to share contaminated needles and by sexual contact. By the 1990s crack cocaine dealers and users who engaged in transactional sex for drugs and/or money were also HIV infected and began spreading AIDS (Edlin et al. 1994).

The drug war drove heroin injectors and crack cocaine dealers and users underground. This intensified their infectiousness, cut them off from medical and public health preventive services, and made them a threat to the entire nation's health (Bowser et al. 2007). Only through special efforts were they reached and the threat they posed mitigated.

Effects on cities

Drug use and dealing made neighbourhoods in which they were centred dangerous to live in and to visit and accelerated their decline as social and physical entities (Aalbers 2006). Property values quickly declined as new residents and investors refused to buy where drugs were sold. Landlords could no longer attract premium renters as only the very poor and most recent immigrants would live there. Banks refused to approve home mortgages or to lend to property owners to make improvements in communities associated with drug dealing. This isolation only attracts more dealers and more addicts.

If nothing was done, residents abandoned their homes and apartments and the area became blighted. At this point, the community died, property values were at their lowest and its decline was complete. Eventually, developers reclaimed the land and rebuilt on it. In the largest US cities many of these communities are now not only being gentrified but are being resettled by a new middle class of primarily young urban professionals eager to give up long commutes and energy-hungry suburban life-styles (Ehrenhalt 2012).

Summary

After some 40 years of effort, it has become clear even to the most ardent supporters of the war on drugs that neither is it a deterrent to drug use and dealing nor does it matter how much money and personnel are devoted to stopping drug-related crime. The war on drugs has become recognized as a failed domestic policy (McCoy and Block 1992; Davenport-Hines and Treadwell 2002) as well as an international failure (GCDP 2011). The supply and demand for illegal drugs has not been diminished; both have in fact steadily increased (Werb et al. 2013).

This criminal-justice approach to the drug problem is simply not working any more than it did during the first prohibition. Meanwhile, the collateral damage of the war on drugs has been enormous to the USA's economy, race relations, public health and cities. Furthermore, city and county governments can no longer finance the war; they are being slowly bankrupted by their court and prison costs. The USA has ended up as the only democracy with the dubious distinction of having the highest rate of imprisonment in the world and little to show for it (Stephan 2004).

Review questions

- Are alcoholic beverages, heroin, cocaine and marijuana the only drugs people have formed addictions to?
- How did governments use alcohol and opium to advance their national interests?

- What was done to prohibit the use of alcohol and what were the outcomes?
- What were the advantages and disadvantages of alcohol prohibition and regulation?
- What were the primary things done to stop drug trafficking and dealing after 1960 and were they any different than the actions taken during the first prohibition?
- Can you briefly describe five outcomes of the US war on drugs?

Further reading

Aldama, F. L. (2006) *Drug Wars: The Political Economy of Narcotics*, Minneapolis, MN: University of Minnesota Press.

Berridge, V. (2004) 'Why alcohol is legal and other drugs are not', *History Today*, 54(5), 18–20.

Buxton, J. (2006) *The Political Economy of Narcotics: Production, Consumption and Global Markets*, Nova Scotia: Fernwood Publishing.

Goodman, J., Lovejoy, P. and Sherratt, A., eds (2007) *Consuming Habits: Global and Historical Perspectives on How Cultures Define Drugs*, 2 edn, London: Routledge.

Keire, M. L. (1998) 'Dope fiends and degenerates: the gendering of addiction in the early twentieth century', *Journal of Social History*, 31(4), 809–22.

Kushner, H. I., Tracy, S. W. and Acker, C. J. (2006) 'Altering American consciousness: the history of alcohol and drug use in the United States, 1800–2000', *Bulletin of the History of Medicine*, 80(1), 115–43.

Mills, J. and Barton, P., eds (2007) *Drugs and Empire: Essays in Modern Imperialism and Intoxication, 1500–1930*, Basingstoke: Palgrave Macmillan.

Mold, A. and Berridge, V. (2007) 'Crisis and opportunity in drug policy: changing the direction of British drug services in the 1980s', *Journal of Policy History*, 19(1), 29–48.

Social Marketing Perspective

4

The first of four explanations of drug use and abuse concerns the availability and marketing of drugs. It stands to reason that one cannot get addicted to a drug that is unavailable. But, once available, use of the drug does not automatically follow. Addiction cannot happen until users are introduced to a drug and then it must be made consistently available. There has to be some sort of initial marketing of an illicit psychoactive drug.

We generally do not think of illegal drugs as reliant on marketing. We know from the short history presented in Chapter 3 that government prohibitions attempt to suppress availability and marketing. We saw how prohibiting alcohol drove its sales and consumption underground, but did not stop its distribution and consumption. Governments that took the alternative route of regulating its availability were more successful in limiting the market for alcoholic beverages and avoiding criminal outcomes. Prohibition and marketing had different impacts on the alcohol market. The social marketing explanation of drug use and abuse is illustrated in Figure 4.1.

In Figure 4.1, the availability of drugs is affected by government intervention which in turn affects how a drug is marketed. Marketing then impacts on the scale of consumption. So, if use of a substance is not declared illicit, there is no need for an illegal market for its product. Any use of the product resulting in dependency is in the open. Availability can be regulated by gov-

Availability ➞ Government intervention ➞ Marketing ➞ Consumption

Figure 4.1   Availability to consumption model for illegal drugs

ernment, and subsequent dependencies can be treated. But an illicit market is created as soon as the substance is declared illegal. The drug's availability is then controlled by those operating underground who wish to break the law (Anderson 2006). It is in their interest to market the drug to make money.

The economics of drug trafficking and dealing

Drug trafficking may violate national and international laws, but it cannot violate the economics of supply and demand (Boivin 2011). The business of illicit drugs is better understood as a market driven by economic limits and constraints (Naylor 2003). When governments attempt to prohibit a drug's availability, they are trying to push potential traffickers' and dealers' costs high enough to eliminate their profits (Brownstein and Taylor 2007). In effect, if the people engaged in this enterprise cannot make enough money to make the risks worth it, their incentive disappears and the market collapses.

We need to look specifically at the behavioural economics of the availability of illicit drugs. We need to answer two questions. First, to what extent has government prohibition and its alternative policies reduced the profits in illicit drug trafficking and dealing? The more profits they can remove the less incentive there is to continue the drug trade. Second, what have traffickers and dealers done to maximize their returns in response to government opposition?

The literature on drug trafficking and dealing generally has a law enforcement emphasis (Inciardi 1981). We already know that this approach alone, while essential, has limited utility. In this chapter, we will focus instead on what has been done in the marketing of illicit drugs to affect consumption. The focus will be on the US market experience since this is the most extensively documented and has the government most deeply committed to prohibition.

Traffickers' and dealers' responses to prohibition

Flexibility in production

Since the 1980s special police have been trained in Colombia to cut down coca crops and to find and destroy processing laboratories. However, they have been met with fierce resistance (Rouse and Arce 2006). Heavily armed troops have to accompany them. And soon they too were met with well-armed resistance. A much more effective and less costly approach in lives and material was to spray the coca crops from the air with herbicides (Buxton 2006). This destroyed the coca plants.

The response of the growers was to plant the crop in smaller and more remote plots of land and frequently to change the locations of crops and laboratories (Rouse and Arce 2006). This made it very difficult to find and spray the crops. It also meant spraying large tracts of land to reach smaller and smaller plots. This turned legitimate farmers and local populations against spraying because the herbicides did not just kill the coca plants: they killed legal crops and made the land infertile for decades.

Another response of planters has been to use the vast territory of Central and South America to move from country-to-country and from one remote area to another to plant and harvest coca. By the time the new locations are discovered and a response can be organized, the planters have already moved across yet another border. This is called the 'balloon effect' of interdiction efforts (ibid.). Planters have gone from Colombia to Bolivia to Peru and now into the Brazilian Amazon. They have unlimited territory across whose borders they keep moving back and forth.

Flexibility in trafficking

The Medellin cartel operated in the open. Its personnel and operations were well known. It was also vertically organized as a hierarchy: growers, processors and traffickers all knew each other (Decker and Chapman 2008). Once the authorities were willing to confront the organization and its violent self-defence, it was relatively easy to dismantle it. Juan Escobar, the feared leader of the cartel, was found by simply monitoring his family's telephone.

By 1997 the Medellin cartel was replaced by the Cali cartel which learned from the Medellin's mistakes (Chepesiuk 2003). In making contracts, great efforts were made to hide the identities of everyone in the organization. Operatives were forbidden to show their wealth, to have loud parties or to call attention to themselves in any way. Ultimately, because of their vertical organization, they were dismantled as well, though with a lot more difficulty. Through surveillance of suspicious locations and persons, the authorities were able to arrest several key operatives who were knowledgeable of the cartel's operations, facilities and personnel. Did Colombian cocaine growing and trafficking stop? The answer is: not at all.

Low-level personnel from the cartels and free-lance planters and traffickers have continued to innovate production and trafficking. Today, the authorities are confronted with organizations that are virtually impossible to break. Instead of hierarchical or vertically integrated organizations, planners and traffickers are now non-hierarchical and fragmented (Lampe 2006; Decker and Chapman 2008). One person plants and does the harvest; a second buys the crop; a third does the processing; and a fourth moves the processed cocaine to an initial trafficker. The drugs may move through the hands of several traffickers en route to market.

The planter knows the first buyer but not the processor. The buyer knows the processor but not the trafficker; and so on. If anyone is caught, they only know who their next-level contact is. There is even a way to make certain that even immediate contacts are unknown. Arrangements can be made to leave the drugs in one place and pick up the payment in another; in which case, there is no need for even face-to-face contact. There is no apparent hierarchy; no one knows who is in charge.

Flexibility in routes

Instead of predictable routes, traffickers ship drugs using many different routes. Cocaine can be flown to a remote Caribbean island and transferred to ships to Europe or small high-speed boats to the USA (Barnes 2002). Radar and on-water interdiction by the US Coast Guard has been avoided by using small submarines and by taking land routes through Mexico (Seelke et al. 2011).

Alternatively, planes can meet a fishing or pleasure boat anywhere on the ocean and drop their cargo (Burns 2002). The boat then returns during a holiday or weekend amidst many other boats. A large amount of drugs can be shipped to a country that does not produce drugs or would not be suspected of being a transit point, such as South Africa, Sweden or Australia. Then, the supply can be easily shipped via container cargo or commercial air transport into the USA and Western Europe. Nigerians were drug couriers in this way until they were discovered (Anonymous 1995).

Flexibility in high-level dealing

The Mafia was the largest and most prominent organized crime group implicated in illicit drug trafficking and dealing (Alexander 1988). Like South American drug cartels, the Mafia was hierarchically organized and run by families. Law enforcement agencies have focused on Mafia families in order to find someone who will provide key information. Since 1990, the Mafia has been removed as a major player in drug dealing in the USA (Reuter 1995). Following this, the police and the US Drug Enforcement Administration have focused on the next most obvious players: ethnic and immigrant street gangs who have been caught trafficking and dealing drugs (Egley et al. 2007). But there is a problem when focusing only on street gangs: they are not sufficiently dispersed to account for most drug trafficking in the USA.

The only people left, based on the literature, are freelance dealers. The non-hierarchical fragmented organization of traffickers now also reflects the organization of domestic drug dealers (Adler 1993). Freelance traffickers pass drugs from one another and then into networks of dealers who then do the same. Middlemen sometimes facilitate these deals. Freelance traffickers and dealers are sufficiently dispersed to supply a large part of the market. And again, people in these networks do not necessarily know one another nor have they met one another face-to-face, making it very difficult for the authorities to break these networks.

Flexibility in street-level dealing

When drugs get to street-level dealers, authorities could rely on dealers having observable routines and using public telephones. This is no longer the case. Drug-for-money exchanges can occur anywhere and anytime, and need not be in person. Street-level dealers now maintain contact with customers via email, mobile phones and text-messages (Ramirez 1993; Barendregt et al. 2006). They also use PayPal, bank cards, automatic payment and wire transfers. Decentralized retail drug dealing means the public and police are given the false impression that it no longer occurs. It also means that inner-city communities are no longer needed as drug supermarkets. Now drug deals can occur at any place. By exercising flexibility and constantly innovating, traffickers and dealers have minimized police disruption of illicit drugs crossing borders and getting into the hands of users.

Restrained and unrestrained markets

The UK, Canada, Australia, the Netherlands, Switzerland and other countries with national health plans all turn out to have what we will call 'restrained' illicit drug markets. They are restrained because dealers can make money only from recreational drug use. Citizens who become dependent on a drug can get treatment and/or prescription maintenance at no out-of-pocket cost. In effect, as soon as a person becomes addicted, the dealer's ability to exploit him or her is minimized. Dealing drugs for profit cannot compete with freely available ones.

An unrestrained illicit drug market occurs when dealers can fully exploit their clients as recreational users and as addicts. A prohibition that cannot effectively stop a drug's profitability at any point in a user's progression to addiction inadvertently leaves an unrestrained market for dealers. If drug dealers in restrained markets figure out how to make addiction profitable, these markets can also be unrestrained. Let's see in detail how an unrestrained market unfolds when prohibition is virtually all that is done to stop drug trafficking and dealing. The USA is the best example.

Unrestrained market: the USA

The first large shipments of heroin entered the US through the port of New York in the 1950s. This consisted of opium grown in Turkey and processed in the south of France near Marseilles by 'The French Connection' (Galante and Sapin 1979). The French police made it difficult to get opium into France, and the American government made it very difficult to get heroin into the USA. As a result, the French Connection devised the first generation of covert measures that initially escaped detection. They smuggled heroin in and money out through hidden panels and false petrol tanks in cars shipped in and then out of

New York. Medical devices, food products and virtually anything shipped from Europe could be discreetly stuffed with heroin. But once in the country, someone had to buy the heroin. Who were these buyers and what happened to the drugs?

Mass marketing of heroin: first wave

By 1960, the heroin showed up in the low-income areas of New York's Harlem (Gootenberg 2003). A small corps of young men went through each community giving away free samples. The give-away continued until some users developed a 'taste' for the drug and wanted more. They were then charged for their continued use. When these users were unable to pay, they had to introduce others to the drug for a fix. Soon, a small army of dealer-addicts appeared with strong incentives to find new users. Who was behind this expansion in dealing? Cuban, Puerto Rican and Mafia gangsters (Galante and Sapin 1979). But the Mafia was the only criminal enterprise at the time with wide enough access, money, organization and muscle to mass market heroin (Alexander 1988; Deitche 2012). Black criminal organizations had neither the money nor willingness to market heroin on such a scale. In fact, they were opposed to its marketing; however, they were soon replaced by more compliant and ambitious black gangsters. The new faces in Harlem managed the new heroin market for the outsiders, though they did not control it (Chepesiuk 2007).

Drug supermarkets

There were reasons for using low-income black communities to distribute heroin. First, ghettos exist not just to segregate religious or racial groups; the purpose of a ghetto is also to exploit its residents. For example, racial segregation limits the choice of housing for blacks, so landlords can charge more for sub-standard housing, just as merchants can charge more for inferior products when the range is poor (Lang 2007). Second, blacks have troubled relations with predominantly white police forces that cannot recognize one black person from another and often engage in brutality (Nelson 2000). Finally, poor black communities are sometimes used as 'red-light' districts for entertainment, gambling and prostitution that would not be allowed in white communities (Heap 2009); heroin dealing became just another item on a list of illegal activities.

During the 1960s, the expansion of the market for heroin beginning in black communities did not stop with New York. The free giving away of heroin until cadres of dealer-addicts formed occurred all across the USA. It appears to have happened from east to west, at first in large and then smaller cities. The scale, cost and complexity of such a targeted expansion of demand for heroin was way beyond the capacity of local gangsters. Furthermore, not all the cities where heroin was marketed had Mafia crime families.

Transition in source

The French Connection could not have fulfilled the 1960s expansion in demand. French and US government cooperation dismantled the French Connection despite its creativity and stealth (Friesendorf 2007). The USA paid Turkish farmers to grow alternative crops, and by 1973 the French police managed to close all the Connection's processing laboratories. Heroin stopped flowing into the USA from France. With the dismantling of the Connection, there was a temporary shortage of heroin in New York and its cost sharply increased. However, soon, French Connection heroin was replaced by that from South East Asia; and this was the heroin that fuelled the rapid national expansion in demand. A new and much larger 'connection' had been made.

The area of South East Asia that has become known as the 'Golden Triangle' (the intersection of Myanmar, Thailand and Laos) has a curious history (Chin 2009). In 1948, the Chinese Revolution led by Mao Tse-tung drove Chiang Kai-shek's Kuomintang Army (KMT) out of China and into Burma (Myanmar). To pay salaries and to buy war material, Chiang Kai-shek's army began trading local opium. By the time the KMT were driven from the Golden Triangle, what had been just a few opium growers had become a whole region of growers, and a few smugglers had become warlords with thousands of well-armed troops (Gibson 2011). The US Central Intelligence Agency (CIA) armed and paid a number of these warlords because they served as proxy fighters against local communists (Chepesiuk 1999).

But the development of opium production in South East Asia did not stop there. After World War II, the Communist Party in Vietnam challenged the continuing French colonial rule (Ho and Bello 2007). The fact that this nationalist challenge came from communists at the height of the Cold War alarmed the US government. It was believed that a communist Vietnam would lead to a communist Indochina. French and American intelligence communities (Service de Documentation Extérieure et de Contre-Espionnage and the CIA) began cultivating tribal clans as counter-insurgent forces to fight the Vietnamese Communists (Chalk 1998). This second group of proxy fighters and their military operations were also paid from local opium production and trafficking.

During the US War in Vietnam, even the South Vietnamese prime ministers, Nguyen Kao Ky, and his successor General Tran Thien Khiem, were alleged to have been heavily involved in the heroin trade (Chepesiuk 1999). Once this trade and trafficking were well established, the French and US authorities promised non-interference to the drug-lords and the Burmese military for their continued support against the communists (McCoy 2003).

It is no coincidence that heroin flooded into the USA from the very region it was fighting a war in and at the exact same time. By 1970, heroin use in the USA had become a national epidemic. It was estimated that in 1971 there were 25,000 to 37,000 American soldiers in Vietnam using heroin (Chepesiuk 1999). There were 300,000 heroin injectors in New York City alone by 1970

(Frank 2000). There were no restraints whatsoever on the marketing and demand for heroin despite the war on drugs.

Mass marketing of cocaine: second wave

Once a mass demand for one illegal drug is established, there is nothing to stop the creation of mass demand for a second. If billions of dollars could be made from heroin, other billions could be made from cocaine. Virtually the entire Cuban upper class fled to south Florida and Miami after the Baptista regime collapsed in 1959 and Fidel Castro came to power (Lopez 1987; Stepick 1992). Among those who fled to the USA were Cuban Mafia figures. Some began working closely with the CIA to assassinate Fidel Castro and overthrow the communist government (Chepesiuk 1999). This culminated in the disastrous Bay of Pigs invasion. They also set up the crime organization, La Compania, whose purpose was to raise money to fund their anti-Castro operations through the sales of heroin and cocaine in the USA (Lee 1996).

It was La Compania that initiated the high demand for cocaine in South America to supply a mass market in the USA. To meet the demand, groups of independent coca growers and smugglers joined together. This was the beginning of the drug cartels, the most ruthless and successful of which was based in Medellin, Colombia. By 1965, Colombians supplied virtually all the cocaine trafficked by Cubans, though by 1980 the Colombian cartels eclipsed the Cubans with their own trafficking into the USA through Colombian immigrant communities in Miami, New York, Chicago and Los Angeles (Chepesiuk 1999).

Here, it is important to note that the money flowing back to Colombia, Peru and Bolivia was a major destabilizing factor. As in South East Asia, the Medellin cartel was able to bribe government officials, the police and military and pay for its own well-armed private army (de la Torre 2008). They even provided social services to poor communities in Medellin and came to rival the national government in power and influence. Their example was not lost on others. Soon, revolutionary groups in Peru and Colombia turned to cocaine production and sales to fund their armies and operations; then right-wing paramilitaries who opposed the revolutionaries and who fought against land reforms did the same (Holmes and de Pineres 2006). The Colombian, Bolivian and Peruvian governments at different times found themselves in a three-way fight between well-financed drug traffickers, right-wing groups and revolutionary movements. However, they did not have the capacity for such a fight and turned to the USA for help.

The USA has provided military assistance to these governments at least since 1999 (Veillette 2006). Thousands of civilians have been killed and there have been hundreds of human rights violations in the cross-fire between militarized interests. Also, as in South East Asia, after 1979, US intelligence was more than simply aware of the role that cocaine trafficking played in funding the operations of the groups they supported. They knew about the long series of human rights violations by the Contras revolutionary movement in Nicaragua in their struggle against the socialist Sandinista government. The US Congress was expressly opposed to the Contras receiving continued funding. But in US Senate hearings, it was disclosed that Oliver North, a member of President Ronald Reagan's National Security Council, and other senior officials were well aware that the Contras were also involved in cocaine smuggling into the USA, to finance their operations, and turned a blind eye (Archive 2011).

Most of the cocaine trafficked by these groups ended up in the USA. But the success of increased cocaine trafficking was not immediate. At first, the huge heroin market stood in the way. When heroin hit its plateau in the 1970s, it was the drug of choice for most addicts. The end of the war in Vietnam, in South East Asia, coincided with an increasing difficulty in trafficking heroin into the USA. After 1980, Afghanistan became the primary source of most opium production and trafficking in the world community (McGowen 2003). But in the USA, a second generation was balking at initiating heroin use. The younger brothers, sisters, children and neighbours of addicts had witnessed its destruction. The heroin 'epidemic' began to wane. The stage was set for a new drug to be marketed to this next generation.

Crack cocaine

At first, cocaine was an unlikely candidate for mass marketing to the next generation because it was too expensive and had limited availability. But all of that changed with crack cocaine. As early as 1974, young people in Lima, Peru, had discovered the following. If bicarbonate of soda was mixed with cocaine and smoked, they could experience an enormous high from a very small amount of cocaine (Webb 1998). Drug traffickers took note. There was now a way to market cocaine to the next generation at a fraction of its previous cost. By 1985, the first social marketing of heroin in US black and Latino ghettos was repeated with crack cocaine, which was given away to get a critical mass of users and was targeted at the anti-heroin generation. Once addicted, like heroin addicts, crack cocaine addicts turned to drug dealing to support their own habits. The advertising pitch this time was that crack was better, cheaper, non-addictive and not heroin. The second wave or 'epidemic' of illegal drug use was underway.

The retail distribution of crack cocaine could have been done in the same way that heroin was trafficked – through networks of covert dealers who discreetly exchanged money for drugs. In heroin dealing, elaborate precautions were taken as to when and where there was the possibility of police surveillance and arrest. So, heroin money-for-drug exchanges took place in alleys, hallways, at the back of bars and restaurants, off-street in houses and apartments, and even through holes in brick walls. It was decided instead to sell crack cocaine directly to large networks of young dealer-users who worked as independent entrepreneurs who were allowed to keep a percentage of their sales (Jacobs 1999).

Suddenly, young people who might otherwise have been unemployed, without job-skills or an education had an opportunity to make large sums of money. Profits from addiction to drugs were taken to a new level where the objective of each dealer was to get as many repeat buyers as possible. Entrepreneurial crack dealing is reputed to have first started in the low-income areas of black South Central Los Angeles in 1988 and became a national phenomenon by 1992 (Webb 1998). The source of this cocaine was a sophisticated network of Colombian traffickers whose products initially came through Miami. The controversy around this beginning and the traffickers is that they are alleged to have been linked to the Nicaraguan Contras and to have operated with at least the knowledge of the CIA (ibid.).

A new way to deal

The number of street-level freelance dealers expanded. Street gangs got involved as well. Virtual armies of young independent dealers took over public spaces in communities already embattled from years of heroin dealing and abuse. The young crack dealers began competing with one another for optimal locations and times to sell. The results were drive-by shootings (Rivlin 1995); a phenomenon unseen in the USA since prohibition.

There was a reason why public sales were so important to young crack cocaine dealers. By far, the most money made was with people who drove into their communities to make volume purchases. These communities continued to serve as drug supermarkets for people in the larger metropolitan areas who were primarily recreational drug users. It turned out that local purchasers and users constituted only a small part of the overall crack market serviced by second and third-level dealers who did not have lucrative public turfs to deal from. Again, it was not necessary to be part of an international drug cartel, domestic gang or criminal organization to make large sums of money trafficking and distributing crack. One could conduct one's own business as a freelance trafficker or dealer.

Conclusion

There is no way to know the extent to which cartels, gangs and organized crime plus freelancers account for drug sales in any one community or city. Press releases from police departments, newspaper articles and television news and documentaries focus on drug busts of street gangs, of low-level drug dealers and of occasional freelance traffickers. The impression given is that one or the other of these groups is responsible for the pervasiveness of illicit drugs in American society after 1960. Every decade or so, there will be a report about the downfall of some organized crime figure and his involvement in drug trafficking or dealing. But, in fact, there is virtually no information about upper-level drug traffickers and distributors.

In reviewing drug busts since 1997, it is rare that any single or even combination of successful raids has resulted in shortages and price increases of either heroin or cocaine (ONDCP 1997–2012). Clearly, the wholesale supply of these drugs is large enough and the number and diversity of entities engaged in trafficking and distribution are extensive enough for interdiction and prohibition efforts to have virtually no effect (Werb et al. 2013). Also, we have to keep in mind that a high demand for these drugs did not just happen, it was created out of initial recreational drug use.

Review questions

■ What is the primary motive for drug trafficking and dealing and what has to be done to eliminate that motive?

■ What have drug traffickers and dealers done to attempt to interdict their drug supplies?

■ Do people who have never used a drug just simply start when it is made available? What must be done to start them using it?

■ How was crack cocaine marketed differently from heroin?

Further reading

Anderson, E. (1998) *Code of the Street: Decency, Violence, and the Moral Life of the Inner City*, New York: W.W. Norton.

Bearc, M. E. (2003) *Critical Reflections on Transnational Organized Crime, Money Laundering and Corruption*, Toronto: University of Toronto Press.

Fabre, G. (2003) *Criminal Prosperity: Drug Trafficking, Money Laundering and Financial Crises after the Cold War*, London: Routledge Curzon.

Jamieson, A. (1994) *Terrorism and Drug Trafficking in the 1990s*, Aldershot: Dartmouth.

Martinez, R., Rosenfeld, R. and Mares, D. (2008) 'Social disorganization, drug market activity, and neighborhood violent crime', *Urban Affairs Review*, 43(6), 846–74.

McCoy, A. W. and Block, A. A., eds (1992) *War on Drugs: Studies in the Failure of U.S. Narcotics Policy*, Boulder, CO: Westview Press.

Natarajan, M. (2006) 'Understanding the structure of a large heroin distribution network: a quantitative analysis of qualitative data', *Journal of Quantitative Criminology*, 22(2), 171–92.

Schiray, M., Geffray, C. and Fabre, G. (2001) *Drug Trafficking: Economic and Social Dimensions*, Oxford: Blackwell; Paris: UNESCO.

Stephens, R. C. (1991) *The Street Addict: A Theory of Heroin Addiction*, Albany, NY: State University of New York Press.

Review questions

Further reading

PART

II

Theoretical Perspectives

Sociological Perspectives

5

Chapter overview

Importance of theory
Structural theories of drug abuse
Social psychological theories of drug abuse
Social explanations: integrating theories and research

There is a second perspective that attempts to explain drug abuse. Sociology is the study of societies, institutions, groups and their impact on individuals. There are many different ways in which societies, institutions and groups can evolve, be organized and managed. These different patterns of social arrangements are referred to as 'social structures' (Blau 1975; Durkheim 1982; Smelser 1988). Central to sociological thinking is the observation that variations in social structures in turn frame individual behaviour.

Our language, ideas, words, names and beliefs are social. That is: our behaviours are largely defined for us. Virtually everything about us and the social world around us existed before us and were defined by others. This is not to say that the individual does not exist or is insignificant. What is pointed out is the extent to which we are social. Individuality is significant to the extent that one comes to realize through time and experience the extent to which one is social and then chooses to work within or outside of that framework. In which case, variations in social environment account for variations in groups and individuals as members of groups. If one's knowledge of the social environment or structures is accurate, then one can anticipate and even predict the attitudes, beliefs, values and behaviours of people who are members of known groups, institutions and societies.

With regard to drug abuse, *one can use drugs in a compulsive manner for purely social reasons and not have either a physical or psychological dependency or motivation*. For example, there are 'social drinkers' who feel compelled to drink alcoholic beverages regularly and heavily only with others. These same drinkers do not need to drink when they are alone. There are also 'social' drug users who use illicit drugs only when they are with others who use them. Likewise, long-term heroin injectors, who lose their drug-using friends or fall out with them for a long enough period of time, can stop using heroin without going into treatment – spontaneous recovery (Waldorf and Biernacki 1979). These examples are instants of social drug use. In reality, it is rare to find compulsive drug users who have only one source of their addiction – be it physiological, psychological or social. Outreach workers and treatment counsellors will tell you that most addictions are multifaceted.

Importance of theory

Theories are important to the study of drug abuse because they offer explanations. Hypotheses derived from theory articulate aspects of drug abuse that can be subject to scientific analyses. Then the scientific method provides us with a way to determine whether or not our theory-driven hypotheses have identified real underlying properties and have accurately characterized them. Theories are useful only if their propositions describe new, unknown and underlying properties and causes, and ultimately can be verified. Accurate theory identifies the necessary and sufficient causes of a behaviour such as drug abuse and enables us to estimate when it will occur and how one might effectively intervene. Theories found not to have such promise fall out of favour and into disuse (Latkin 2010). Let us explore the social theories that might help us to understand drug abuse.

Structural theories of drug abuse

Social conflict theory

Perhaps social conflict theory can in some way explain drug abuse. This theory holds that societies are divided by distinct classes of people. When these classes have unequal access and control of material and non-material resources, such as political power, class conflict occurs (Bottomore and Ruben 1964). Until inequality between classes is resolved, there will be conflict. New conflict theories since Karl Marx's have varied in the number of classes proposed and the conditions under which conflict occurs (Dahrendorf 1954; Skocpol 1980). They also vary in the extent to which class conflict is considered inevitable and that class resources are material (capital) or non-material (social capital, such as specialized knowledge or values) (Bourdieu 1972).

Conflict theory and drug abuse
There are illustrations of the use of conflict theory in drug abuse research. If arrests were based strictly upon drug use or violations of the law, then arrests should be randomly spread among drug users in all social classes. A research team found that actual arrests in the USA were highly selective by race (blacks) and were concentrated among the most economically disadvantaged (Lo 2003). Drug users from higher social classes ran virtually no risk of arrest. A

follow-up study was more specific (Parker and Maggard 2005). Between 1980 and 1990, the greater the shift away from labour-intensive manufacturing jobs, the higher the drug use arrest rates for blacks, even when their actual drug use had not increased. In contrast, downturns in white employment and even increased drug use were not matched with increased arrests. In effect, structural or class position predicts the extent to which drug abuse in the USA is associated with race and economic disadvantage. Whether one actually abuses drugs is secondary to police profiling and public fear of blacks and the poor.

Critiques of conflict theories suggest that conflict is not always inherent or apparent between distinct classes (Dahrendorf 1954). Groups and individuals can subjectively identify with a class that they may not objectively or materially be members of. It is also possible to have conflicts and differences within classes that override differences between classes.

Anomie and strain theory

Emile Durkheim presented a hypothesis to explain increased rates of suicide (Durkheim 1951). Specifically, there is a gap between individual expectations regarding social and economic mobility and what the same individual actually achieves. The wider the gap, the higher the rates of frustration, and the greater the sense of failure, which can lead to suicide in societies that most encourage individual achievement and responsibility. This condition is called 'anomie'. In its extreme, alienated persons can feel as if they are invisible, worthless and without meaning, purpose and a sense of self.

In Western countries with Protestant work ethics, there is a very high cultural emphasis on success in business, measured by income and public recognition (Gupta et al. 2011). This emphasis motivates many to work long and hard to succeed. But the fact is there are structural limits on how many hard workers can actually achieve societal goals since the reward structure is hierarchically arranged. Very few can actually attain sufficient money and recognition to be considered successful. This theory recognizes a fundamental reality of any social world: everyone does not have an equal opportunity to succeed legitimately. No matter how deserving and talented individuals may be, if they do not know what to do and how to do it, are without the right mentors, sponsors and sufficient resources, the chances that they will become 'successful' are limited.

Robert K. Merton (1938) clarified and focused on an essential feature of Durkheim's notion of anomie. There is a 'strain' or a gap between available opportunities and individual expectations and outcomes. To recognize this fact, or even to be vaguely aware of it, is to produce anomie (Agnew 1992a, 1992b).

Alienation and drug abuse
In a study of college student alcohol consumption, researchers found that students who were struggling academically reported significantly higher levels of

depression and were more likely to engage in non-medical use of prescription stimulants than students who were not struggling (Ford and Schroeder 2009). The struggling students believed that drugs would help them to study longer, retain more, improve their grades and avert failure of expectations. In a second study, investigators interviewed over 5,000 adolescents aged 15 to 16 from 83 neighbourhoods in Iceland (Bernburg et al. 2009). Those with normative family expectations but who had disrupted family lives and weak ties to parents were much more likely to smoke cigarettes, drink heavily and use cannabis than those with strong family ties.

In these studies illustrating alienation and strain, it is assumed that parents, and schools, convey effectively and completely societal expectations and that adolescents' failure in social relations with parents and/or school is seen as a failure to meet societal expectation. Yet it is possible to be alienated from school and parents and still succeed, as it is possible to do well in school, remain close to parents and still fail to meet societal expectations. Perhaps the socialization and influence of social actors other than parents and school were underestimated.

Reference groups

What is the best way to find out what a person thinks, believes and will or will not do? The answer is: find out their reference groups (Sherif 1964; Hyman and Singer 1968). We engage in society as members of groups, not as individuals. Groups are the basic building blocks of a social order. We cannot get to the level of social organization that we now enjoy as aggregates of unorganized individuals. Groups are significant because members subordinate their individuality to the group and internalize the group's attitudes, beliefs and values as their own (Merton and Kitt 1950). Here we are not referring to groups that you voluntarily join or drop out of. The groups discussed here are the basis of all one's taken-for-granted identities. One starts out as a member of a family, community, gender, faith, place and nationality. Then one learns later about one's class, race, marital status, occupation and generation. For instance, political affiliations and voting patterns more often than not follow social group affiliations, although voting is about individual choice (Koch 1995).

Implicit in every reference group are roles – specific sets of responsibilities and duties that one is expected to fulfil (Biddle 1979). Roles are assigned and then internalized. For example, in families, specific roles are mother, father, child, daughter, son, youngest, oldest, brother, sister, uncle, grandmother, etc. These roles are already defined for us; you watch others perform them, learn them, practise them in play, anticipate them and at the appropriate time are expected to play that role. In school, it is the same. One learns roles and plays them out: smart, clown, geek, dummy, athlete. The bottom line is that the individual plays out her or his roles within reference groups that are part of larger groups within a social order.

Reference groups and drug abuse

A sample of over 3,000 college students at two universities was asked about marijuana use (LaBrie et al. 2011). Those who abstained from marijuana did not think many other students abstained from drug use as well. They believed most other students were generally more permissive in using drugs than they were. In contrast, students who used marijuana occasionally, or regularly, believed that there was no difference in their and their closest friends' attitudes toward the drug. Heavy users believed that they had much higher approval of their marijuana use from close friends and even from families. What we learned from this research is that it mattered to each group how they were viewed by their peers, and the heavier the drug use the more it mattered.

In another study, young adults with low social integration in their Baltimore community were found to have no specific mainstream reference group (athletic, church, school or recreational centre) that they identified with in their neighbourhood (Green 2010). The same young people were later found to have significantly higher drug use as adults than those who were well integrated in the neighbourhood as youths. In effect, a non-drug using reference in one's teens appears essential to abstinence from drugs as an adult.

Perhaps reference group theory is an improvement over anomie and social conflict theories because it is more focused and more narrowly specifies a possible source of motivation for drug use and abuse. But it is also possible that reference groups may not be the only motivation. However, there is another closely related structural theory that might be a better candidate – social control.

Social control theory

Social control theory is the study of the conditionality of social order and focuses on incomplete socialization as a cause of deviance (Winfree et al. 2007). A key observation of social control theorists is that there are two forms of social control (Ross 1969). The first is the more powerful form of control. It comes through individual internalization of societal norms and values. We learn to act without a second thought to the thousands of norms and values for particular social circumstances such as walking streets, driving a car, using money, eating in public or riding public transportation. The second form of social control is external, as in passing a law and using formal punitive measures and force. If anyone violates the law, he or she should be arrested and punished in this form of control. You get compliance by a massive show of force; you put thousands of police and armed troops on the streets and dare anyone to break the law. This is a much less effective way to control the public than by having wide acceptance of norms and values. External control is limited; if enough people choose to confront the police and the troops, these authorities will be ineffective at maintaining social order.

Social control theory and drug abuse

More recent formulations of social control theory have focused on aspects of social bonding between adolescents and socialization agents such as parents and schools (Hirschi 1969). 'Incomplete bonding' explains delinquency and criminal behaviour as illustrated in the following study. In the 2005 (US) National Survey on Drug Use and Health (a nationally representative sample of persons aged 12 and older), researchers found the following: adolescents with strong bonding to family and school were much less likely to report non-medical prescription drug use (Ford 2009). Those with weak bonding were much more likely to use prescription drugs inappropriately. In another illustration of ineffective social control, 165 Canadian adults were asked about their awareness of laws against smoking cannabis and if they felt bound by the law (Brochu et al. 2011). Their responses were that these laws were 'absurd, harsh, excessive and ridiculous'. The laws were just on paper, but did not apply to real life – they clearly had not internalized the law.

A weakness of anomie and social control is that they both focus on societal expectations and norms as central points of reference. Anyone who does not meet these expectations (strained) or has not internalized them (bonded) is hypothesized, as in anomie, to be lacking in sufficient social controls to remain committed to mainstream society. In effect, these are necessary but not sufficient conditions to explain deviance such as drug abuse. Here as well, there may be other sources and better explanations. Maybe, instead of societal expectations and norms, a more powerful explanation of drug abuse might be found by focusing on the conditions and circumstances of drug abusers, such as subcultures.

Subcultures

The concept of culture is taken directly from social anthropology and can be defined as the taken-for-granted assumptions about how society is and should be organized and about one's place within society (Schwartz 1972; Gelder 2005). Culture is our map and commonly held vision of the society we are immersed in. With regard to culture, we are like fish in water. If you have never been out of the water, do you know that you are wet? The answer is 'no'. If you have never jumped out or been pulled out of your culture, you have no idea whether you are in water or are wet.

What makes culture interesting is that it is possible simultaneously to have multiple cultural affiliations – to swim in several different kinds of water. Multiculturalism is obvious in immigrant households where the primary culture and language might be Chinese and Mandarin or Brazilian and Portuguese and the secondary culture and language might be Canadian and English. Or the multiple cultural affiliations may not be as obvious as in having family roots in Sicily and Ireland, but growing up in New Jersey or spending one's formative years in London and Northern California – a virtual mix of ethnic and regional cultures. There may be a third and even fourth sub-identity.

Participation in multiple cultures and identities is not equal. One has major identities, and secondary ones referred to as 'subcultures' (Fischer 1995). Furthermore, subcultures can be complimentary, in conflict with one another, in conflict with the major culture or simply apart from one's primary culture.

The idea of subcultures can then be used to explain any deviant behaviour such as drug abuse. Youth gangs were the earliest examples of deviant subcultures studied by sociologists (Thrasher 1933) and drug addicts were second (Stephens 1991; Golub et al. 2005). This is because the concept of subculture has several important insights about gangs and drug abusers. First, their delinquency or drug use is shaped and motivated directly by the group, and only secondarily by general society. The group is a subculture because it has its own norms, beliefs, values, a hierarchy and a division of labour. The group has its own explanations and justification for drug dealing and using drugs. In effect, any one individual's drug use is an outcome and even requirement of membership and engagement in a drug-using subculture. These individuals are a part of a drug-using world within a larger world that is at odds with one another.

Subcultures and drug abuse
Teams of investigators interviewed over 300 prostitutes, drug dealers and homeless people in Miami, Chicago, Harlem, San Francisco and Los Angeles, Denver, Newark and Philadelphia (Ratner 1993). Respondents described the formation of a crack cocaine dealing and using subculture where expectations were formed and behaviours were selected and repeated by dealers, between dealers and users, and among users. The expectation of transactional sex is one such norm where sex was bartered for drugs, and rape became expected for non-payment of debts. In another study, 45 crystal methamphetamine users were recruited and interviewed in Sydney, Australia (Degenhardt and Topp 2003). It turns out that meth users were part of a long-running party scene in which a variety of drugs had been used. Users kept each other informed about drug effects and there were elaborate precautions and preparations made in the event that someone overdosed or was in danger from drug side effects. The information flow, precautions and preparations were only possible because a subculture had evolved among party-going users.

Discussion of structural theories

None of these structural theories are mutually exclusive. In anomie and strain theories, societal expectations sit squarely in the mind of those who have failed (in anomie) to bridge the gap (strained) between expectation and performance. Social control explains the same societal norms as does anomie and strain but in terms of the outcomes of the extent of bonding between adolescents and societal representatives such as schools and parents. In effect, anomie and strain place social structure in the people who experience it, while social control puts it in the relationship between them and societal agents. Reference groups and subcultures attempt to explain the same phenomenon – how it is possible to have small numbers of people whose behaviour is blatantly contrary to societal norms and expectations and who are viewed as deviants. In reference groups the deviance comes with membership of the deviant group, while the notion of subculture focuses on the norms, rules and worldview of the deviant group.

One can see in the development of structural theory a movement toward greater specificity of cause from large class divisions to small groups – reference groups and subcultures. The strengths of these theories with reference to drug abuse are: (1) that they provide the big picture or the social context for human behaviour; and (2) they explain how small groups can end up in conflict and in defiance of general social norms and expectations. The weakness or limits of structural theories are: (1) that they presume that societies are single and well-integrated social systems, even if segments are in conflict with one another, and that all members know the rules and expectations even if they do not or cannot follow them; and (2) they explain human behaviour in aggregate as a function of group membership and identification. These theories do not explain individual behaviour. Next, we will review sociological theories that attempt to explain the effects of social structures and influence on individuals. These are social psychological approaches.

Social psychological theories of drug abuse

At the core of social psychology is the concept of 'symbolic interaction', attributed to Max Weber and George Herbert Mead (1977). Herbert Blumer, a student of Mead, defined the term. Symbolic interaction is defined as: individuals responding to what they perceive about others based upon the meanings they attribute to their perceptions (Blumer 1969). These meanings change and are rechanged through social interactions. It is important to note that the medium of perception consists of symbols such as facial images, body movements, language, graphic designs, specialized vocabulary or clothing for specific occasions. All encounters and interactions with others are understood through symbols and images that are imbued with meaning.

Alfred Lindesmith, who worked under Herbert Blumer, first applied this theory to drug abuse in the USA. It was Lindesmith's view that addicts derived no pleasure from their drug use and were compelled to use a drug out of fear of withdrawal. Addiction was essentially a disease in which the addict was compelled to use drugs (Lindesmith 1938). When Lindesmith's view was published, it was roundly condemned because it did not conform to the image of addicts as criminals. The Federal Bureau of Narcotics attempted to suppress Lindesmith's work and ignore its policy implications (Keys 2008). But despite government opposition, his book, *Opiate Addiction* (1947), has been used by researchers and practitioners for over 60 years and has been a starting point for a number of social psychological theories derived from symbolic interaction. The oldest of these social psychological theories is labelling theory.

Labelling theory

The notion of societal 'tagging' or labelling of specific behaviours and people as deviant can be traced back to the writing of Edwin Lemert and Frank Tannenbaum in the 1930s, though it is Howard Becker who fully articulated labelling theory. Becker wrote (1963, p. 9): '*social groups create deviance by making rules whose infraction creates deviance*'. In other words, individuals who are thought to violate the rule are separated from society and are labelled 'outsiders'. In these cases, what is rejected and considered deviant is not inherent in the violator or in his or her actions. The deviance is due to the rules and sanctions – the label – that arbitrators of society have imposed upon the action and actor. Labels are socially constructed and reconstructed by the group; the violator does not have the capacity to label him or herself in the eyes of others.

Furthermore, once labelled, the violation and the person tied to the violation are stigmatized for further societal condemnation (Goffman 1963). The social psychology of labelling theory is that violators internalize the label and the stigma, and then see themselves that way. So, 'I use drugs because I am an addict (and criminal)' – there are no other reasons. So declared deviant actors identify themselves with the stigma and come together with similarly stigmatized others.

Labelling theory and drug abuse

Individuals were interviewed who were considered already deviant because they were physically disabled (Goulden et al. 2001). This is primary deviance. They were also found to be highly susceptible to becoming addicted to drugs – secondary deviance. Key to their increasing dependencies as disabled and as addicts was their progressively deeper internalization of stigma associated with each identity. In other words, one stigma and label can lead to a second stigma and label. In a second study, Danish adolescents, aged 15–16, were interviewed in 28 focus groups (Ostergaard 2009). As there are stages to pass in becoming a marijuana user (Becker 1953), the investigators found similar stages to becoming heavy alcohol users. The process starts with the demystification of the risks associated with alcohol followed by learning to enjoy losing control while drinking. Once engaged in heavy drinking, identification as such and the stigma associated with it are quickly internalized.

Critically, one of a number of problems with labelling theory is that it is more applicable and convincing after the fact – *ex post facto*. One cannot predict an action or outcome from this theory; one can only see it after the fact. Also, based upon symbolic interaction, two people can perceive the same label differently. Labelling theory assumes that there is a consensus of perceptions on what constitutes deviance and who the deviants are. That is: those who wish to enforce the rules and their definition of 'deviant' and those who will be stigmatized as deviant perceive the same label and meaning. What happens if such a consensus does not exist as in the case where a government insists that marijuana use is illegal and deviant, but a sizeable proportion of the general public disagrees? In this circumstance, marijuana smokers can defy the label and will not be effectively stigmatized. In labelling theory, the potential and flexibility inherent in variations of perception and symbols are not used. The next theory does not limit itself in this way.

Social learning theory

Formulated by the psychologist Albert Bandura (1977), social learning proposes that one learns all behaviours, deviant or otherwise, in three structured ways: (1) by careful observation of live models that demonstrate the behaviour that will subsequently be imitated; (2) by verbal instruction in which a specific behaviour is outlined and described in detail; and then (3) symbolically where real or fictional characters demonstrate the behaviour. The latter can occur in any medium such as in books, on radio, television, the Internet and even in one's imagination. Social learning suggests that the sources of learned behaviours are virtually infinite, where no two individuals necessarily have the same sources and developmental history. In which case, two individuals who are dependent on drugs can have arrived at their drug use from different sources and may be sustained in their drug use by very different processes. There is no need for a label and stigma to explain their behaviour and identity. In this theory the full flexibility of symbolic interaction is utilized.

Social learning and drug abuse

Puerto Rican adolescents from public and private schools in San Juan, Puerto Rico, were asked about cigarette, alcohol and marijuana use (Miller et al. 2008). Participants who perceived greater peer approval of substance use were more likely to use all three substances than participants who did not perceive such approval. This finding could be explained by reference groups or subcultures. But what this study pointed out is that the mechanics of drug use were not simply peer influence. The investigators isolated the pathway by which these young people's drug use was facilitated. Peer and parental approval facilitated selective teen learning of how to acquire and use cigarettes, alcohol and marijuana.

Like reference groups and labelling theory, social learning theory is *ex post facto*. But social learning is much more flexible in attributing cause than labelling theory. It can be applied in ambiguous situations where a consensus between authorities and the public may not exist on what causes drug use. But like labelling theory, social learning explains the social context of drug abuse after the fact. Each structural theory reviewed here may have identified some important conditions for drug use, but none of them are sufficient explanations that can predict who in advance will use and become dependent upon drugs. The next theory, social networks, may take us a step closer.

Social networks

When we are able to identify the people who facilitate social learning, or describe the people who label some type of behaviour and stigmatize persons who act out that behaviour, we identify these people by their roles – i.e. peers, parents, teachers, authorities or mentors. We are saying that the source of labelling or social learning is some specific aggregate of people, when, in fact, the social influence may be coming from only a few individuals who play these roles. Actors who are able to label others may just have higher social capital and influence.

Social network theory can specify these differences. By specifying which specific relationship, and the frequency and nature of the contact between a single individual and everyone they have contact with, we are able to lay out a social network in a much more thorough and precise way than any theory reviewed so far. 'Nodes' become actors within a network and 'ties' are the relationships between actors (Scott 1991). A unique capacity of social network analysis is the ability to map graphically nodes and ties between parents, peers, etc. in someone's network (Wasserman and Galaskiewicz 1994). That is: we can explore to what extent relations (ties) between specific parents and peers affect our research subject and influence whether or not they, for example, use drugs. Through social networks we are able to map out the source, frequency and attributes of the specific social influences on an individual.

Social networks and drug abuse

A social network of 49 Vietnamese injection drug users (IDUs) and 150 IDUs of other ethnicities were mapped and analysed in Melbourne, Australia (Aitken et al. 2008). The purpose of the study was to determine the extent to which hepatitis C had infected their networks. The Vietnamese IDUs were much more interconnected than the other IDUs. Each was a member of at least one dense sub-network of injectors. For this reason, the Vietnamese IDUs were at much higher risk of infection. The networks of the other IDUs were much more dispersed which reduced their hepatitis risk. Without social network analysis, this qualitative distinction in networks with clear epidemiological implications would have been missed. Prevention efforts for the Vietnamese IDUs needed to be approached differently than for the others.

In another study, 426 young opiate users in Yunnan province, China, were recruited and interviewed about their risk of sexually transmitting the human immunodeficiency virus (HIV) to partners (Li et al. 2011). Opiate users with multiple sexual partners took significantly higher risks of acquiring HIV than those without multiple partners. Through interconnected sexual networks in which there was very little condom use, there was a very high likelihood that HIV was passing between partners in the networks. A general educational intervention would not be effective in this case. An intervention that targets specific opiate-user networks would. Interventions at the level of specific social networks are desperately needed to prevent an HIV/AIDS pandemic in the province.

Social explanations: integrating theories and research

It is also apparent from the research using these theories that no one of them is sufficient to explain the causes of drug use and dependency. Research exclusively using one or the other theory is not going to advance our understanding of drug abuse – only specific aspects of it. The field would be at an impasse without a way to go beyond these limits.

Fortunately, we are not at an impasse and have a way to proceed that is largely methodological. If each theory focuses on some distinct aspect of social structure, why not test them together and simultaneously? We want to determine which theory is the best explanation and what are the relationships between theories. So, instead of single theories trying to explain drug abuse, we have the combined strength of several. Perhaps, by combining them, we will get closer to specifying the necessary and sufficient conditions to explain drug abuse and even to predict it.

There are several studies that have done precisely this sort of comparative analysis. What are they and what did they find? In the first, a large sample of adolescents in grades 7 to 12 in the US Midwest was interviewed regarding their drug use (Akers and Lee 1999). Analysis of their responses revealed that marijuana use increased with age. Variables from social learning and social control or social bonding were used to explain this increase. Although variables in each theory were significantly related to increasing marijuana use by age, the social learning variables were collectively stronger predictors. In a second study using 2006 Monitoring the Future Survey data (a national survey given annually in the USA to young adults in secondary schools and colleges), the authors explored non-prescription drug use using social control and social learning variables (Higgins et al. 2009). Again, social learning was the best overall predictor.

In a second Monitoring the Future Survey, social bonding and social learning variables were used to explore lifetime methamphetamine use (Stanley and Lo 2009). The results showed that methamphetamine use increased when social bonding was weakest and social learning was strongest. In effect, social bonding has an impact that is mediated through social learning. Occasionally, one or the other theory is more useful in explaining drug use for different subgroups. Based upon the US National Household Survey of Drug Abuse, an investigator tested the efficacy of general strain, social learning and self-control theories in explaining tobacco, alcohol and marijuana use among 18 to 25-year-old respondents (Preston et al. 2006). He found that psychological strain, social learning and low self-control were all significantly related to chronic drug use. However, social strain was a better predictor of chronic drug use for minorities, while social learning was the best predictor for non-minority group members.

Review questions

- What is the importance of using theory to explain drug abuse?
- What do structural theories explain and how are they used to explain drug abuse?

- How is social conflict theory different from anomie or strain theory?
- How do reference group, social control and subculture theories explain drug abuse?
- How are social psychological theories different from structural theories?
- How do labelling, social learning and network theories explain drug abuse?
- Are any of these theories mutually exclusive? Do any overlap?

Further reading

Denham, B. E. (2008) 'Folk devils, news icons and the construction of moral panics', *Journalism Studies*, 9(6), 945–61.

Fullilove, M. T., Heon, V., Jimenez, W., Parsons, C., Green, L. L. and Fullilove, R. E. (1998) 'Injury and anomie: effects of violence on an inner-city community', *American Journal of Public Health*, 88(6), 924–7.

Goode, E. (1973) *The Drug Phenomenon: Social Aspects of Drug Taking*, Indianapolis, IN: Bobbs-Merrill.

Hawdon, J. (2005) *Drug and Alcohol Consumption as Functions of Social Structures: A Cross-cultural Sociology*, Mellen Studies in Sociology, vol. 47, Lewiston, NY: Edwin Mellen Press.

Mohamed, A. R. and Fritsvold, E. (2006) 'Damn, it feels good to be a gangsta: the social organization of the illicit drug trade servicing a private college campus', *Deviant Behavior*, 27(1), 97–125.

O'Donnell, I. (2005) 'Violence and social change in the Republic of Ireland', *International Journal of the Sociology of Law*, 33(2), 101–17.

Wallace-Wells, B. and Magnuson, E. (2007) 'How America lost the war on drugs', *Rolling Stone*, (1041), 90–119.

Criminological Perspectives 6

Chapter overview

- The sociology of deviance
- From deviance to normalization
- Drugs and crime
- New criminologies of everyday life
- Conclusion

A third perspective on drug use has come from criminology. Criminology is the study of crime and deviance and responses to criminality. It has been an influential perspective on drug-taking since one of its core purposes is to help explain why people break societal rules and choose to act in ways that may be considered as 'deviant', or contrary to conventional norms of behaviour. Early criminological contributions to explaining drug use drew heavily on sociology. We will not repeat the account of sociological explanations set out in the previous chapter but instead will focus on how these early beginnings provided a foundation for a criminology of drug use that has become an important way of thinking about, and trying to explain, drug use.

One interesting point to note about criminological perspectives is that the emergence of a radical criminology, based within academic institutions in the 1950s and 1960s, coincided with the expansion of youth drug-taking in many developed Western economies. This has meant that the post-war criminology of drug use has had a radical orientation right from the start. Indeed, as we will see, a 'traditional' criminological perspective on the issue which could inform criminal justice policy and practice only really developed later on. The traditional perspectives to which the early criminology positioned itself as an alternative were in fact those developed largely within the 'psy' sciences.

The sociology of deviance

In the 1960s, early North American criminology was for a brief time transformed by the emergence of what became known as the 'new deviancy theories'. In keeping with the spirit of the times, the new deviancy theorists were committed to 'appreciating' crime, deviance and rule-breaking from the perspective of the 'deviants'. So, rather than seeing criminality as dysfunctional or pathological, and criminals as troublesome or abnormal wrongdoers, the new deviancy theorists set out to understand the world as seen by the rule-breakers themselves. As such, it provides an additional or complementary perspective to evidence from research conducted from within other frameworks. By the same token, its weakness is that it understands drug-taking *only* from the viewpoint of the rule-breakers.

Arguably the single most influential contributor to this radical new approach was Howard Becker; his 1963 book *Outsiders* became one of the most cited works ever in the discipline. *Outsiders* included reprints of two earlier pieces on drug-taking which in effect kick-started a new criminology of drug use. Drawing on research carried out in the 1950s, Becker argued that becoming a marijuana user had little or nothing to do with pre-existing personality or psychological traits. Instead, he suggested the process could best be described as one of learning how to get high:

> An individual will be able to use marihuana for pleasure only when he: (1) learns to smoke it in a way that will produce real effects; (2) learns to recognise the effects and connect them with drug use; and (3) learns to enjoy the sensations he perceives. (Becker 1963, p. 235)

In other words, according to Becker, it was only through actual experience that the motivation to use started to develop. This radically subverts the conventional idea that motivation *precedes* initiation into drug use and that the causes of drug-taking can be understood in terms of individual antecedent deficits or weaknesses. In the second reprinted piece, he takes this analysis further to look at how 'beginners' can go on to become regular users. Becker argued that it was through participation in a subculture of drug use that the social forces that might otherwise constrain or limit use could be overcome. Within a subculture of marijuana smoking, not only could participants get ready access to the drug, but they would also have a space where use did not need to be kept secret and where a ready set of moral justifications for breaking conventional societal prohibitions could be learnt. So Becker's account claimed to explain not only initiation into smoking marijuana but also how this could develop into a regular and sustained activity within a drug-taking subculture.

Other work in this vein, which drew on Becker and the new deviancy perspective, included Harold Finestone's famous essay, 'Cats, kicks and color', which examined the subcultural world of young African American heroin users in Chicago (Finestone 1964). Finestone explored how taking on the role of the 'cool cat' immersed in a heroin lifestyle provided a way of dealing with the pains of segregation and discrimination in American society in the 1960s. This idea of 'delinquent subcultures', a term coined by Albert Cohen (1957), as creative solutions to the difficulties experienced by marginalized groups was part of a broader and rich stream of subcultural theory within criminology in the 1960s and 1970s.

Another seminal work that followed in Becker's wake was British criminologist Jock Young's book *The Drugtakers* (1971). In many respects, Young's work provided the fullest account of a criminology of drug use from the new deviancy perspective. His central aim was to uncover and understand the *meaning* attached to drug use, by users, their peers and wider society. Echoing Finestone, Young argued that drug use provides an apparent solution to a range of problems experienced by different groups in society. Within each group, the meanings of that drug use, and the related drug-taking practices that emerge, are shaped and reshaped by the specific social, economic and cultural position of the group. So, for example, cannabis smoking amongst middle-class students in Notting Hill in West London in the late 1960s is very different from the smoking of the same drug by black jazz musicians in 1940s New York City. In this way, Young downplayed the significance of pharmacological effects which had traditionally been at the centre of attempts to explain drug use – and, indeed, which remain key to certain types of explanations today. Instead, he highlighted the social and cultural context.

A further distinctive feature of Young's contribution was the emphasis he placed on social reaction. Drawing on Becker's (and Edwin Lemert's) notion of labelling theory, he described how a process of what he termed 'deviancy amplification' operated. In brief, he argued that increased media scrutiny of, and police attention towards, young people's drug use turned out to be counter-productive. By serving to heighten feelings of alienation from mainstream society, and to increase a sense of community and shared identity among young people, the social reaction to drug use tended to prolong and deepen involvement in drug-taking subcultures. In other words, social disapproval was not only ineffective, it actually made the 'problem' worse. We place the word 'problem' in scare quotes here because, of course, from the perspective of young people, their drug-taking was in fact a *solution* to some of the broader problems and difficulties they were experiencing in society.

The new deviancy theories laid the foundation for a radical criminology of drug use. As we have seen, scholars like Becker, Finestone, Young and others painted a picture of youthful drug-taking that in most respects was the exact opposite of the conventional view, revolving around three central claims:

- Motivation to experiment with drugs is generally not caused by pre-existing personality traits or individual psychological 'weaknesses'; rather, it is a learned experience (people 'learn how to get high').
- For some social groups, drug use is a meaningful activity that may be understood as beneficial or positive for them.
- Social condemnation of drug-taking, including police enforcement of the drug laws, is often counter-productive.

The implications of this perspective are obviously challenging. In the closing chapter of *The Drugtakers*, Jock Young explored some of these, setting out what he described as 'ten rules' for delineating a path towards a 'sane and just drugs policy'. We need not look at all of these here but three of them, in particular, illustrate well the powerful implications of these new deviancy perspectives on drug use. Rule 3 asserted that we must 'avoid designating behaviour as sickness'. He suggested that disease models, and the treatment modalities which derive from them, undermine individual responsibility and so, consequently and somewhat ironically, help to cause the very problems they are meant to prevent, such as relapse.

Rule 7 stated that policy-makers ought to attempt to 'maintain cultures'. By this, Young meant, and here Becker's influence is most obvious, that it was within drug subcultures that practices of 'safe' drug-taking were learnt and passed on to new 'entrants'. Young argued that to 'harass and undermine' existing subcultures risked removing the primary source of norms and values which actually limit more dangerous consumption practices and encourage self-regulation. Rule 8 called for 'positive propaganda', suggesting that 'misleading and inaccurate' information which exaggerated risk undermined the credibility of anything that figures of authority said. For Young, it was only information that was rooted in the values of the subculture and 'told the truth' from that perspective that was likely to be able to have any educational impact at all.

This is all heady stuff! So it is surprising to note that after this explosion of new thinking and radical ideas about drug use in the 1960s, this early criminological perspective rapidly disappeared from view. In fact, Jock Young's book published in 1971 turned out in retrospect to be almost the final contribution to this phase of scholarship. Nevertheless, the legacy of this work has continued to be influential. Recent research, for example on youth dance cultures and drug-taking in San Francisco, without citing their work, clearly owes a heavy debt to the likes of Becker and Finestone in its adoption of an 'appreciative' stance to the study of 'raves' and dance parties (Hunt et al. 2010). Indeed, this illustrates how the idea of the importance of understanding drug cultures in their own terms has become almost mainstream and no longer directly connected with the new deviancy theories of half a century ago. In this sense, this early contribution has left an indelible footprint on the criminology of drug use.

From deviance to normalization

One obvious hallmark of new deviancy approaches to the criminology of drug use was the idea that drug-taking was a deviant, minority activity. As patterns of use changed over subsequent decades, and youthful experimentation with drugs like marijuana became more commonplace, the usefulness of 'deviancy' perspectives started to be questioned. Put simply, if young people taking drugs was no longer so exceptional, what sense did it make to understand it as an unusual or underground or deviant pursuit?

The strongest challenge to the deviancy framework came from a group of researchers led by Howard Parker who were based at the University of

Manchester in the UK. Parker and his colleagues carried out a longitudinal study of young people in the north west of England. The baseline data involved a survey of nearly 800 14-year-olds undertaken in 1991, with the cohort then followed up at intervals, with the latest wave in 2005 (Parker et al. 1998; Aldridge et al. 2011). Based on their emerging findings from the early phases of the study, they argued that, by the mid-1990s, drug-taking in England had undergone a process of *normalization*, moving 'from the margins *towards* the centre of youth culture' (Parker et al. 1998). They set out five dimensions of normalization:

1   *Availability*. Ready access to drugs is an obvious prerequisite to any idea of normalization. Sustained increases in availability have been found in numerous studies. Parker's team found that by age 16, around 80 per cent had been in 'drug offer situations' (Parker et al. 2002). This contrasted powerfully with drug scenes in earlier decades where being able to get hold of drugs was something restricted to the small number of those 'in the know' who were involved in the relatively hidden subculture. An important finding from Parker's study was that this widespread availability was not a result of aggressive or predatory drug dealing (the stereotypical 'drug pusher' at the school or college gates), as some media or political accounts wanted to claim, but rather was facilitated by friendship networks. The practice of 'sorting' friends or acquaintances by acquiring and distributing drugs to them became a central feature of drug-taking amongst young people.

2   *Drug trying rates*. Rates of drug trying indicate levels of experimentation with drugs, in answer to the question 'Have you ever taken ...?' Even if many young experimenters only try a drug once or twice and then never again, it is an indication that drug-taking has become normalized, according to Parker et al. In their study, they found that around half of their sample reported trying drugs at least once, mostly cannabis (Parker et al. 1998, 2002). This perhaps was the strongest indicator of all in support of the normalization claim. If half of young people were trying something, how could it possibly be understood or viewed as 'abnormal' or unusual? The 50 per cent figure found in the north west of England turned out to be at the higher end, compared to rates in other parts of the UK, but on a par with those found in studies of young people in North America (SAMHSA 2011).

3   *Drug use rates*. As we have already observed, a number of young people who experiment with drugs turn out to be 'one-off' triers who do not go on to become regular consumers. This indicates that it is important to know how many are regular or current users. This is not so easy to measure exactly, but a proxy indicator is usually taken as 'use in the last month'. Reviewing a range of studies, as well as drawing on their own findings, Parker et al. (2002) suggested that around one-quarter of young adults were 'current' users, mainly of cannabis but also including significant levels

of stimulants. Although a less dramatic figure than the 50 per cent experimentation rate, this level of regular drug-taking represents a transformed picture compared to previous decades.

4   *Peer accommodation.* With drug-trying rates approaching one in two, it is inevitable that non-drug-using young people will have contact with drug-taking peers. In contrast to the situation of earlier decades, where drug subcultures were hidden and involved a very small minority of youths, Parker's study showed that awareness of, and encounters with, drugs and drug-taking had become commonplace by the 1990s. An important question, then, is how abstainers or former triers view their drug-taking peers. If they remain highly negative and critical in their attitudes, this would be a serious limitation of any idea of normalization. In fact, they found quite high levels of tolerance and accommodation of others' drug use. Put simply, for many young people, it was not problematic that friends or acquaintances used drugs, even if they themselves did not. This tolerance extended primarily to cannabis smoking and, to a lesser degree, to ecstasy. Strongly negative attitudes to the use of drugs like heroin remained very evident. Distinctions were also drawn between 'sensible' recreational use and 'excessive' consumption, with the former viewed as reasonably acceptable, the latter clearly not. According to Parker, this all indicated that the broad claim of peer accommodation was supported by their study but that this was a reasoned and discriminating tolerance which distinguished between acceptable and unacceptable behaviour. In other words, young people and young adults who are themselves abstainers seem to respect the right of their peers to use (some) drugs 'sensibly'.

5   *Cultural accommodation of drug use.* The fifth and final dimension of normalization is much harder to substantiate or confirm. To what extent does society as a whole tolerate sensible recreational drug-taking? One set of evidence that Parker and colleagues pointed to was the increasing level of references to drugs in TV programmes, comedy and films. The same distinctions that we have just described also appeared to be drawn between more or less dangerous drugs and between sensible and excessive consumption. They also argued that it had started to become possible for high-status or high-profile individuals, such as politicians, to admit to previous drug-taking without this automatically proving disastrous for their careers, as would have been the case in previous decades. Here we could contrast two statements by US presidential candidates. In 1992, Bill Clinton admitted on the campaign trail that he had once smoked marijuana but insisted he 'didn't inhale'. Barack Obama, on the other hand, made a point in 2006 of saying that he had inhaled, adding: 'that was the point'. It is hard to imagine even Clinton's equivocal confession being made by a candidate in, say, the 1960s or earlier, let alone Obama's outright admission. Perhaps, then, despite the continuing hysteria about some aspects and types of drug consumption, we can see a certain level of cultural accommodation of drug use.

The normalization thesis has not been without its critics. Shiner and Newburn (1997, 1999) have argued that Parker and colleagues have exaggerated the degree of change that has taken place and that drug use remains a minority pursuit within youth culture and one that is viewed negatively by the majority. Nevertheless, despite these criticisms, the prevailing view today, some 20 years since the idea was first articulated, is that young people's experience of drugs in many Western developed countries has been transformed in the last couple of decades. Studies from around Europe (Zobel and Gotz 2011), in the USA (Hunt et al. 2010) and elsewhere have repeatedly substantiated Parker's findings. Further, the idea of a move 'from the margins to the mainstream' appears to capture the nature of this transformation quite well, even if there is disagreement about the precise scale or scope of this change. The language of 'deviance' used by Becker and others simply no longer fits in the way that it once did.

Drugs and crime

One of the most consistent research findings in criminology has been the association between drugs and crime (Bennett et al. 2008) and this has become an important area of focus for criminological perspectives on drug use in recent decades. The basic evidence for this association is stark and seemingly unarguable: go to any prison anywhere and you will find a disproportionate number of people who use drugs or have drug-related problems, compared to peers in the general population; go to any police station and you will find the same in police cells; and go to any treatment service and many of the people you will encounter will have some kind of criminal history.

Perhaps one of the most sustained and thorough programmes to establish and explore this link has been the Drug Abuse Monitoring research which has been conducted in many countries around the world, originating in the USA in the 1980s under the banner of the Drug Use Forecasting programme. The studies all involve interviewing and drug testing booked arrestees in jails or police stations. They are intended to paint a picture of the extent of drug use at the entry point or gateway into the criminal justice system (Taylor 2002). The most recent sweep of arrestee surveys across the USA shows variations between sites in the nature of drug-crime problems but consistently demonstrates that the association exists and is significant in scale. In Chicago, for example, in 2009, 82 per cent of arrestees tested positive for the presence of a substance in their system at the time of arrest (ONDCP 2010).

If the drug–crime association is very evident, the standard explanation for it is equally clear: people with relatively expensive drug habits, and with low legitimate incomes, find themselves driven to crime to pay for their drugs – in other words, stealing to 'feed their habit'. This is known as the 'economic necessity' model. It corresponds to one part of what, according to Stevens (2011), has become the most frequently cited work on the drug–crime link: a famous paper by Goldstein (1985). Goldstein's paper, based on his research in New York City in the 1980s, focuses on what he calls the 'drugs/violence nexus', and proposes a tripartite explanatory framework:

1 *Psychopharmacological.* Some psychoactive substances can increase aggression and reduce inhibitions in ways that might raise the risk of violence.
2 *Economic-compulsive.* Addicted users are compelled to fund their habit by committing income-generating crime.
3 *Systemic.* Drug markets are unregulated by law and so are inherently violent, as this is the only means for participants to regulate their business.

As Stevens (2011) notes, surprisingly this framework has not been widely tested empirically. A study by Inciardi (1990) in Miami examined connections between crack use and violence among young people and concluded that involvement with crack heightened pre-existing propensities to deviance and criminality. Much of the violence they uncovered was carried out against fellow crack dealers, suggesting some support for the systemic explanation. Menard and Mihalic (2001), drawing on longitudinal data from youth surveys, also found that systemic violence within drug markets was the explanation most supported by the data.

It is this economic necessity model of the drug–crime link that has come to form an orthodoxy in the field which has proved highly influential on police and criminal justice policy and practice. The development of drug courts, beginning in Miami in the late 1980s and subsequently becoming an international phenomenon, was based squarely on this idea. The spread of drug interventions within criminal justice systems has become one of the prevailing features of drug policy around many parts of the world (Seddon et al. 2012). It is here that criminology has arguably had its greatest influence on mainstream practice.

This mainstream view, represented by Goldstein's influential framework, has inevitably come under scrutiny and challenge. From the 1990s, criminologists have found the picture to be less clear-cut than this, suggesting that the relationship does not go just in one direction (Seddon 2000, 2006). One puzzle is that longitudinal studies tend to show that initiation into crime often precedes the first drug use. This seems odd if it is drug-taking that is supposed to lead to crime. We also know that when people stop drug use, this is not always followed by complete desistance from crime. Again, this is perplexing if the offending is meant to be drug-driven. All this has led some criminologists to turn the drugs-cause-crime models on their head and argue that it is actually involvement in crime that leads to drug-taking (Auld et al. 1986). The argument here is that it is through participation in a criminal lifestyle and criminal networks that people first encounter drugs like heroin and crack cocaine. In this sense, it is criminality that leads to drug involvement and not the other way round.

Another strand of thinking takes a different tack and has suggested that the association between drugs and crime is rooted in the fact that both are linked to other factors that they have in common, notably socio-economic disadvantage (Seddon 2006). In other words, the fact that they co-occur is not because one causes the other but rather because they share a common foundation. This was a possibility that Menard and Mihalic (2001) also raised. This type of explanation starts to look most compelling when we examine the evidence at the community level. It has been a repeated finding that drug and crime problems tend to be found in the poorest neighbourhoods, where they sit alongside a range of other social and economic difficulties, including unemployment, low educational attainment and poor health. In other words, multiple problems, including drugs and crime, often coalesce or cluster in the poorest communities, reinforcing each other and accumulating to create an experience of multiple disadvantages (Pearson 1987; Seddon 2006). This 'urban clustering' effect first emerged in a British context in the 1980s, but could be seen several decades earlier in the USA through the classic study, *The Road to H*, by Isidor Chein and colleagues. This study described the interconnections between heroin, crime and poverty in New York City in the 1950s (Chein et al. 1964).

There are then three main models which seek to explain the drug–crime association:

1   Drugs cause crime (or the economic necessity model).
2   Crime causes drugs.
3   Drugs and crime are related to a third common factor (or set of factors).

More recent research has pointed to two important further qualifications about the seemingly universal drugs–crime association. First, in describing the drug–crime link, *specificity* is essential. There is no blanket connection between the broad categories of 'drugs' and 'crime'. Rather, what we are typically talking about are associations between particular drug-taking practices and particular forms of criminality – for example, between frequent heroin injecting and prolific shoplifting. In an important contribution, based on a study of nearly 5,000 arrestees, Bennett and Holloway (2007) show how there are in fact multiple drug–crime connections, rather than a single relationship. They argue that this diversity requires researchers and policy-makers to disaggregate or break down the relationship between drugs and crime in order to understand the quite different connections from which it is made.

Second, these specific links and multiple connections also have to be clearly *located in time and space*. The current crime of choice for crack-cocaine users in Baltimore is not necessarily the same as for their counterparts in New York City or, for that matter, Sydney or Cape Town. As well as varying by place, these connections also change over time. In England, for example, local heroin outbreaks in the 1980s were associated with rapid rises in domestic burglary and theft from vehicles (Parker and Newcombe 1987). Today, this is much less the case – the most common crime committed by heroin users is shoplifting.

And in earlier historical periods, there was no association between drug-taking and crime at all. Even as recently as the 1970s, an official study in England and Wales found that a clear majority of opiate users had no criminal history and, even among the minority with convictions, many of these related to only drug possession offences (Mott 1975).

So criminologists have shown how this consistent and widespread link between drugs and crime is, in fact, more complex than first meets the eye. In relation to drug policy, it remains extremely important. Indeed, after the HIV scares of the mid- to late 1980s, it has arguably been the drug–crime issue which has most strongly shaped the development of drug policy in many countries around the world (Seddon et al. 2012). The spectre of the drug-driven offender causing havoc in local communities has been a potent image for politicians to draw on.

New criminologies of everyday life

Since the 1990s, criminology has taken a new turn. The leading criminologist David Garland (2001a) has described this shift as the emergence of a new style of criminological thinking. He terms this new genre the 'new criminologies of everyday life'. He describes these criminologies as a related set of 'ways of thinking' about crime which together makes up a new framework which has been vitally important in the development of crime policy in both the USA and the UK.

For Garland, the common starting point for this new style of thinking is the 'premise that crime is a normal, commonplace aspect of modern society' (ibid., p. 128). In other words, it requires no special personality, pathology or abnormality and cannot be explained in terms of troubled development or 'bad' character. It is simply a particular form of behaviour which conforms to standard 'motivational patterns'.

In this mode of thinking, the criminal is viewed not as a 'deviant' but rather as a human actor who has simply taken a particular pathway of choice or set of options which involve breaking certain rules (the criminal law). And, crucially, his or her decision-making can be understood in exactly the same way as all human decision-making. That is as the product of the weighing up of costs and benefits in order to reach a decision about the 'best' course of action. For Garland, this 'rational choice' model of human behaviour has lent itself to some new directions in crime policy. The focus is now on 'shifting risks, redistributing costs, and creating disincentives' (Garland 2001a, p. 129) and moving away from older approaches based solely on punishment or correction of deviant individuals.

The influence of this development in criminology on our understandings of drug use has not been directly or explicitly set out. Nevertheless, it is quite striking and important. The normalization work discussed above was premised on a similar view about the importance of understanding drug-taking as an activity not especially different from most others. Indeed, Parker and his colleagues even talk about young people going through a process of 'cost–benefit risk assessment' in deciding 'how far to go to "buzz" and get "out of it" via alcohol or illicit drugs' (Parker et al. 1998, p. 159). This fits very closely with Garland's 'new criminologies of everyday life'.

The idea that drug-taking might be the product of a more or less rational decision is, of course, a challenging one. But perhaps it is one many might accept in relation to the type of youthful, usually short-lived, experimentation with recreational drugs that Parker and others describe. For a teenager, for example, the decision to start smoking cannabis moderately may not be a terribly irrational decision. Then, the subsequent choice by many such people to reduce or stop this smoking as they progress through young adulthood and take on new responsibilities (college, job, relationship and parenthood) may be seen as equally 'rational'. What about addictive or problematic use of substances like heroin or crack cocaine or methamphetamine?

Surely it makes no sense to see these behaviours, too, as 'rational'? Yet this is exactly what was suggested in a provocative paper co-written 25 years ago by the famous Chicago economist, Gary Becker (Becker and Murphy 1988), developing from his earlier paper on crime (1968). Setting out what they describe as a 'rational theory of addiction', Becker and Murphy argue that even the most addictive behaviour can still be understood and modelled using the same basic assumptions about rationality and utility maximization that underpin all economic perspectives on human behaviour. Well-observed phenomena in the general addiction literature like 'tolerance', 'reinforcement', 'binges' and even 'going cold turkey' are all reinterpreted within their framework. Although the theory has never hit the mainstream, for perhaps obvious reasons, other scholars have sought to develop the insights that a rational perspective highlights (Vuchinich and Heather 2003).

While the Becker and Murphy perspective might be seen as intellectually radical and unlikely to interest anyone outside academia, in fact we can see its profound influence in policy developments around the world. At a basic level, one of the perennial areas of debate on law enforcement policies and the policing of drug markets has been about whether there is a good or bad outcome to increasing the price of drugs within a given local market. Is a successful enforcement operation one which, for example, affects availability to such an extent that it makes a rock of crack significantly more expensive for a time? Or is a positive outcome one that may lead to reductions in levels of crack use? Or, conversely, does it ratchet up levels of violence in that market, as parties fight more fiercely over valuable commodities which have suddenly become scarcer? Or does it simply mean that buyers have to commit more property crimes to generate money to buy crack at its new higher price? Such debates all take place on the economic terrain set out by Becker and his colleagues – in which, to continue our example, crack consumers make rational decisions about their drug-related behaviour in the face of the specific social and economic contexts they are living in.

Drug markets are, of course, obvious places where we might expect to see the ideas of economists having import. But we can also see the influence of such economic styles of thinking in other areas of drug policy. A recent proposal in the UK, for example, suggests that recipients of social security benefits for the unemployed who are identified as dependent on drugs or alcohol should be drug-tested and required to attend an appointment at a treatment centre. Those who refuse the appointment, or who do not show up, should have their benefit payments reduced or stopped. Putting the rights and wrongs of the policy to one side, we can see very clearly that this is built on an understanding that dependent drug users, or alcoholics, are capable of weighing up the impacts of the 'sticks' and 'carrots' involved here and making rational decisions about their behaviour. The policy assumption is that many, or even a majority, will decide that it is better to go along to the treatment appointment than risk losing their benefit money. Such a policy could not be proposed if it were believed that dependent drug or alcohol consumers were irrational or 'out of control' or unable to think clearly enough to make reasoned decisions.

In certain respects, this is a quite remarkable perspective which flies in the face of many other mainstream theories of drug use and addiction, as outlined in other chapters in this book. Indeed, one of the hallmarks of the very concept of addiction has long been held to be the notion that an addicted person is no longer able to choose freely how to act. What else could addiction mean? This view has underpinned the classic disease model for many years. Jellinek's landmark book, *The Disease Concept of Alcoholism* (1960), for instance, made 'loss of control' the defining characteristic of the disease. For Jellinek, if you could control your consumption or related behaviour, you were not suffering from the disease. By seeing drug-taking and drug addiction as, fundamentally, 'normal' behaviour, in the sense of activities which can be understood as the product of normal reasoning and decision-making processes, this long tradition of thinking about drug and alcohol problems has been turned on its head.

There are further implications which illustrate the implicit acceptance of rational models into the mainstream. Pathological models of addiction, which viewed it as a symptom of an underlying problem or deficit of personality or bio-psycho-social functioning, were closely linked with prevailing approaches to treatment, which sought to address, alleviate or manage these deficiencies. More recently, new treatment interventions have been developed which are clearly based on rather different perspectives on the nature of the problems, perspectives that would be more familiar to Becker than Jellinek.

One good example is the emergence of what is known as 'contingency management' (Petry 2012). This is the simple idea that offering users of treatment services monetary incentives like shopping vouchers can be an effective way of achieving desired behavioural outcomes. One example is the idea that giving vouchers for the achievement of negative drug-test results will reduce levels of use of street drugs. Similarly, although more controversial, access to affordable housing and work opportunities have been made contingent on negative drug tests (Milby et al. 2003). Therapists have also used vouchers to reinforce the development of social skills and activities (Iguchi et al. 1997). A meta-analysis of the research evidence carried out by Prendergast et al. (2006) found strong support for the effectiveness of contingency management as an approach for reducing drug use and improving attendance and retention in drug treatment programmes.

It is evident, then, that these new styles of thinking identified by Garland as operating in the field of criminology have been particularly, and arguably unexpectedly, influential and important in the area of drug and alcohol policy and practice. Behaviour that for some may be viewed as the epitome of irrationality turns out to be usefully framed as rational.

Conclusion

The contribution of criminological perspectives on drug and alcohol use has been an interesting area over the last 50 years. Bookended by two very different Beckers – Howard and Gary – we have seen that approaches that seek to understand drug-taking in particular as rule-breaking have been potent sources of new ideas about the subject. We cannot talk about a criminology of drug use in the sense of a single approach to, or coherent set of ideas about, the issue. But we can nevertheless identify some profoundly important ideas that have been developed by criminologists, or by others with an interest in crime and its control. It therefore represents a perspective that needs to be incorporated in any broad-based understanding of the topic, and which is distinctive in its own right.

Even though many criminologists may self-identify as sociologists, or at least as sociologically inclined scholars, their contributions in this field cannot be reduced to those of sociology. This is no doubt because of the strong focus there has been within this body of work in grappling with the question of why individuals break laws or norms about conduct. From Howard Becker and Harold Finestone through to Howard Parker and Gary Becker, this has proved to be the core of criminological inquiry. In common with criminology more generally, it is also evident that Anglo-American research and thinking has dominated this set of perspectives. For example, and somewhat surprisingly, a distinctive European criminology of drug use has not really emerged to date.

Review questions

- What does Howard Becker mean when he says that marijuana users 'learn how to get high'?
- According to Young, why is social disapproval of young people's drug use (including increased police attention) counter-productive?
- What are the five dimensions of normalization? Can drug-taking be said to be 'normalized' if it remains a minority activity?

■ What are the three main models of the drug–crime link?
■ Can we understand drug-taking and drug addiction as rational behaviour?

Further reading

Aldridge, J., Measham, F. and Williams, L. (2011) *Illegal Leisure Revisited: Changing Patterns of Alcohol and Drug Use in Adolescents and Young Adults*, Abingdon: Routledge.
Seddon, T., Williams, L. and Ralphs, R. (2012) *Tough Choices: Risk, Security and the Criminalization of Drug Policy*, Clarendon Studies in Criminology, Oxford: Oxford University Press.
Shiner, M. (2009) *Drug Use and Social Change: The Distortion of History*, Basingstoke: Palgrave Macmillan.
Stevens, A. (2011) *Drugs, Crime and Public Health: The Political Economy of Drug Policy*, Abingdon: Routledge-Cavendish.
Walters, G. (2013) *Drugs, Crime, and their Relationships: Theory, Research, Practice, and Policy*, Sudbury, MA: Jones & Bartlett.

Psychological Perspectives

7

The psychology of drug abuse attempts to answer the question: 'Why do some individuals use illegal drugs and others, who live in the same environment, do not?' While nations differ on the prevalence of drug use, the prevalence of problematic drug use among individuals within countries also varies. What accounts for these individual variations? In this chapter we will examine psychological explanations for problematic drug use at the individual level.

A central consensus among those who experience drug dependency, and those who study it, is that loss of control is at the heart of problematic drug use. Long-term users and professionals alike describe addiction as the individuals no longer being able to determine their own drug use: they are compelled to use, even when it no longer brings pleasure, and even when continued use ruins their lives and harms their families and communities. A second common characteristic of those who are addicted is that they deny that they are dependent even when there is an abundance of obvious physical evidence that they are. Perhaps there are factors outside of a person's awareness that are at play here.

Factors that act on us without our conscious awareness has been a central theme in psychology since Sigmund Freud first connected his patients' physical complaints to their unconscious conflicts in the late 19th century. The work of unconscious factors has been found in research on problematic drug use. For example, children exposed to childhood adversities, including physical or sex abuse, are more likely to become drug users as adults and not remember what drove them early in life to drug abuse (Nomura et al. 2012). Many of those in treatment for substance abuse have been found to have psychiatric disorders that they were unaware of (Fergusson et al. 2008). Studies using random samples of adults in several countries have found a link between psychiatric impairment and substance abuse (Cheung et al. 2010; Fenton et al. 2012). Similar studies have found unconscious psychiatric processes closely related to problematic drug use in Australia (Teesson et al. 2010), England and Wales (Frisher et al. 2004), Germany (Bischof et al. 2005) and the USA (Harrington et al. 2011).

While the sum of all these studies points to a link between psychiatric disorder and drug use, the problem is: which comes first, the chicken or the egg? Do people turn to drug use to ease their pain from psychiatric disorder – *the self-medication hypothesis* – or does drug use lead to psychiatric disorder? Even when this problem became the focus of study, the majority of those with psychiatric problems did not go on to develop problems with alcohol and drugs (Timko and Moos 2002). Something else must be operating to produce the numbers of individuals who develop drug problems, as we saw is the case with nations in Chapter 2. What are the explanations that psychologists have developed to explain this mystery?

Psychodynamic approaches

Sigmund Freud is generally credited with the discovery of psychodynamic models of drug abuse (Brickman 1988). Trained as a neurologist in Austria in the late 1800s, Freud first sought to link all disorders to biological processes in the brain. However, after working with Charcot and others in Paris, he began to investigate the borderline of consciousness made possible by hypnosis. Charcot had begun to link physical illness to mental states by using hypnosis. Attempts were made to treat mental states like depression also by hypnosis, but with little success. When Freud returned to Austria, he discovered that by just listening to clients talk about their lives, feelings and dreams their symptoms sometimes improved. He wrote a series of case histories of his clients, using what he called 'the talking cure'.

Psychodynamic

Freud's neurological training led him to postulate that mental illness began in childhood as part of the normal developmental path from infant to adulthood. He thought all children developed patterns of dealing with the stress of growing up based on how well their parents provided love and support. He further believed that the difficulties many experienced in growing up were, as in hypnosis, not available to an individual's consciousness, but could be revealed to the individual through therapy. When a person develops *insight* into developmental issues hidden from consciousness, their symptoms are mitigated. The process of discovery, whereby the therapist acts as a guide, Freud believed, was lengthy, but ultimately led to freedom from impulses and thoughts that caused pain and suffering. Freud named his approach 'psychodynamic' because he believed it allowed feelings hidden from the conscious mind to be brought to consciousness, where they could no longer cause trouble (Mitchell and Black 1995).

Evidence

In the 19th and early 20th centuries, cases studies from individuals diagnosed by Freud and his followers were accepted as evidence of the link between unobserved unconscious processes and mental illness (Edelson 1985). Therapy conducted by skilled practitioners appeared to relieve some symptoms of mental illness for some clients. This was considered proof of the underlying processes and effectiveness of the therapy.

Promise

Freud's theories revolutionized how mental illness was defined and treated throughout Europe and the USA. His theory brought order to a confused system of classifying disorders that bridged physical symptoms with thought disturbances. No longer were individuals who were addicted to drugs placed indefinitely in sanitoriums where they received little more than custodial care. Exploring unconscious conflicts led to some effective treatments for some individuals.

Critique

Certain features of Freud's approach were controversial. First, Freud believed all individuals went through the same developmental processes because everyone's underlying biology is the same. Current biology does not support his beliefs. Second, his theories were developed before modern anthropology was able to show that all cultures do not use the same arrangements for child care and guidance (Arnfred 2005). Third, Freud's approach makes it impossible to verify independently claims of success. This has led many to assert that psychodynamic evidence is unscientific (Hale 1995). A modern scientific approach, critics contend, must allow for independent verification of claims. Fourth, if the developmental model Freud described is universal, we would expect the same rates of drug use and abuse in all cultures. As we saw in Chapter 2, there are huge differences between countries on the use of alcohol and drugs and similarly huge differences in rates of substance use disorder (Degenhardt et al. 2011).

Self-medication

Freud's followers split into several groups in the middle of the 20th century. These include Harry Stack Sullivan, Melanie Klein and Karen Horney. Karen Horney, trained in Germany before World War II, moved to the USA in 1932. She disagreed with Freud's model that coping with biological drives was the cause of mental disorder. Instead, she emphasized that children sometimes develop anxious ways of dealing with relationships as a result of their early experiences with their parents; no biological basis was necessary for such learning (Sayers 1993).

Horney began to emphasize how people develop patterns of relating to others in early childhood, and then retain mental representations of those relationships. These mental models then influence how one feels about oneself, and also impacts on how people function in new relationships. Some people have early experiences with parents and guardians that leave them with life-long problems with their own self-esteem. Everyone needs to develop ways of meeting their own needs, and also to respond to the needs of others. When an individual develops unhealthy patterns, the emphasis is purely on the self. They are preoccupied with maintaining their self-image, often at the expense of those around them. Psychologists of the self term these individuals 'narcissists'. According to this model, narcissists turn to alcohol or drugs to cope with the constant stress of trying to maintain an exaggerated sense of self.

Evidence

Psychologists from the self-medication tradition focus on how individuals either feel too much anxiety or none at all. Alcohol or drugs serve to medicate the anxiety or to put individuals in touch with their own feelings (Khantzian 1997; Hall and Queener 2007; Robinson et al. 2011). In a nationally representative sample of 34,653 adults in the USA, self-medication was linked to the onset of substance use disorders. Those with anxiety disorders at their first interview were more than twice as likely to develop a substance use disorder during the three years before their final interview (Robinson et al. 2011).

Promise

Linking addiction to the process of self-medication has great promise for understanding why drugs have such appeal for some individuals. It is clear that among those who seek treatment for addiction, many suffer from some psychic pain. It is clear that many who have survived traumatic experiences have turned to drugs or alcohol when they later experience anxiety or depression due to these earlier experiences. The ways in which people cope with trauma or anxiety serve as pathways to addiction.

Critique

While therapists providing care to some addicts report problems of self-medication as common, it is unclear as to how many with self-medication issues go on to develop problems with drugs or alcohol. Indeed, surveys have repeatedly shown that the majority of those with an anxiety or even depressive disorder *do not become addicts* (Grant 1995). While it is true that those with such disorders are more likely to develop addiction, the majority do not. It may be that among *those who seek* treatment for addiction, many use drugs to self-medicate.

Attachment theory

British psychoanalyst John Bowlby is generally credited with articulating the post-Freudian theory of *attachment*. Having observed thousands of British children separated from their parents during World War II, Bowlby began to investigate the effects of such separation on child development. Rather than focus on biologically based drives, Bowlby saw the need for all children to develop a healthy relationship with their guardians. He named this process the 'attachment behavioural system'. This line of thinking draws from research on how children develop a sense of security (Bowlby 2008).

When a parent or guardian responds consistently to the child's needs, the child develops a healthy mental representation of the self and the guardian. If the guardian is inconsistent or indifferent to the child's needs, the child develops an internally unhealthy working model of the world that persists throughout life. An unhealthy internal working model, according to this theory, will often lead to lifelong difficulties in establishing a trusting relationship with others. The theory holds that the primary task for any infant is to develop a trusting bond with their caregiver, usually the mother. Closely related to problems of trust and intimacy, children with insecure attachment models are much more likely to develop problems with fear and anxiety.

Evidence

A series of studies conducted by Ainsworth served to provide direct empirical support for attachment theory. Using observation, Ainsworth and colleagues were able to show how children behave when they are separated from their parents in a laboratory setting. About 70 per cent displayed a 'secure' style. They reacted to the parent's departure, but were not overly upset by it. They went back to playing. Another 20 per cent displayed an 'anxious-avoidant' style, characterized by not paying much attention to the mother's departure or return. The third group was termed 'anxious-ambivalent': those who cried, wanting both to be comforted and also to be let go of (Ainsworth 1991).

A body of research has provided support for this approach (Schindler et al. 2009) and found that those with attachment issues were more likely to abuse drugs (Caspers et al. 2006). These findings were replicated in five European cities among adolescents aged 14–15 (McArdle et al. 2002), and among persons entering substance abuse treatment in England (Peel 2010), among alcoholics in Belgium (Sivolap Iu 2010) and among German adolescents with a substance use disorder (SUD) (Fergusson and Horwood 1997).

Promise

Attachment theory rests on a scientific basis. Unlike various unconscious processes, attachment can be reliably measured, both in children and adults. One does not have to be a skilled therapist to uncover attachment difficulties.

Critique

Again, the majority of those with attachment difficulties do *not go on to develop a substance abuse disorder*. The great differences in rates of substance use disorders between the USA, Canada and Mexico cannot be explained by assuming that parenting varies amongst the countries. Parents are not three or four times more indifferent to their children in Buffalo, New York, as compared with Toronto, Ontario. Parents are not more loving and attentive in Mexico City than in California, yet the rates of substance use disorders in California dwarf those in Mexico.

A trauma-related approach: adverse childhood experiences

In contrast to lifelong psychological problems stemming from parenting, trauma-focused theory looks at specific experiences that can compromise the psychological health of children, adolescents and adults. A series of studies have shown links between adverse childhood events – such as the death of a parent, a natural disaster, childhood sex abuse or neglect by parents – and later illegal drug use and heavy drinking among adolescents and young adults (Madruga et al. 2011; Nash et al. 2011). Trauma-focused approaches emphasize that it is not just the trauma that is at the genesis of addiction. How people cope or fail to cope with trauma is equally important. According to this model, individuals develop a series of protective psychological habits to minimize the pain of the trauma, and these habits, in turn, serve to make them vulnerable to addiction.

Evidence

In the USA interviewers asked a random sample of adults a series of questions about childhood adversities, such as death of a parent, parental mental illness or drug abuse, child sex abuse or neglect. Those who reported these kinds of adversities were more than twice as likely to have a current problem with alcohol or drugs (Murphy et al. 2010) than were those who were exposed to traumas such as a natural disaster (Washio et al. 2011). In another study, adolescents who had experienced traumatic life events were much more likely to smoke cigarettes as well as abuse prescription drugs (Anda et al. 1999, 2007). Adverse events included: verbal, physical or sexual abuse; having a mentally ill household member, a household member in prison or a substance-abusing household member; parental divorce or separation; and witnessing domestic violence.

Childhood sex abuse (CSA) has been shown to predict many cases of substance abuse and dependence (Huang et al. 2011). This is particularly the case when parents do not believe the child, or, worse, allow the abuse to continue. Survivors are likely to become substance abusers later in life. The trauma associated with surviving CSA is so common among those seeking treatment for

SUD that some programmes screen for such experiences and develop specific treatment modes to handle clients with these experiences. For example, 26 per cent of heroin users seen in Shanghai, China, reported CSA (Wang et al. 2010). In South Africa, exposure to violence, parental neglect and CSA were prevalent among those with SUD ((Jewkes et al. 2010). In our own study of injection drug users in California, about a third reported CSA (Bowser et al. 2003).

Promise

Linking adverse childhood experiences to drug use allows for scientific analysis. We need not guess about the childhood experienced by addicts, nor do we need lengthy psychiatric interviews to establish linkages. Adverse experiences can be conceptualized in the medical model of stress and coping. Medical studies have shown that stress alone can cause physical illness (Boscarino 2004). It is easy to explain that physical illness and stress can be linked to mental illness without need for unconscious processes or poor parenting. Providing education about how to handle stress has been shown to be effective in numerous medical studies of chronic disease patients (Wadsworth et al. 2011; Sherman et al. 2012).

Critique

The evidence still leaves plenty of room for speculation. While many of those who experience problems in their early development go on to develop problems with alcohol or other drugs, again *the vast majority do not*. In a study of childhood-adverse events conducted in five US states, among 26,229 adults, 59 per cent reported at least one such event, while 8.7 per cent reported five or more (Staff 2010). Even though more than half survived these adverse events in childhood, nowhere near the expected proportion went on to develop problems of substance abuse. Further, studies of US soldiers in Vietnam showed many exposed to horrific trauma began using heroin during their time in the war zone. However, when they returned to the USA, few continued their heroin careers (Robins and Slobodyan 2003).

Social learning

Cognitive psychologists have challenged psychology's preoccupation with individual parent–child disruption as the leading cause of adult problems. Instead, these researchers point out that most people learn how to handle their emotions from watching and imitating the adults around them. People are social beings. We are raised from infancy as part of families, groups, tribes and nations. Each of these has its customs, much of which is imparted by observation of adults. Given an opportunity, children will imitate what they see. In a series of studies, psychologist Albert Bandura was able to demonstrate that children exposed to an adult model imitated that model. They did so even when they were given no reward or encouragement by their parents (Bandura 1983).

One is reminded by the aftermath of young boys who return home after viewing a karate feature film at the movies. While they receive no encouragement from their parents, they proceed to imitate kicks and punches with great enthusiasm. Furthermore, every society uses social pressure to get its members to behave in preferred ways. Whether it is table manners, our dress, how close we stand to one another or how we handle our emotions, our society sets rules, and sanctions against those who break them. To get along, we adopt the habits of those around us. We conform. Consciousness is not required for us to conform to the habits of those around us. We seem to do so automatically.

Evidence

Adolescents face particular difficulty with conformity. When they are searching for role models to emulate, they are particularly vulnerable to the feelings of their friends. If their friends are smoking and drinking, they feel pressure to do so as well – which does not require a poor parenting experience or childhood adversity. Social pressure is all that is required for many people to start using legal as well as illegal drugs.

Bandura (1999) insists that addiction is learned and can be unlearned. When the circumstances under which drug use is initiated are examined, we often find the most important factor in adolescent drug use is their peer environment. When parents and peers use tobacco, so do adolescents (Kelly et al. 2011). The best predictor of adolescent tobacco use is how many of their friends use it. The more friends who use a drug, the more likely the individual will be to use it (Pollard et al. 2010).

Promise

Young people typically begin using drugs when they are adolescents or early adults. Social learning explanations show that drug use does not require trauma, poor parenting or psychiatric disorder. If a child observes an adult model using drugs to handle difficult emotional situations, it is likely that he or she will grow up to imitate that behaviour when confronted with a similar situation. On the other hand, anything learned can be unlearned. People develop a sense of what Bandura called 'self-efficacy' about making changes in their habits; and when their sense of self-efficacy changes, they discontinue drug use (Kuusisto et al. 2011). These beliefs are central to the social cognitive approach to substance abuse. Bandura urges that greater attention needs to be directed to personal beliefs about drug use and social pressure to use drugs. These are the factors that enable an individual to refuse offers to use drugs from friends. Further, social learning can explain why there are such great differences between countries and groups within countries, without assuming parenting or traumatic experiences are causal.

Critique

The friendship network explanation shows promise as to why many try both legal and illegal substances. If self-efficacy explanations rely on current beliefs, what role, if any, do prior beliefs, personal history and experiences play in current behaviours? This explanation does not address such influences. Also, while social learning may explain why adolescents try illegal drugs or alcohol, it does not explain why some individuals use a drug a few times and discontinue, while others in their same friendship network go on to develop addiction.

Learning theory and behaviourism

The Russian scientist Ivan Pavlov became the first to demonstrate the fundaments of learning behavior (Zinbarg and Griffith 2008). When his dog was being fed, a tiny bell attached to the door from which the food came rang first. After a while the dog began salivating as soon as the bell rang, even when food was not presented. Pavlov labelled this pairing 'classical conditioning', a process by which incidental objects (like the bell ring) come to induce automatic responses. The animal had learned that the bell ring signalled food was on the way, and so he began to salivate for the food.

Pavlov further found that when the bell was presented before an electric shock, the animal reacted to the bell in the same way he did to the shock: by withdrawing his paw. The bell alone produced an automatic response. If the bell was repeatedly rung, and no food was produced, eventually the habit ceased – a process Pavlov called 'extinction'. Conditioning studies with animals have established principles of learning which have been applied to humans.

In the USA, John B. Watson paired a negative stimulus such as a loud unpleasant noise with the simultaneous presence of a small furry animal. In doing so, the children learned to fear small furry animals. This fear he termed 'conditioned emotional reaction' (Moore 2011). Watson and the behaviourists believed that anxieties were not derived from parenting or biological drives, but learnt from experiences. Behaviourists do not say that thoughts and consciousness do not play a role in learning, but that the role they play is not as large as we would like. If we carefully study the behaviour of children and adults, it is possible to isolate specific and conditioned emotional reactions and then to devise a series of sessions so as to unlearn the behaviour.

B. F. Skinner replicated Pavlov's and Watson's research with small animals in laboratory settings to further demonstrate how rewards come to shape particular behaviour (Schlinger 2011). He termed this learning process 'successive approximation' and termed the rewards 'reinforcers'. For example, to get an animal to jump over a stool, he provided rewards each time it approached the stool. Then rewards were given for getting on the stool; then for climbing over the stool. Finally rewards were only given for leaping over the stool altogether.

Through this process of shaping, the animal could be taught whatever the experimenter wanted.

Skinner felt the same processes were present in human learning. Parents give rewards in the form of praise, encouragement, hugs or food when a child performs the behaviour the parents want to see repeated, like brushing one's teeth. After enough instances of this successive approximation, teeth brushing becomes an automatic habit. Behavioural assessment seeks to examine environmental cues as to what rewards clients receive from drug use. Then, strategies are devised to alter the behaviour by changing the rewards, so that drug use is no longer rewarding. Behaviourists insist this automatic use of drugs or alcohol or tobacco can be reduced, using principles drawn from behaviourism (Drummond 2001).

Promise

A learning theory approach has great appeal. There is no need to search for unconscious processes as the cause. Instead this approach says attention needs to be directed at the rewards associated with drug use. Cultures differ widely on how people learn to cope with the stresses of life, its tragedies and disappointments. Those differences may be explained as learned traditions. The belief is that anything learned can be unlearned, including drug addiction.

Critique

Behaviourism has great power and precision in describing how animals learn habits, but it is much less successful in explaining how people develop drug use habits. What one learns and the source of one's learning are not unidimensional. The sources can be physical, cognitive, fictional and purely imaginary. Therefore, to find and isolate the source and content of learning is exceedingly difficult.

Evidence

While an animal or person demonstrates what they have been taught, the efficiency of learning theory is self-evident. While behaviourists seldom direct attention to thinking, a series of recent studies on drug dependent persons have shown that just changing their thinking about drug use can have powerful impacts (McHugh et al. 2010).

Cognitive psychology

Cognitive psychologists hold that perceptions and cognitive awareness can play the same role in learning as social behaviour and physical conditions. Learning does not require modelling other people or physical stimuli to condition behaviour. Learning can occur through perception and cognition, including through dreams, imagination, visions and even through misperception. The South African psychiatrist Joseph Wolpe is generally credited with demonstrating that conditions like extreme anxiety can be treated, not with talk therapy, but with systematic desensitization (Wolpe 1973; Head and Gross 2009). Fearful perceptions are what are unlearned, rather than behaviours or behavioural cues.

Once a person has developed a fear of some object, such as a fear of being in elevators, a series of unlearning trials can be used. This approach assumes that people have learned, via conditioning, beliefs and perceptions that lead to a fear response in an elevator. Perhaps at some time in their life they experienced an unpleasant event associated with an elevator, or of being in a confined place, or they thought they had had such an experience. Through systematic desensitization, they learn there is no connection between the fear emotion and being in a confined elevator.

If an individual has learned to cope with feelings of anxiety by using alcohol or drugs, the cognitive behavioural approach can be used to de-establish the connection between relief from anxiety and drug use. A skilled therapist first locates the cognitive context in which that connection has been established and then helps the client focus on the emotions underlying the need to use alcohol or drugs and prepares a series of homework assignments to break the connection. A strong working alliance with the client is essential – there has to be trust for the treatment to work.

Evidence and promise

Cognitive behavioural scientists have provided evidence that cognitive learning is the basis treatment for addiction – from cigarettes to heroin (Beck 1991; McHugh et al. 2010; de Haan et al. 2011).

Critique

We must rely on a person's current beliefs and conditioned emotions: we do not know that they were there when that person starting using drugs. They may have come afterwards. It may be that the cognitive beliefs and emotional conditioning were learned after drug use began. Individuals may have learned to deny their problems with addiction and then adopted beliefs in support of this denial.

Family systems

All of the psychological approaches we have described thus far place their attention on the individual. In contrast, family systems theory sees the problem of substance abuse as a problem within family functioning. Family therapists believe individuals play roles within their families, and these roles exert powerful influences on behaviour, influences that are almost never known by the individual (Cox and Paley 2003). Many roles are designed to maintain the balances among family members so that the family unit can continue to survive. Maintaining balance is termed 'homeostatic balance'. Drug addiction on the part of one or more members serves, paradoxically, to keep the family together. In some families there are forces pulling it apart. The addict's behaviour serves to draw attention away from that ongoing crisis or potential for imbalance and onto the addict's difficulties: it is a diversion and a distraction. Stanton and Todd (1982) document common features of families where one member is a heroin addict:

1　There is multi-generational substance abuse (sometimes, grandfathers as well as fathers have problems with alcohol).
2　The addict is quite close to his or her family, either through living with the family even though an adult, or through frequent contact.
3　The mother maintains a close symbiotic relationship with her addict son/daughter.
4　Drug addiction serves to prevent the addict from moving away from the family to establish a stable family of his or her own.
5　The symptom of addiction serves to divert attention away from ongoing problems in the family that might cause it to dissolve.

According to this model, the addict develops a pattern of 'pseudo-individuation'. While a young adult is expected to grow up and develop a life and family of his or her own, the symptom of addiction prevents this process from occurring, while the family blames the addiction. Instead of becoming an individuated adult, the addict maintains his or her status psychologically as a troubled child, one the parents periodically have to rescue because of his drug addiction. Paradoxically, the addict cannot give up the role of the 'addict', because abstinence from drugs requires the family again to confront problems which may cause it to fall apart. The addict is literally dying so that the family can live (Stanton and Todd 1982).

Promise and evidence

Separation from the family becomes an issue for late adolescents, and that is precisely the time most develop problems of alcohol or drug addiction. A series of studies have confirmed that adolescents, who may repeatedly fail individual therapy for addiction, succeed when the entire family is engaged in treatment (Rowe 2012). The sudden death of closely bonded relatives during critical developmental years (prior to age 13) was found to be very common in the backgrounds of severely addicted drug users (Coleman 1981) and highly correlated to HIV high-risk behaviours through injected drug use (Bowser et al. 2003). When family therapists treat the entire family, rather than just the adolescent, the results have been very promising (Liddle et al. 2009; Rowe 2012).

Critique

As with prior theories, family relations and roles explain addiction for some drug abusers but not for all. There are people dependent on drugs due to causes that have nothing to do with their family relations. How do we explain addiction among people who had no early losses or did not grow up in close family systems? There are drug users who also blame their families for their addiction and cite early loss of friends and relatives as explanations of their plight. In these cases, there may be no family influences and expected roles that keep an addicted member dependent. What seems plausible and convincing may not in fact be accurate or adequate.

Summary

While people with substance abuse problems frequently have other psychiatric disorders, the vast majority of persons with such disorders do not go on to substance abuse. While many people exposed to trauma as children or adults develop substance abuse problems, the majority do not. While individuals with attachment disorders are more likely to develop a substance use disorder than others with more positive attachments, the majority do not develop such problems. Families facing long-standing problems that threaten them with dissolution are more likely to cope via having an adolescent as an addict, but the majority does not. Behaviour-based models provide a compelling explanation, but evidence is lacking on the connection between learning and drug use across the many cultures, where variations are large and unexplained. What we have are some models that explain some drug use for some people, but leave the majority still unexplained.

Modern research has begun to shed light on the persistent linkages between psychological functioning and the development of alcohol or other drug abuse. Yet, much remains to be explored. No study has met the 'gold standard' for research: that is when all of the necessary and sufficient causal factors have been identified and accounted for. One cannot randomly assign an individual to grow up in a problem family. For ethical reasons no scientist is going to give alcohol or drugs to subjects to see who does or does not develop an addiction. We must rely, instead, on studies of people who have various characteristics or experiences, and examine what proportion become drug users and what nonusers. It can very well be that some other influence causes both psychiatric disorder and problems with alcohol and drugs.

Review questions

- What are four common beliefs about the causes of illegal drug use?
- Why do some scientists believe addiction is outside of conscious control for users?
- Discuss the evidence that mental disorder is the immediate cause of drug use for the majority of users.
- State some of the problems scientists have encountered when explaining drug use by way of Freud's theories?
- Why, according to Karen Horney's theory, do individuals become narcissists? How does this lead to drug use?
- Do most people with problems of depression or anxiety go on to develop substance use disorders?
- How does trauma lead to drug use?
- What happened to the majority of US soldiers who used heroin during their service in the Vietnam War?
- Why do people use drugs according to family systems theory?

Further reading

Mitchell, S.A. and Black, M.J. (1995) *Freud and Beyond: A History of Modern Psychoanalytic Thought*, New York: Basic Books.

Robinson, J., Sareen, J., Cox, B.J. and Bolton J.M. (2011) 'Role of self medication in the development of co-morbid anxiety and substance use disorders: a longitudinal investigation', *Archive of General Psychiatry*, 68(8), 800–7.

Rogers, C. (1961) *On Becoming a Person: A Therapist's View of Psychotherapy*, London: Constable.

Stanton, M.D. and Todd T.C. (1982) *The Family Therapy of Drug Abuse and Addiction*, New York: Guilford.

Physiological Perspectives

8

To review: drug use is being able to take a drug once, twice or over a period of time and then to stop at will. Use becomes abuse when a user cannot stop using even after the personal, social and financial damage of continued use becomes self-evident (APA 1994). The key term that distinguishes use from abuse is 'compulsion' or 'addiction'. The power of addictive behaviour far exceeds the voluntary exercise of will power over mild compulsion. In compulsive drug abuse users are also preoccupied with getting more drugs and then using them. They build their daily routines around their drug use. Everything else, including job, bills, personal hygiene, friends, family and even children, becomes secondary.

The problem is that compulsive use disorder is not an either–or dichotomy as believed in the moral-ethical perspective. This disorder ranges on a continuum. At one end, there are no symptoms whatsoever: at the other end, the symptoms are apparent and severe. What explains compulsive behaviour? Availability, social, criminological and psychological explanations have provided some necessary correlants. But none have provided both necessary and sufficient conditions – the highest criteria for scientific causation. There is a fifth area closely related to the psychological that some scientists believe holds great promise both to explain more thoroughly and eventually to treat mental illness and addictions (Kraly 2009). It is recent knowledge derived from brain physiology that underpins this hope.

The physical correlates of drug abuse

Addiction begins in the pleasure centre in the brain. It turns out that all of the ways in which we experience joy, pleasure, pain, boredom, comfort and discomfort are controlled by a combination of the nucleus accumbens, where we experience highs and depressions, and the septum pellucidium and hypothalamus (or 'pleasure centre') of the brain (Kandel 2000; Carlson 2007). Nerves run to the pleasure centre from throughout the body and from other areas of the brain. It is like a box, and all the wiring related to pleasure and pain converge and connect to the box. Because of this highly centralized 'wiring', we assume that the underlying mechanics behind qualitatively different experiences of pleasure and pain are the same.

What makes experiences different are variations in the signals running across the wiring – the neural network. So, the signals running to the pleasure centre from observing a bed of roses and seeing beauty in them are very different from the signals going to the pleasure centre from getting hit with a soccer or baseball. Note that the pleasure centre is not the only place that varied neural signals, marking different experiences, run to. There are hundreds if not thousands of other such centres and of neural networks running to and from different areas of the brain carrying vital signals controlling body functions, muscle activities, perceptions, intelligence and memory.

The fact that nerves are like wires carrying signals to the pleasure centre of the brain seems straightforward. But what makes this system both more interesting and complex than simple wiring is that the electrical signals carried across the nerves have to be transmitted from one nerve to the next. Depending on where the signal originates and its purpose, its routing from one nerve to the next may be different from the prior or next signal. It is very much like a bus or train route. Multiple signals can go across a common nerve yet be routed to several different nerves going to different centres. So, the transmission of electrical signals from one nerve to the next is not direct like connecting two wires together to make one unbroken electrical circuit.

At the end of each nerve is a connector called a synapse. Each synapse has on it a series of transmission nodes called receptors. The signal has to come down a nerve to the synapse and be transmitted from that nerve's receptors. From the receptors the signal has to cross a narrow gap to another set of receptors on a synapse of the next nerve where the signal continues its circuit, and so on. The transmission of electrical signals from one synapse to the next, between receptors of different nerves, is done through chemicals called neurotransmitters (see a representation in Figure 8.1).

It is estimated that the adult brain has approximately 100 to 500 billion synapses and that there are at least ten different types of neurotransmitters regulating the types and functions of neural transmissions across all of the different kinds of synapses in the body and brain (Reith 1997). One key neurotransmitter is dopamine which regulates the body's motor system, reward and cognition, and endocrines. Another key neurotransmitter is serotonin which regulates mood, satiety, body temperature and sleep. We now have enough neurophysiology to have a basic understanding of drug addiction.

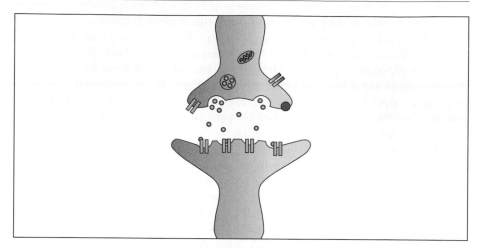

Figure 8.1 Synapse, receptor and neurotransmitters

How physiological drug addiction works

What we take into the body in the way of food and fluids provides it with basic nutrients based upon diets derived over thousands of years. The various body systems could not work without essential nutrients such as potassium, sulphur, zinc, iodine or lithium (Kiple and Ornelas 2000). This is true for the nervous system as well, which has a particular need for vitamin C, niacin (B3) and calcium in order to keep the electrical signals moving through the nerves and to maintain the chemical neurotransmitters located between synapses and receptors. This complex neural system is affected by three types of psychotropic drugs – drugs that can alter one's mental state. A drug type is based upon the nervous system's reaction to them. There are:

- *Depressants*, such as alcohol, heroin, morphine, codeine and barbiturates;
- *Stimulants*, such as amphetamines, nicotine, caffeine, cocaine and crack cocaine;
- *Hallucinogens*, such as LSD, mescaline, peyote, angel dust (PCP) and ketamine.

Researchers are not quite certain about cannabis: it has been classified as a stimulant and depressant (Murray 1986), though it can also act like a hallucinogen.

Effects of depressants

Depressants such as alcohol inhibit the nervous system, decreasing awareness, sensitivity and consciousness. They mute physical stimuli and allow a temporary escape from psychological stress and anxiety. The first time a person takes a sufficient amount of a depressant it changes the chemistry of the neurotransmitters leading to the pleasure centre of the brain, the specific effect being a reduction of the size of the electrical charges that cross the synapses. When this happens the person experiences a euphoria or high. They are slightly numbed to stimuli; their reaction timing is slowed; their inhibitions drop, so they may say and do things that they would not ordinarily. Their speech may become slurred or they might just pass-out. When they stop using the drug and its effects wear off, the neurotransmitters return to normal. As this adjustment takes place, they may feel discomfort (a hangover). They have had an experience where they have chemically altered their mental state, were temporarily relieved of their worries and concerns and may have even enjoyed themselves despite the hangover.

If the neurotransmitters return to normal after each time one takes a depressant, one is very fortunate. One simply 'used' the drug. Addiction happens when the synapses between the nerves adjust their number of receptors in response to the drug. The synapses *increase* the number of receptors to try to increase the electrical charges crossing the gap between them in order to return back to normal. In other words, the nervous system adjusts itself to the drug as if its presence were permanent. The new 'normal' is now dependent on the depressant drug as a permanent feature affecting the number of receptors. What is remarkable when this adjustment happens is the body's attempt to maintain homeostasis or balance of the electrical charge crossing the synapses. The body wants predictability in its functions, especially in its neuro-activity.

When a depressant such as heroin is in the system, the number of receptors on the synapses leading to the pleasure centre of the brain increases, and the person has to maintain the same level of the depressant in his or her system in

Opioids			
Category and Name	Examples of Commercial and Street Names	DEA Schedule	How Administered
Heroin	*Diacetylmorphine*: smack, horse, brown sugar, dope, H, junk, skag, white horse, China white; cheese (with OTC cold medicine and antihistamine)	I ?	Injected, smoked, snorted
Opium	Laudanum, paregoric: big O, black stuff, block, gum, hop	II, III, V ?	Swallowed, smoked
Acute Effects – Euphoria; drowsiness; impaired coordination; dizziness; confusion; nausea; sedation, feeling of heaviness in the body, slowed or arrested breathing			
Health Risks – Constipation; endocarditis; hepatitis; HIV; addiction; fatal overdose			

Figure 8.2 Commonly abused drugs: opioids

Source: National Institute on Drug Abuse (www.drugabuse.gov/drugs-abuse/commonly-abused-drugs/).

Alcohol			
Category and Name	Examples of Commercial and Street Names	DEA Schedule	How Administered
Alcohol (ethyl alcohol)	Found in liquor, beer, and wine	Not scheduled	Swallowed
Acute Effects – In low doses, euphoria, mild stimulation, relaxation, lowered inhibitions; in higher doses, drowsiness, slurred speech, nausea, emotional volatility, loss of coordination, visual distortions, impaired memory, sexual dysfunction, loss of consciousness **Health Risks** – Increased risk of injuries, violence, fetal damage (in pregnant women); depression; neurologic deficits; hypertension; liver and heart disease; addiction; fatal overdose			

Figure 8.3   Commonly abused drugs: alcohol

Source: National Institute on Drug Abuse (www.drugabuse.gov/drugs-abuse/commonly-abused-drugs/).

order to feel normal. Once a person is addicted, they do not experience the same 'high' that they did initially. People who are addicted testify that the first high they experienced was the best and every time they used the drug thereafter was a nearly futile attempt to experience the same high again. In time, they have to use the drug simply to feel normal. If for some reason they stop taking the drug, their neural system goes into shock. The electrical charges between synapses increase above the drug-induced normal, due to the increased numbers of receptors. The person now experiences crippling pain throughout their body, nausea, cold-sweat, psychological disorientation, nightmares, inability to sleep, even loss of control of their bladder and anus. Assuming that one does not return to the addictive drug, these symptoms may last from three days to several weeks until the synapses reduce the number of receptors back to the old normal – or close to it. One can now see why a person with an addiction will do almost anything to avoid going through withdrawal.

Effects of stimulants

Stimulants excite the nervous system, producing greater temporary alertness, sensitivity and arousal. In doing so, they increase blood pressure and heart rate. Drugs are not the only source of stimulation: well seasoned foods and exciting experiences are forms of stimulation (Schivelbusch 1992). The path to addiction here is virtually the same as that for depressants, except, instead of depressing the nerves that lead to the brain's pleasure centre, stimulants excite them. They change the chemistry of the neurotransmitters, resulting in an amplification of the electrical charges that pass from synapse to synapse. The person taking the stimulant experiences increased energy and sensitivity. They can be paranoid, believing that people are talking about them and conspiring

Stimulants			
Category and Name	**Examples of Commercial and Street Names**	**DEA Schedule**	**How Administered**
Cocaine	*Cocaine hydrochloride*: blow, bump,C, candy Charlie, coke, crack, flake, rock, snow, toot	II ?	Snorted, smoked, injected
Ampheta-mine	*Biphetamine, Dexedrine*: bennies, black beauties, crosses, hearts, LA turnaround, speed, truck drivers, uppers	II ?	Swallowed, snorted, smoked, injected
Metham-phetamine	*Desoxyn*: meth, ice, crank, chalk, crystal, fire, glass, go fast, speed	II ?	Swallowed, snorted, smoked, injected

Acute Effects – Increased heart rate, blood pressure, body temperature, metabolism; feelings of exhilaration; increased energy, mental alertness; tremors; reduced appetite; irritability; anxiety; panic; paranoia; violent behaviour; psychosis

Health Risks – Weight loss, insomnia; cardiac or cardiovascular complications; stroke; seizures; addiction

Also, for cocaine – Nasal damage from snorting

Also, for methamphetamine – Severe dental problems

Figure 8.4 Commonly abused drugs: stimulants

Source: National Institute on Drug Abuse (www.drugabuse.gov/drugs-abuse/commonly-abused-drugs/).

against them and others. They are constantly busy and almost never sleep.

When the drug wears off, if they are lucky they return to normal and just have a hangover. They feel dehydrated, sleep deprived, exhausted and disoriented. If they are unlucky, their nervous system adjusts to the presence of the stimulant in their neurotransmitters by *decreasing* the number of receptors on their synapses. Their nervous system tries to reduce the size of the electrical charges passing from synapse to synapse. Their new normal now requires the permanent presence of the stimulant in their system. Withdrawal will throw them into the same physical and mental hell as is experienced by someone withdrawing from a depressant. Their withdrawal symptoms will last until their nervous system increases the receptors to a new normal.

Effects of hallucinogens

Hallucinogens disconnect the user from ordinary perception and psychology. This disconnection can be either temporary or permanent. With hallucinogens, the mind is disassociated from reality, emotions or expected consciousness (Beyerstein and Laing 2003). Less is known about how hallucinogens affect the brain than depressants or stimulants. This is because the nervous system appears to have a predictable reaction to depressants and stimulants in which it adjusts to their presence, whereas hallucinogens appear to interfere with the electrical impulses passing across the synapses by increasing or decreasing signal strength, breaking the signal up or blocking the electrical charge altogether. Hallucinogens appear to do much the same with neurotransmitters. They change their chemistry to increase or decrease the electrical impulses crossing the synapses, much like depressants or stimulants (it is not clear or predictable which they will do). But hallucinogens can also stop the signal completely or redirect them to a nerve system that the signal was not intended for.

So, the person who takes an hallucinogen can have out-of-body experiences, delusions, feel depersonalized, and see, feel, touch, hear and talk to colours, ideas and things no one else can. Or in the case of PCP they initially just experience a sense of unity and peace with all other people and things. Other users have traumatic psychic experiences such as being pursued and devoured by demons and wild animals, being cut up alive or of being eaten, or possessed by devils. The outcomes of taking a hallucinogen are totally unpredictable.

Stimulants			
Category and Name	Examples of Commercial and Street Names	DEA Schedule	How Administered
LSD	*Lysergic acid diethylamide*: acid, blotter, cubes, microdot yellow sunshine, blue heaven	I ?	Swallowed, absorbed through mouth tissues
Mescaline	Buttons, cactus, mesc, peyote	I ?	Swallowed, smoked,
Psilocybin	Magic mushrooms, purple passion, shrooms, little smoke	I ?	Swallowed,

Acute Effects – Altered states of perception and feeling; hallucinations; nausea

Also, for LSD – Increased body temperature, heart rate, blood pressure; loss of appetite; sweating; sleeplessness; numbness, dizziness, weakness, tremors; impulsive behaviour; rapid shifts in emotion

Also, for Psilocybin – Nervousness; paranoia; panic

Health Risks, for LSD – Flashbacks, Hallucinogen Persisting Perception Disorder

Figure 8.5   Commonly abused drugs: hallucinogens

Source: National Institute on Drug Abuse (www.drugabuse.gov/drugs-abuse/commonly-abused-drugs/).

Hopefully, as the drug wears off, the nervous system returns to normal. But with hallucinogens the neural system may not. Neuro-signals and transmitter chemistry may be so badly thrown off that the user's nervous system cannot return to normal, especially for those with prior family or personal histories of psychotic disorders. Signals remain scrambled, selective transmissions remain blocked and the neurotransmitters' chemistry remains permanently altered. When this happens, at best the user becomes a different person by virtue of some brain damage. At worst they are rendered completely insane – unable to communicate with anyone else or to behave in an acceptable fashion in society.

Scientists who have studied the negative impacts of hallucinogens on users do not know whether or not the user is addicted. This is so because no one has been able to record all of the physiological changes that hallucinogens induce; nor are they able to interview sufficient numbers of users who did not lose their mind and forget about their experience while on the drug. It would be unethical to give people such drugs to study their reactions. One dose can render some people permanently insane. It happens often enough for there to be too small a pool of long-term users to study who can talk about their experience (Johnson et al. 2008).

Role of dopamine

What we have described thus far are the mechanics of drug addiction and dependency for the major types of drugs. What has not been explained is why some people develop dependencies while others do not. The answer to this question is thought to lie in the variations of the body's ability to produce and regulate dopamine (Blum et al. 2012). Addiction is considered a brain disorder due to impairment of the 'reward circuitry'. People whose bodies do not produce enough dopamine are highly vulnerable to drug abuse and other compulsive behaviours. In effect, they are compelled to seek out substances to boost their deficient dopamine functioning. So drugs like cocaine can stimulate the release of two to ten times the amount of dopamine in physiological systems which are initially deficient in it. Drugs such as alcohol can depress the release of dopamine thereby stimulating the body to produce more of it to correct the deficiency. Correcting this impairment in reward circuitry is particularly critical if drug treatment is to work (Fishbein and Tarter 2009). Those who complete treatment and have this underlying impairment in dopamine functioning have a very high probability of relapse – returning to their original drug abuse.

Factors affecting addiction

Tolerance

After explaining the mechanics of addiction, we now have to describe how addictions vary. They do so because of varying physical tolerances. Tolerance is when one's reaction to a drug decreases and higher dosages are needed to obtain the same effect (Sharp 1984). Some people have such low tolerance for specific drugs that the first time they use any of them, they are immediately addicted. Their synapses and receptors make an immediate adjustment to the need for the drug as a new and dependent norm. At the other extreme are people who can take a drug in heavy doses for years and never develop a physical need or dependency. People at these extreme ends of the tolerance continuum are rare. Most of us have physical tolerances in which it is unlikely that we will become immediately addicted, though each person has a specific probability of exposure that indicates the extent to which they might develop a physical dependency. The more often one takes a drug, especially in high dosages and purity, the closer one gets to one's point of tolerance where dependency can develop and where a dopamine deficiency can be triggered.

Another characteristic of tolerance is that it does not stay at the same point. Once an addiction is triggered, tolerance can progressively increase (Ehrman et al. 1992). Some can go for years with the same tolerance level and be satisfied with the same amount of a drug. Then suddenly users find their tolerance increasing. Once this happens they need more and more of the same drug to maintain their normality until their tolerance level stabilizes again. If tolerance continues to increase, the dependent person can be 'driven to the (street) curve' – to have to make the choice between recovery or homelessness or suicide. They have to choose between going into detoxification and treatment or killing themselves with the drug. They will have to acquire and consume an impossible amount of the drug and, if they succeed, they will at some point overdose.

There are also some people whose tolerance for some unknown reason decreases and they need less and less of the same drug until they can go without using it entirely. This is referred to as 'spontaneous recovery' (Price et al. 2001).

Modes of acquisition

There are four modes of drug use which are increasingly efficient in getting drugs into the blood system. The least efficient way is to *ingest* a drug. That is to swallow a drug and have it go through the digestive system (e.g. alcohol and pills). Only a small percentage of the original amount, as little as 15 per cent, will survive the chemicals in the digestive track and pass into the blood stream. The next level is to *snort* the drug and have it pass through the membranes of the nose (e.g. using powdered cocaine). This is much more efficient than through digestion. An even more efficient way to get more of a drug into the blood system is to *inhale* it. By smoking the drug, one turns it into a gas and it can then more easily pass into the blood through the lungs (e.g. marijuana and crack cocaine). Finally, the most efficient way is to *inject* it into a vein. This way 100 per cent of the drug reaches the blood system without any loss due to body barriers.

Purity

There is a third factor that affects addiction: the purity of a drug. If a person develops an addiction to a prescription drug, we at least know the amount he or she is addicted to. We can also assume that the drug is pure because it has been produced under strict pharmaceutical standards. In contrast, purity is a real problem with illegal drugs bought and sold on the streets because they are generally 'cut' or 'stepped on'. This means that they have been mixed with other materials which reduce their purity to increase the profitability of each sale. These other materials have included cooking flour, baby powder, rat poison and detergent. Marijuana is notorious for being cut with common grass, leaves and weeds.

Poly-drug use

Until the late 1980s, most illegal drug users preferred, and were addicted to, only one drug. They may have tried others but returned to a preferred one. In recent years, drug abusers are more likely to be poly-drug users: they regularly use more than one addictive drug, such as cocaine or heroin (Leri 2003). What makes poly-drug use complex is that users may now have addictions to multiple drugs. One could take a drug for years that one has a high tolerance for and not develop a dependency on it. But it may take only a few hits of another drug that one has a low tolerance of for dependency to occur. This is why poly-drug use is especially dangerous and, as we will see later, is so problematic in treatment.

Genetic predisposition

Another important factor in drug abuse is genetic inheritance, which provides a predisposition to varied levels of tolerance to drugs. The nervous system's sensitivity to specific drugs and tolerance is thought to be coded in one's genes. While geneticists have not yet identified the genes associated with addiction, there is evidence that such a disposition exists from studies of twins (Zickler 1999).

Two types of twins have been monitored: identical twins born with exactly the same genetic make-up and fraternal twins born at the same time to the same mother but with differing genetic make-ups. Comparisons of these two sorts of twins are as close as scientists can get to isolating the differential impact of early environment and physical inheritance on the course of a human life. For identical twins, the *in utero* environment and physical inheritance were the same for both. For fraternal twins, the *in utero* environments are the same but they have different genetic inheritances. In which case, identical twins should abuse drugs at approximately the same rate, and fraternal twins should have comparatively discordant rates of abuse.

A team of investigators found that genetic inheritance plays a major role in the progression from cocaine or marijuana use to abuse and dependence based upon female twins (Kendler and Prescott 1998). Significantly more pairs of identical twins used, abused and were dependent on drugs than fraternal twins. In which case, it appears that abuse and dependence are highly heritable.

Examples of physiological research on drug abuse

In several studies a magnetic resonance imaging machine (MRI) was used to compare the brain functioning of a sample of amphetamine users with non-users (Berman et al. 2008). The users included a sample of respondents who were exposed to amphetamine *in utero*. Across these studies, physical brain structural abnormalities in the frontal lobe were consistently found in amphetamine users exposed *in utero*. The same structural differences were not found among non-users. These findings were consistent, even when a variety of imaging techniques were used.

These findings suggest that the depression, aggression and social isolation associated with amphetamine use may not be just outcomes of the drug's toxicity but point to some changes in the brain (Homer et al. 2008). The same techniques were used to find the brain pathways by which cannabis use can trigger psychosis and other serious symptoms of mental illness (Fergusson et al. 2006). The chemical 9-tetrahydrocannabinol binds to specific cannabinoid receptors in the brain with an outcome of changes in perception, cognition and functioning. It is also possible that nicotine addiction can be broken by using nicotinic receptor agonists and antagonists to block the pathways by which nicotine dependency is reinforced in the brain (Rose 2008).

It is assumed that many people who are dependent upon drugs can resist using them if craving for their drug of choice were eliminated. There is research underway that would be advanced with knowledge of the neural pathways by which one craves drugs. Clinical research to date suggests that either craving is not as important as we think in predicting relapse or we do not know enough yet to understand the connection between drug craving and relapse (Drummond et al. 2000). Research is needed on where craving functions in the brain, the dynamics of craving, factors that influence craving and how it might be better measured.

Recently, this first question of where craving takes place has been answered for heroin use. By using functional magnetic resonance imaging (fMRI), the brain sites for heroin craving were identified by comparing a sample of heroin users with non-users (Li et al. 2012). The heroin users were given heroin-related cues while the non-users were given neutral cues. In another study, a central cue, and a trigger for drug craving for people addicted to illicit drugs, was money. Seeing paper money, and touching and handling it, are all cues and a reinforcement to craving drugs. Cocaine abusers and non-abusers were shown increasing denominations of dollar bills (Konova et al. 2012). An MRI was used to record brain activity for both groups. The cocaine users had very distinct response patterns in the sensori-motor striatum of the brain compared to non-users. The more severe was the cocaine abusers' dependency, the more pronounced their neural response pattern and the more distinct they were in comparison to non-users. What these studies have done is locate the sites in the brain that should be the focus of more intense study that might in turn show how we could devise effective barriers to craving and physical dependency.

Looking forward

In the USA, The National Institute on Drug Abuse is the primary federal agency charged with research on drug addiction and abuse. It also sets the agenda and direction for the study of drug dependency for the US scientific community and the programmes it funds. As of 2009, most of the agency's funds committed to science are directed toward improving our understanding of the physiology and biochemistry of drug addiction. Clearly, an area of great potential and hope is that of obtaining a better understanding of the nervous system and the variations in the body's production of chemical neurotransmitters to the brain's pleasure centre. The area that now receives the most funding and has the most promise is the development of vaccines that will suppress or eliminate physical addiction (Orson et al. 2008).

In one approach under development, antibodies of these vaccines will attach to a drug's molecules forming another molecule that is too large to cross the blood-brain barrier easily; in doing so, these vaccines will slow the drug's entry into the brain, reducing if not preventing the addictive euphoria. This would be a major breakthrough and is currently in clinical trials and may not be very far away. But there are a number of challenges (Kantak 2003). First, there is tremendous individual variability in antibody formation; second, a vaccine can be structurally very different from the drug it is designed to block; third, it can inadvertently have the same effect on dependency for some other drug or food than the one it is intended to block; fourth, a vaccine can have no impact on craving and not serve as a barrier to relapse. Examples of several drugs in clinical trials are:

- Buprenorphine: for heroin craving.
- Ibogaine: blocks physical craving and psychological dependencies.
- Acamprosate: for alcohol and depression.
- Disulfiram (antabuse): for alcohol aversion.

While the physical basis of drug addiction is fascinating and straightforward, it is a rare dependent person whose only basis of addiction is physical. If and when a medicine is developed that will eliminate physical dependency for one or more drugs, it will improve detoxification of those who wish to end their physical drug dependency. It will no longer be necessary for a severely drug dependent person to experience the pain and suffering of withdrawal. If they take their medicine, they may be able to avoid withdrawal altogether.

Whether this medicine will provide a permanent cure or will have to be taken indefinitely remains to be seen. The point is it will address only the physical aspect of addiction. The other sources of dependency remain – the social, criminal, supply and availability, and the psychological.

Review questions

- Briefly describe how the physiology of addiction works.
- What do depressants do that are different from what stimulants do?
- How are hallucinogens different from depressants and stimulants?
- What are the five factors that vary the extent to which a person will become addicted to a substance? Can you describe why each is a factor?
- If a drug is developed that can efficiently counter the physiology of addiction, will the problem of drug abuse be solved? If so, why? If not, why?

Further reading

Amsel, A. (1989) *Behaviorism, Neobehaviorism and Cognitivism in Learning theory: Historical and Contemporary Perspectives*, Hillsdale, NJ: Erlbaum Associates.

Cohen, J. A., Perel, J. M. and DeBellis, M. D., Friedman, M.J. and Putnam, F.W. (2002) 'Treating traumatized children: clinical implications of the psychobiology of post-traumatic stress disorder', *Trauma, Violence & Abuse*, 3(2), 91–108.

Dean, E. T. (1997) *Shook Over Hell: Post-Traumatic Stress, Vietnam and the Civil War*, Cambridge, MA: Harvard University Press.

Fields, R. D. (2010) *The Other Brain: From Dementia to Schizophrenia, How New Discoveries about the Brain are Revolutionizing Medicine and Science*, New York: Simon & Schuster.

Martin-Santos, R., Fagundo, A. B., Crippa, J. A., Atakan, Z., Bhattacharyya, S., Allen, P., Fusar-Poli, P., Borgwardt, S., Seal, M., Busatto, G. F. and McGuire, P. (2010) 'Neuroimaging in Cannabis Use: A Systematic Review of the Literature', *Psychological Medicine*, 40(3), 383–98.

Scott, K. F. (2009) *The Unwell Brain: Understanding the Psychobiology of Mental Health*, New York and London: W.W. Norton.

PART

III

Responses

Public Policy: Criminal Justice

9

Chapter overview

■ Importance of public policy in drug use and addiction
■ Historical development of the criminal justice approach
■ Has criminalization worked? Reviewing the evidence
■ Criminal justice and international human rights
■ Alternatives to criminalization: global drug law reform experiments
■ Conclusion

Public policies are the principles, objectives, goals and priorities that governments use to fulfil their mandate to advance the public good (Dye 2012). With regard to social problems such as drug addiction, public policies are what each government believes are their best courses of action to lessen or solve the problem. Public policies are ideally the outcome of public debate and the formation of consensuses among voters who are represented by elected officials. Public policies are informed by: actions taken in the past to address similar problems; national culture, religious beliefs and popular biases; more recently, international treaties and consensuses; and by scientific findings. A nation's priorities are more often expressed in terms of its public policies even when those policies are not formally articulated.

As is the case with all rationalizations, articulated public policy as expressions of national priorities may not match what a government actually does – its operative policy. When there is contention, debate, lack of consensus and changes in administrations due to unsettled points of view, government action – operative policies – may differ from expressed policies. A good way to test the extent to which the operative policy matches expressed policy is to study government expenditures. In effect, public policy, both expressed and operative, is apparent in what a government increases or decreases spending on. New policies reflecting new priorities are generally followed by new matching expenditures; discredited policies are generally evident by the defunding of activities that reflect former policies.

Importance of public policy in drug use and addiction

Every action taken on a meaningful scale above the level of the individual is an outcome of public policies. The money used to fund scientific research, to devise treatments and preventions and to operate the courts and fund police services are all outcomes of public policy. With regard to alcohol, tobacco and drug abuse in the world community today, a central issue is the balance between addressing this problem as a criminal justice issue or as a medical and public health issue. Some have defined these as competing and opposite approaches. Still others are developing a perspective that sees the medical or criminal approach as having specific and differing roles and emphases that can be complementary. What is driving the need to work out the balance between the two approaches is the pragmatic necessity to determine the most effective way to address the national and global problem of drug use and abuse.

The purpose of this chapter and the one that follows is to explore the ways in which national states have used public policy to address the problem of drug use and abuse. Our purpose is also to estimate where they are in seeking a balance between criminal justice, medicine and public health as tools to confront the problem of addiction in society. Ultimately, we want to identify and understand the most effective public policies that can be used to address the challenges that drug use and abuse pose to modern societies. In this chapter, we focus on what has been, in many respects, the dominant approach over the last 100 years or more: criminalization. In Chapter 10, we examine the principal alternative to a criminal justice approach: a public policy based on public health and the goal of harm reduction.

In this chapter we begin by explaining the historical development of the criminal law/justice approach, showing how it is in fact embedded in a fundamental way within drug policy. We then appraise the evidence for the effectiveness of this approach, before setting out some alternative legal frameworks that have been developed in different parts of the world which seek to move away from the use of criminal sanctions and penalties.

Historical development of the criminal justice approach

A drug policy approach built on the criminal law and its enforcement through the criminal justice system is sometimes described as the fighting of a 'war on drugs'. This was a phrase coined by US President Nixon in 1971, although commentators often date the start of this 'war' ten years earlier to the 1961 United Nations Single Convention on Narcotic Drugs. From this perspective, this has been a war fought for just over 50 years.

Arguably, however, this is too narrow a historical vision, if we are to understand properly the development of the criminal justice approach. We suggest that a more important year to look at is actually 1909, rather than 1961, as it was in that year that the first international meeting took place in Shanghai to discuss a new approach to the perceived opium problem in the Far East. Further international meetings were held in the next couple of years, culminating in the signing of the International Opium Convention at The Hague in 1912, an agreement which formed the blueprint for the global drug prohibition system. Importantly, the 1912 Convention broadened out the focus from just opium to include morphine and cocaine, and also looked beyond the Far East to the worldwide situation.

Built in to this global system, created in the first couple of decades of the 20th century, was the use of the criminal law and criminal penalties to regulate the trade and consumption of this particular set of psychoactive substances. The US Harrison Narcotics Tax Act of 1914 is a good example of this, as it provided for fines of up to $2,000 and prison sentences of up to five years for violations of its regulations.

So we can say that the century-old global drug prohibition system is based on a criminal justice framework. It seeks to use the criminal law to regulate, and ultimately eliminate, the transnational drug trade. We will consider in the next section how effective this has been. Before that, we will make one further observation which points to how fundamental the criminalization approach is to drug policy. We have already described how the global prohibition system was constructed in the early 20th century. It has been suggested that prior to that the concept of a 'drug' in our modern sense did not really exist (Porter 1996; Seddon 2010).

In the 19th century, 'drug' simply meant medication or medicine. The idea of 'drugs' in the sense that we are concerned with in this book is a 'twentieth-century coinage' (Porter 1996). But more than that, it is a coinage that was invented as part of the creation of this new legal category of prohibited psychoactive substances (Seddon 2010). Substances that are called 'drugs' share little in common, other than how they are regulated (like the categories of 'over-the-counter' or 'prescribed' medicines). Indeed, new ones get added to the category over time. In other words, the very term 'drug' is linked to a public policy based on criminalization – drugs and criminal justice are two sides of the same coin. This also gives us a clue as to why it has proved so difficult to decouple the two.

Has criminalization worked? Reviewing the evidence

The purpose of a prohibition approach is elimination – of a commodity or service or behaviour. We can ask a very simple question then of the global drug prohibition system: how close has the drug trade and drug consumption come to being extinguished or eliminated during the course of the last 100 years? As ever, answering this is not quite so straightforward; but we will review here the available evidence.

Generally, in evaluating the effectiveness of any policy or programme, we want to try to compare outcomes with the counter-factual scenario, that is, with the outcomes that would have been produced had that policy never been implemented. In other words, we want to find out what difference the policy has made. This is not so easy with a global system that has been in place for such a long time. Nevertheless, there are a number of sources of evidence we can draw on to begin to answer this question.

Judged against the toughest measure – elimination of the drug trade and non-medical consumption of controlled drugs – we can certainly say that criminalization has failed. Estimates of the number of current drug users vary but run to hundreds of millions worldwide (Room and Reuter 2012). If we look at trends over time, the picture looks even worse. Particularly since the 1961 Single Convention, often taken as the point at which the criminal justice approach ratcheted up several notches, levels of drug consumption globally have increased significantly and drug markets have spread across the world to new regions which had previously largely been untouched by the trade, notably Asia, Eastern Europe and, more recently, Africa. To put it simply, in virtually every part of the world, proportionately more people are taking illegal drugs now than was the case 50 years ago. In the UK, for example, in 1964 there were 342 heroin addicts notified to the Home Office (Spear 1969), whilst by 2012 it is estimated there were around 300,000. A similar picture holds in many other parts of the world – the UK is by no means an outlier. Increases of this scale are astonishing and indicate that the headline for the prohibition story is overwhelmingly negative.

But prevalence is just one part of the picture. A more sophisticated way of assessing the effectiveness of criminalization is suggested by MacCoun and Reuter (2011). They argue that *numbers* of users is only one relevant dimension to look at in appraising policy. They propose a threefold framework for evaluating different policy approaches to drugs:

Total Harm = *Harmfulness* (average harm per dose) × *Prevalence* (number of users) × *Intensity* (number of doses per user)

This framework is helpful because it reminds us that policy action can be effective in relation to one dimension (e.g. reducing prevalence) whilst at the same time being counter-productive for another (e.g. harmfulness). It is the overall harm that ought to be our focus. This is important to remember when we look more closely at the evidence on the effects of criminal law sanctions and enforcement.

As MacCoun and Reuter (2011, pp. 64–5) state, enforcing the drug laws could potentially reduce consumption levels, through a mix of deterrence (using fear of punishment to put people off) or incapacitation (taking people out of communities by locking them up in prison). However, the evidence is not positive. On deterrence, it is a basic principle that certainty of sanctions is generally more important than their severity – knowing you have a high chance of getting caught deters more effectively than there being heavy penalties which are rarely invoked. This is something that intense enforcement activity can deliver, in theory. Yet a sizeable body of research has concluded that even the certainty of sanctions only has a modest deterrent effect in the context of drug use.

Studies and evidence

A meta-analysis by Pratt et al. (2006), aggregating findings from across multiple studies, suggested an average effect for certainty on self-reported consumption of −0.171 and for severity of −0.049. These are very small effects. The deterrent benefits of enforcement are further undermined by research on the wider impact of high-intensity enforcement action. Miron (1999) analysed homicide rates in the USA in relation to expenditure on drug enforcement and concluded that more enforcement is associated with higher levels of violence. Studies in Florida (Benson and Rasmussen 1991) and New York State (Shepard and Blackley 2005) found drug arrest rates were linked to increases in property crime, as prioritizing drug enforcement inevitably diverts finite police resources away from other crime-control activity. There is also a considerable amount of research on the policing of drug markets which points to further negative effects. A review of the evidence by Kerr et al. (2005) concluded that enforcement action by the police, aimed at disrupting drug markets, produces considerable collateral damage by disrupting access to health care and increasing risk behaviours (e.g. sharing of injecting equipment).

On incapacitation, the impact of enforcement looks even less positive, based on the limited evidence we have (MacCoun and Reuter 2011). Whilst it might be imagined that taking users or dealers off the street should reduce the scale of the problem, even if only temporarily, this appears not to be the case to any measurable extent. This has been found to be particularly the case in relation to drug sellers where an often-observed replacement effect seems to occur, whereby arrested and imprisoned dealers are simply replaced by others who step in and fill their shoes (Saner et al. 1995).

Criminal law enforcement might also lead to an indirect impact on drug use by affecting prices within drug markets. We might anticipate that police crackdowns on drug selling would raise prices and that, in turn, might be expected to dampen down demand. After all, a higher price for a drug is a certain cost to be incurred before it can be consumed, in contrast to the 'costs' associated with being arrested, for example, which is something that happens only rarely. The evidence here is relatively clear: drug consumption is sensitive to variations in price. For cannabis, the price 'elasticity of demand', as economists call it, is similar to that for alcohol and tobacco – for every 1 per cent increase in prices, there is a corresponding −0.5 reduction in demand (Gallet and List 2003; Wagenaar et al. 2009; Kilmer et al. 2010). For other drugs, like heroin and cocaine, the evidence is less clear but suggests that demand is also affected by price though maybe less than for other substances (MacCoun and Reuter 2011).

This is the good news from a policy perspective – use can be discouraged by increasing prices. The bad news is that efforts at law enforcement, border controls and other supply-reduction measures have been 'spectacularly ineffective at achieving this goal', as MacCoun and Reuter (2011, p. 66) bluntly put it. Taking the example of the USA, they note that prices have dropped in recent decades, whilst enforcement activity has increased – yet consumption has been broadly stable. This suggests that the criminal justice approach is seriously flawed, measured against its own objectives. Basov et al. (2001) draw similar conclusions, pointing also to the considerable cost of these increases in law enforcement which appear to have had little or no impact.

Harvard economist Jeffrey Miron argues that the effect of prohibition on keeping prices high (and therefore demand lower) has been overstated. In a careful analysis, he concludes that the price of cocaine in an illicit market is only between two and four times the price that it would be in a legal market, and for heroin six to 19 times (Miron 2003). Standard estimations are many times higher than that – Miron (2003) states that for heroin it is usually suggested that the black-market price is hundreds of times higher than the legal market price would be. Assuming that price is an important mechanism, this casts further doubt on the ability of a policy approach based on criminalization and law enforcement to tackle consumption effectively.

Miron has also done interesting work on alcohol prohibition, using historical data, which is instructive for us. The 13-year experiment in the USA with the prohibition of alcohol, between 1920 and 1933, provides a useful source of evidence for thinking about the impact of the criminalization of psychoactive substances. Drawing on multiple data sources, Miron and Zwiebel (1991) claim that from their analysis three main conclusions can be made about the effectiveness of the experiment:

1   Prohibition had a strong short-term impact on alcohol consumption, reducing it to about 30 per cent of pre-prohibition levels in the period immediately after prohibition.
2   Consumption levels rebounded quite quickly and by the mid-1920s had risen to between 60 and 70 per cent of pre-prohibition levels.
3   After prohibition was lifted at the end of 1933, alcohol consumption levels did increase, but not significantly.

Miron and Zwiebel (1991) also observe that alcohol prohibition provided a significant opportunity for the expansion of organized criminal activity. This reminds us of another important consideration when reviewing the effectiveness of the criminalization of drugs, that is, the question of unintended consequences or side effects. Here, the scorecard for the criminal law paradigm of prohibition is overwhelmingly negative. There is good evidence that it has contributed to the global spread of HIV (and other blood-borne viruses) (Room and Reuter 2012), that it fuels property and violent crime in communities (Bennett et al. 2008), motivates the corruption of officials and boosts organized crime (Reuter et al. 2009). It also entails enormous costs for the criminal justice system, from the policing of drug markets through to the incarceration of drug offenders within the prison system.

It seems reasonably clear, then, that a policy approach oriented around the enforcement of the criminal law through criminal justice agencies has not achieved its self-proclaimed goal of eliminating, or even reducing, the scale of the drug trade or levels of drug consumption. Indeed, on the contrary, the global drug market is bigger now than it was 50 years ago when the UN Single Convention on Narcotic Drugs was drawn up in 1961. And, on top of this, not only has it not worked, it has created along the way some quite serious negative side effects. In other words, more than just failing to solve the problem, it has actually made things worse.

Critiquing the critique

At this stage in our review of the evidence for the effectiveness of a criminal justice approach, we should acknowledge an important counter-argument. As MacCoun and Reuter (2011) are at pains to remind us, it is highly likely that the removal of prohibition, that is any form of decriminalization or legalization, would increase aggregate consumption levels. The increase might not be as substantial as some commentators would claim but, nevertheless, the evidence points us towards the conclusion that some level of increase would be an almost inevitable consequence of such a shift.

Put simply, there would be more people smoking cannabis, snorting cocaine powder, injecting heroin and so on. For some, this is enough to outweigh any concerns about the failures of the criminal justice approach – it may not work terribly well but the alternative is even worse. But, here, it is important to go back to MacCoun and Reuter's tripartite framework for evaluating policy that we described above. It may be true that moving away from prohibition would increase *prevalence*, but it is also highly likely that it would reduce *harmfulness*, that is, average harm per dose. Alternatively, a legal supply of unadulterated heroin of known purity, for example, would lower the risks of overdose. What is not clear at all is what the net effect would be on total harm. Would the reduction in harmfulness counteract or exceed the increase in prevalence? We simply do not know. In this sense, despite the power of the critical evidence against the criminal justice approach – and critiques of prohibition are plentiful and fairly damning – we cannot give a definitive answer to this question.

Criminal justice and international human rights

So far, we have been evaluating the criminal justice approach from an instrumental perspective, that is, in terms of whether it 'works' in achieving certain outcomes. It is also the case that, right from its origins a century ago, prohibition has not just been about outcomes. In general, criminalization tends to be applied to behaviour that is seen as morally undesirable or wrong – and this is certainly the case for drugs. As a result, drug policy and drug interventions are not always solely oriented towards reducing or eliminating the drug trade and drug consumption. Sometimes, or to some degree, they are *punitive*, designed to communicate social disapproval of immoral behaviour and/or to exact retribution against wrongdoers. We can see this reasonably clearly in a number of areas. In the context of street policing, for example, there is a considerable amount of evidence that police treatment of drug users is often shaped by the strong negative views about them.

A recent study showing this was made by Sarang et al. (2010) who examined police practice in three Russian cities and found it to be characterized by the deliberate production of fear and terror amongst injecting drug users. Another area is the prison system. Incarceration of drug users is obviously partly intended to operate as a deterrent but, arguably, when applied on the scale it is in some countries, it takes on a punitive character too (Bewley-Taylor et al. 2009). Perhaps the best example of this is the USA, where the robust execution of a 'war on drugs' has helped to fill federal and state prisons in what has been termed an era of mass imprisonment (Garland 2001b). At the very extreme end of the punitiveness of the criminal justice approach is the use in a number of countries of the death penalty for drug users.

According to Gallahue (2011), there are 32 countries or territories where the death penalty is permitted by law, although there are most likely less than 15 where executions have actually taken place in the last five years – these include China, Iran and Saudi Arabia. These countries are clearly out of step with international human rights standards. They might be seen, therefore, as extreme cases, though we suggest that they would be more accurately viewed as being at one end of the continuum that is the criminal justice approach to public policy on drugs.

Alternatives to criminalization: global drug law reform experiments

Toward decriminalization

The perceived and actual failures of the criminal-law prohibition approach have led many countries to experiment with different policies. Some of these are defined by law, that is, they involve legislative change, whilst others are based on changing how the law is enforced. All remain rooted in a law-based paradigm in the sense that they see legal categories and a legal framework as central to public policy on drugs and addiction. In this section, we review some of these alternatives and their effectiveness as policy measures.

Drug law reform experiments have grown in number over the last decade. Indeed, Rosmarin and Eastwood (2012) describe this trend as a 'quiet revolution' and claim that at least 25 countries now have formal decriminalization policies. We can identify early policy moves in this direction as far back as the 1970s. In Spain, for example, a ruling by the Spanish Supreme Court in 1974 held that drug consumption and possession were not criminal offences, a decision later formally enshrined in law in 1982 (ibid., p. 34). In the Netherlands, a 1976 law which distinguished between 'hard' and 'soft' drugs eventually led to the famous 'coffee shop' system through which cannabis could be sold in small amounts (ibid., pp. 25–6). Much of this approach was based on guidance about enforcement priorities, rather than actual legal change. Italy also first decriminalized drug possession in the 1970s, although its drug laws and policy have fluctuated quite widely in the decades since then (ibid., pp. 23–4).

Outside Europe, another early pioneer of decriminalization was Australia. South Australia's Cannabis Expiation Notice scheme, for example, began in 1987 and involved the use of civil fines for possession of small amounts of cannabis (ibid., pp. 15–16). In Uruguay, a decriminalization principle – that drug possession for personal use was not a criminal offence – was formally enshrined in law in 1974 (ibid., p. 33).

From the 1990s and into the 21st century, there has been a flourishing of experiments of this kind. Across Europe, several countries have joined the early pioneers and now include Belgium, Germany and Portgual, as well as a number of Eastern European countries, from the Czech Republic to Poland. The other main regions which have followed this path are South America and some states in the USA. Countries in the former include Argentina, Brazil, Chile, Colombia, Paraguay, Peru and Uruguay. In the USA, whilst there has been no move towards decriminalization at the federal level, several states have introduced cannabis decriminalization schemes, including California, Colorado and Washington.

To give more of a flavour of what these alternative policies look like, we will now examine in more detail three particular examples from Portugal, California and the Czech Republic, respectively. The Portuguese policy has been one of the most widely discussed in recent years, especially across Europe but also around the world (ibid., pp. 28–30). In 2001, in response to a perceived national drug problem, Portugal decriminalized personal use and possession of all drugs. Individuals found in possession of defined amounts were to be dealt with administratively by referral to a three-person panel with a diverse range of responses/sanctions at its disposal – from referral to treatment to suspension of the person's driving licence to issuing a fine. The panel also had the option of suspending proceedings and imposing no sanction at all.

According to Rosmarin and Eastwood (2012, p. 28), over 6,000 cases were dealt with administratively by these panels between 2002 and 2009, with around six in every ten cases resulting in suspension of proceedings for non-dependent use. Use of 'punitive' sanctions – fines, restrictions on movement, licence suspensions – remains low but has gradually increased over the years, from just 3 per cent in 2002 to around 14 per cent in 2009. Around three-quarters of all the cases concern cannabis, with 11 per cent involving heroin and 6 per cent cocaine.

The Portugal experiment is significant and interesting in several respects. Unlike many such approaches, it is legally defined and is not just based on altering enforcement priorities. Unusually, it applies to all drugs and not just cannabis. It was also accompanied by significant investment in health and welfare provision, which is an important aspect of the policy. As might be expected, it has proved controversial and there has been considerable debate about what the impact has been. Perhaps the most measured assessment has come from Hughes and Stevens (2010, 2012) who reach four main conclusions, albeit with certain caveats about the quality of evidence available:

1 The policy did not lead to significant rises in drug consumption.
2 There has been a reduction in levels of problem use, including injecting.
3 There have been significant reductions in the transmission of HIV and tuberculosis amongst drug users.
4 The number of drug-related deaths has fallen.

The third and fourth findings are believed to be closely linked to the investment in health services that accompanied the legal changes. Perhaps the single most important finding is the first, as this was the fear that some commentators had when the policy was first initiated. That is, there would be an explosion of drug use, especially amongst young people. That this has not happened, as far as we can tell, is a key lesson, and the Portuguese example continues to be central within debates about drug law and policy reform.

A very different example of an alternative to the criminal justice approach is Proposition 36 in California (Rosmarin and Eastwood 2012, p. 36). This was approved in a state-wide vote in 2000. It applies to cannabis only and provides for non-violent first- or second-time possession offences to be dealt with by community treatment rather than imprisonment. Offenders have to be convicted or plead guilty to apply, so it is not a legally defined decriminalization initiative in the way that Portugal's is. Nevertheless, in the context of the heavy use of custodial sentences in the USA that we have described, it represents a radical alternative to the typical approach. In 2011, funding for treatment programmes associated with Proposition 36 was cut, resulting in eligible offenders either being released without any treatment or being placed on long waiting lists.

The evaluation of Proposition 36 by researchers at the University of California at Los Angeles (UCLA) (Urada et al. 2009) concluded the following:

1 Those offenders who completed treatment had reduced drug use, committed less crime, were less likely to be homeless and had improved employment rates.
2 Aggregate falls in recent years in drug, property and violent crimes have been steeper in California than nationally.
3 Treatment completion rates are low with significantly more than half of entrants failing to complete.
4 Re-arrest rates are high, with around half of offenders being arrested for a further drug offence within 30 months.

Despite this quite mixed picture of success, the UCLA evaluation also concluded that Proposition 36 had saved the state of California around $1 billion over a five-year period, a result of reductions in criminal justice costs. It remains to be seen whether the 2011 cuts to treatment will significantly change this picture. In the present economic climate, any potential savings are clearly important for policy-makers to consider.

Our third example is much more recent. In 2010, the Czech Republic decriminalized possession of all illegal drugs (Rosmarin and Eastwood 2012, p. 21). This policy had its origins in a research study a decade earlier which had concluded that a punitive drug policy was failing to stem the availability of drugs and that levels of consumption, and of drug-related problems, were rising significantly. The new legislation provided that possession of amounts deemed to be for personal use should be dealt with administratively, rather than with a criminal charge. From 2011, on-the-spot fines could also be issued, in a similar way as for minor traffic violations.

Although it is too early to assess properly the impact of the decriminalization, there has so far not been any significant expansion of the drug problem in the Republic, or in levels of consumption which, as in Portugal, had been the principal fear of opponents of the change. An interesting possibility is that the Czech initiative might herald similar developments in other Eastern European states. This is a region which has traditionally followed 'tough' punitive approaches, not only in drug policy but more widely across the criminal justice field. A recent development in Poland in late 2011 – giving prosecutors the discretion to discontinue prosecution for low-level possession – might be a small indication that Eastern Europe is on the brink of change.

Assessing drug law reform experiments

In their report on the various decriminalization experiments from around the world, Rosmarin and Eastwood (2012) make a broadly positive assessment of their impact. They suggest that at the very least what they term the 'doomsday predictions' – that is, that decriminalization leads to significant rises in consumption – have proved incorrect. They also argue that there have been benefits in relation to reducing criminal justice costs, directing users to treatment and avoiding the negative impacts for users of acquiring a criminal record. They conclude that the best approach involves combining decriminalization with investment in health and welfare provision and in treatment services.

This approach points towards the importance of *balancing* criminal justice and public health approaches, rather than treating them as polar opposites. A slightly less wholehearted evaluation is offered by MacCoun and Reuter (2011). They argue that it is actually not possible to show that full legalization is socially beneficial overall and that therefore the real public policy challenge is to make prohibition 'work better'. In this regard, they argue for less incarceration, more treatment, more targeted ('smarter') enforcement and investment in harm-reduction provision. This, they suggest, represents a more deliverable and politically feasible programme for change, in contrast to more radical proposals which they describe as 'seductive' but highly unlikely to be implemented in the foreseeable future.

Conclusion

The century-long prohibition experiment, built on criminalization and a criminal justice approach, has not been an auspicious success. It has certainly failed to eliminate the global drug trade. Indeed, to the contrary, levels of drug consumption have increased significantly in the last several decades. And, on top of this, criminalization has been seen to lead to a range of negative side effects which contribute to the undermining of the wider public policy goals of health, security and safety, whilst costing an enormous amount of public money. At its most extreme, it has even contravened international human rights standards.

It is this track record that has led to sustained calls for a new approach and the development of alternative legal and regulatory frameworks that do not rely on the criminal law and criminal justice agencies. A number of experimental 'decriminalization' initiatives have been developed. Nevertheless, the potential risks of full-blown legalization of drugs are also strongly felt in many quarters: can we be certain that the likely increases in consumption rates would not outweigh any benefits from decriminalizing? Partly for this reason, policymakers have tended to focus more on developing strategies, policies and interventions, that can improve public health and welfare, from within the existing prohibition framework. It is to these important efforts that we now turn our attention in the next chapter.

Review questions

■ When did the 'war on drugs' begin? What happened in the years 1912, 1961 and 1971?

■ By what measures should we assess whether prohibition has worked? Has it?

■ How many countries currently permit the use of the death penalty for drug users?

■ What was the Portuguese decriminalization policy? How successful has it been?

Further reading

Gallahue, P. (2011) *The Death Penalty for Drug Offences: Global Overview 2011*, London: Harm Reduction International.
MacCoun, R. and Reuter, P. (2011) 'Assessing drug prohibition and its alternatives: a guide for agnostics', *Annual Review of Law & Social Science*, 7, 61–78.
Nadelmann, E. (1992) 'Thinking seriously about alternatives to drug prohibition', *Daedalus*, 121(3), 85–132.
Rosmarin, A. and Eastwood, N. (2012) *A Quiet Revolution: Drug Decriminalisation Policies in Practice across the Globe*, London: Release.

Public Policy: Public Health Responses

10

Chapter overview

- Public health policy: harm reduction
- Harm reduction interventions
- Public policy and drug abuse in China
- Public policy and drug abuse in the USA
- Public policy and drug abuse in the UK
- Public policy and drug abuse in Australia
- Public policy and drug abuse in Canada
- Public policy and drug abuse in the Netherlands
- Public policy and drug abuse in Switzerland
- Some comparative points

A consequence of international conventions is that countries have worked together to determine which drugs should be banned for non-medical use (Coulson and Caulkins 2012). Generally, drugs initially developed for medical use but which find their way into criminal use are selected for inclusion in the 'schedule A' of banned drugs. Once a drug is selected, there is a 12- to 18-month delay for policy-makers to get sufficient information on the possible danger the drug poses to the public if not regulated. This information comes from the medical research community and law enforcement. Drugs banned in common by the UN, the USA, the UK, Canada, Australia and New Zealand include not just heroin, cocaine and marijuana, but include drugs unfamiliar to the public, such as 2C-T-7, DMA, GHL, ketamine, oripavine, MPPP and 2C-B.

Critics of the international conventions point out that they have failed to achieve their main purpose – to stop the movement of illicit psychoactive drugs from one country to the next. An unintended consequence of these conventions and tight regulation of schedule A drugs is that important drugs are unavailable for legitimate medical use outside of the developed world (Room and Reuter 2012). These are most needed in Asia, Africa and Latin and South America. Other critics point out that countries such as Peru, Somalia, Afghanistan, Myanmar and India (Charles and Britto 2001) have had to criminalize century-old cultural traditions where cannabis, coca leaves and opiates have been managed and used without apparent harm.

Public health policy: harm reduction

A public policy approach which has developed as an alternative to criminalizing drug use and unconditional abstinence is referred to as 'harm reduction' or 'harm minimization'. The basic premise of harm reduction is that addiction is not some moral failure or failure of rationality, which should be punished as a legal violation (Marlatt et al. 2011), but is a compulsive disorder that should be recognized and treated as such. *In which case, harm reduction or minimization is any action taken to minimize the harm from behaviour that could be destructive to the user or other people and that does not first require abstinence from drugs.* This definition was sharpened by the necessity to respond effectively to the AIDS epidemic (Ball 2007). Drug dependent persons should continue to be accepted and treated at whatever phase of addiction they are in. Harm reduction is about helping dependent persons to control their dependency and allow them to live as normal a life as possible until they are ready and able to abstain from drugs.

The harm-reduction approach grows out of the recognition that societal reactions to drug abuse can reinforce the harm caused by addiction and cause harm in its own right (Reuter et al. 2009). The prohibition against drugs creates a market and the gangs and criminal enterprises to service that market. Harm reduction is also pragmatic – the focus is on what can be done that is effective to control drug use and reduce its consequential harm. The following are examples of harm-reduction interventions that have been devised to reduce some specific harm associated with addiction and drug use. These interventions were pioneered as public health measures in the Netherlands.

Harm-reduction interventions

Heroin maintenance

One way to divert people addicted to heroin away from drug dealers is for their addiction to be treated by a specially trained physician. The doctor determines their maintenance dosage and provides prescriptions for heroin or a substitute to be legally filled at a pharmacy (Haemmig 1995). In this way, the dosage and purity of the drug can be guaranteed, avoiding the fillers, impurities and variations in dosage of street drugs. The doctor can progressively reduce a user's heroin dosage until the user is drug free. In countries that have heroin maintenance, the state pays the cost of the doctors and prescriptions.

Cannabis cafés

In the Netherlands, people who use cannabis have an alternative to using illicit marijuana. A small number of cafés are allowed to sell over-the-counter cannabis for use on the premises (Lemming 2012). There is a limit to the amount purchased, and foreign nationals are now prohibited from ordering it. Prices are kept low in comparison to street prices, and purity is assured. The cafés are also safe and more attractive places to use than the streets. In recent years a user identification and purchase tracking system has been set up to prevent multiple purchases from different cafés on the same day.

Legalized prostitution

In a number of countries, prostitution in specific locations has been legalized (Weitzer 2011). The basic premise is that criminalization of prostitution does not stop it, but only drives it underground and has negative health and social consequences for all involved. Sex workers are routinely tested for sexually transmitted diseases, are provided with condoms and counselling, and are allowed to claim their income as legal wages. Their access to medical care serves as a platform for social services – food, shelter, legal aid and child care. Prostitutes who might also be drug users can get drug counselling, referrals and treatment.

Safe sex and condom distribution

A common feature in public toilets, train and bus stations and outside of pharmacies in many European countries are free condom dispensers. Condoms are made available for free and are conveniently located to encourage safe sex. For those who are sexually active, condoms are also effective for birth control and as barriers to the transmission of sexually transmitted diseases (US CDC 2010).

Street outreach

Street outreach consists of training as health outreach workers people familiar with the streets in specific communities where drug abusers congregate (Wiebel et al. 1996). Their task is to find drug abusers, establish a rapport with them and provide them with essential information to prevent HIV infections. In time, their service expands to include condoms, food and referrals to health care and to treatment. Street outreach has been shown to be effective in reducing over-dosing, the transmission of HIV and STDs, and has led to a number of drug abusers going into recovery (Colón et al. 1995; Rudolph et al. 2011).

Needle exchange

Injectors contract HIV through sharing needles and syringes already used by others who were infected with the virus. A residue of the prior user's infected blood remains in the needle and syringe which is then injected into the next user with their drugs, and so on. In needle exchanges, the injector exchanges needles that are likely to be contaminated for the same number of clean and sterile needles (Guydish et al. 1998; Kerr et al. 2009). In doing so, potentially HIV contaminated needles are taken out of circulation. The more this exchange is used, the fewer contaminated needles there are in circulation and the lower the likelihood that users will contract HIV and other blood-borne diseases.

Safe injection sites

Drug injectors vary in their skill and technique. Many do considerable damage, developing sores and abscesses and becoming infected by repeated use of blunt needles in the same location. Many inject in public and are apt to discard used needles in parks, back alleys, on the streets and in play grounds. One way to address all these problems is to have safe, clean and private places where injectors may come and, if needed, get counselling on better injection techniques from health professionals (Dolan et al. 2000). Safe injection sites are another opportunity to engage drug abusers, keep them informed and provide them with referrals.

Critique of harm-reduction interventions

It should be noted that harm-reduction interventions are very specific as to whom they reach and what they will do. This is one reason why they have proven to be effective. But this effectiveness is limited to the specific drug users they reach and who use their services repeatedly (Ritter and Cameron 2006). This means that unless harm reduction is implemented to scale, it will not reach the majority of drug abusers and make a difference in the overall problem.

With the harm-reduction or minimization strategies outlined, we can now ask the following questions. To what extent have selective countries in the global community used harm-reduction interventions? How have they balanced their older prohibition public policies with the opportunity to address the problem of drug abuse through harm reduction? We will start with China and English-speaking countries that are the least advanced in harm reduction and end with Switzerland and the Netherlands which are the most advanced.

Public policy and drug abuse in China

Despite the threat of severe punishment, it is estimated that from one to eight million people were active illicit drug users in 2004. Based upon 1.3 billion people this is a prevalence of 0.08 to 0.62 per cent of the population (Devaney et al. 2007). China is also estimated to have at least 1.9 million injection drug users (Aceijas et al. 2006). The public policy response well into the 1990s was to pass new laws and regulations with increasingly severe penalties against drug sales and use and to increase efforts to eradicate domestic cultivation of opiates (Chen and Huang 2007). Millions of police have been employed but they have not stopped drug trafficking, cultivation or a rapid increase in the prevalence of illicit drug use and abuse. Drug-free communities are one alternative where users are integrated into a community with a larger number of people who do not use drugs and who will be especially vigilant to keep drug dealing out of the community. In theory, with zero supply and no encouragement or reinforcement, drug abusers eventually lose the habit and learn to live a normal drug-free life.

Harm reduction in China

In recent years, the Chinese government has come officially to endorse harm reduction as a supplement to their continued drug war policies. The HIV/AIDS epidemic brought them to this measure. When it became apparent that there was such an epidemic in China, driven by injection drug users, it was very clear that something effective had to be done to stop it (Hammett et al. 2008). A pragmatic approach was taken to adapt successful measures from overseas. Needle exchanges and methadone maintenance have been implemented in a limited number of locations.

Interviews of injection drug users in southern China have revealed that both men and women use the needle exchange (Lau et al. 2005). Most of the exchange users share needles with friends, spouses and acquaintances, but few sterilize their needles properly. Many are commercial sex workers who use condoms inconsistently with clients, spouses and other regular and irregular sex partners. Very few are aware of and concerned with contracting HIV or STDs. This is striking evidence that educational and outreach efforts are also needed along with needle exchanges. Besides sex workers, there are millions of migrant workers and internal migrants who engage in HIV high-risk behaviour and who are at high risk of using drugs and contracting HIV through sexual exchanges.

Public policy and drug abuse in the USA

The mass marketing of heroin in the USA during the 1960s was initially seen as a local police problem. The Federal Bureau of Narcotics that was so instrumental in setting the prohibition policies prior to World War II was merged and reorganized twice. The US government's lead agency for narcotics fell into relative obscurity until it became the Drug Enforcement Administration in 1973 with President Nixon's declaration of war against drugs (Ferraiolo 2007). From the 1960s and the Kennedy administration to the second Reagan administration in the mid-1980s, there was no presidential advisor, cabinet officer or any other official with the authority to plan, set budgets or direct a national drug policy (Smith 1990).

From 1961 to 1988 there were 20 major studies and reports from federal committees, special presidential taskforces, national commissions, national drug policy boards and strategy councils (ibid.). They assessed every aspect of the growing problem of drug trafficking and drug use in the USA. All of these reports called for a centrally executed national policy and for research that would better inform national policy. None of these reports mentioned harm reduction. The Reagan administration (1981–89) did just the opposite of what the numerous reports called for. The primary responsibility and funding for drug abuse prevention and treatment of alcohol and mental health was transferred from federal agencies to the 50 state governments (ibid.). The argument in favour of this arrangement was that state agencies were closer to the problem and would be more effective than federal agencies.

In 1972 the National Institute on Drug Abuse (NIDA) was founded to serve as the research arm of US public policy on drugs (ibid.). This included management of national programmes for drug treatment, training and prevention. Then, in 1982, NIDA treatment and prevention responsibilities were transferred into block grants to the 50 states. This effectively separated government research from treatment and prevention. By 1989 the lack of a coordinated federal response to drugs was finally addressed in the 1988 Anti-Drug Abuse Act. The White House Office of the National Drug Control Policy (ONDCP) was established with goals to develop policies and coordinate all aspects of the federal response to illicit drugs. Since its inception this office has focused primarily on the supply side of the problem and, until recently, vehemently rejected harm reduction (McCaffrey 1999). Only in the Obama administration have new resources been given to treatment (ONDCP 2012).

Harm reduction in the USA

Frustration has mounted with the lack of an effective national response to drug abuse and for the continued single-minded and expensive emphasis on a war on drugs. A consensus has formed even in the law enforcement community that the USA cannot arrest its way out of the drug problem (Staff 2011). Even the current ONDCP emphasizes treatment over incarceration. The most populated state, California, has passed a state law to legalize the use of marijuana for medical purposes with proposition 215 in 1996 and with proposition 36 in 2000. People convicted of drug possession would be offered treatment in lieu of jail (VanderWaal et al. 2006). Seventeen other states have passed similar laws. These state laws are largely symbolic since state law cannot supersede federal law.

The public health and medical communities have arrived at their own consensus that drug addiction is a disease and should be treated as such. Treatment in the USA reaches only about 7.6 per cent of those who need it (Staff 2011). It is the most cost-effective response to drug abuse and, therefore, needs to be greatly increased. Needle exchanges, started as acts of civil disobedience by health professionals, and non-abstinence-based treatment have also been proven to be effective and cost efficient (Kerr et al. 2010; Strike et al. 2011). Finally, a number of state and public health organizations have urged that harm reduction should be seriously considered as part of a new proactive national response (McBride et al. 2009; Marlatt et al. 2011). The barrier to implementing such programmes is the current impasse in political decision-making and opposition to any alternative to the drug war from religious, rural and Southern conservatives in Congress who vehemently oppose any legislation that even considers a change.

Public policy and drug abuse in the UK

By the 1950s, a new drug epidemic was underway which was at first attributed to black West Indian and African immigrants who patronized 'blues clubs' where African American musicians played (Yates 2002). Then, by the 1960s, a much larger domestic drug market appeared with white British youth as its primary clients. In 1961, 'The First Brain Report' estimated the number of addicts in the UK and declared there was no significant increase in their number since the 1950s (Brain et al. 1961). Then, a London pharmacist testified that he alone had dispensed heroin and cocaine to that stated number of customers. Soon afterward, a law was passed that heroin and cocaine could be prescribed only by psychiatrists with special licences from the Home Office.

The 1971 Misuse of Drugs Act was passed and consolidated existing illicit drug prohibitions (Yates 2002). Police efforts to reduce supplies (drug trafficking) were expanded, but so also was treatment. A ministerial drug taskforce was set up with a UK Anti-drugs Coordinator. It was not until 1998 that the British government spelled out a ten-year plan in *Tackling Drugs to Build a Better Britain*. Enforcement would continue to pursue the trafficking of more harmful drugs such as heroin and cocaine, though prevention and treatment were also further enhanced through partnerships between education and health agencies to deliver services at the local level (Lafrenière 2001). A new National Treatment Agency for Substance Abusers was set up to execute the National Health Service's comprehensive demand reduction strategy. The goal of the strategy was to double the number of people in treatment and to offer a comprehensive range of services (Rassool 2006).

Harm reduction in the UK

Substitution heroin under the chemical names diamorphine and diacetylmorphine have been legally prescribed on a wide scale in the UK since 2008 (Metrebian et al. 2006). It is hoped that, by maintaining the most seriously addicted persons on prescription, crime rates would be reduced. Since 1960, a nagging question has been why so many people turned to heavy drug use in the first place. Interviews of a range of policy-makers, treatment providers and drug users show a link between poor housing and education, poor health, property crimes and problematic drug use (MacGregor and Thickett 2011). The most dangerous drugs are sold as a source of income and are used mentally to escape communities with the highest concentration of poverty and social problems – the inner cities and outer estates. Adolescents who left school and were unemployed were found to be the most drug involved; those still in school and who clearly had a career ahead of them were the least involved (Egginton and Parker 2002).

Between 1995 and 2005 prison time was tripled for those convicted of drug crimes, and treatment resources linked to the criminal justice system increased dramatically. Treatment may now cover 58 per cent of problematic illicit drug users (Reuter and Stevens 2008). Recently, drug-related crimes have started to decline. One reason for this massive increase in treatment amidst redoubled prohibition efforts has been the need also to address the HIV/AIDS epidemic driven by heroin injectors (Hughes 2001).

The debate in the UK over the most effective approach has been between being 'hard on drugs' (prohibition) or being 'soft on drugs' (harm reduction or outright legalization). But neither approach addresses poverty and inequality as the underlying factors. Critiques of current policy suggest that it does not go far enough in using harm reduction despite international evidence that this is more effective than prohibition (McKeganey 2007).

Public policy and drug abuse in Australia

Many Australians believe that their country is too remote and has too few people to be part of global drug trafficking, and that there are more than enough indigenous plants with psychoactive properties to satisfy curiosity. Nevertheless, Australia signed all the anti-drug international conventions, though it did not outlaw heroin use and possession until 1953 (Wodak 1997). As it turns out, Australia is not too vast or too remote to have a heroin problem. The country has large urban centres, not unlike other developed countries, and is, in fact, closer to the Golden Triangle than Europe or the USA. Since the 1960s, heroin use and other illicit drugs have steadily climbed. The response was the first National Drug Plan in 1985 which called for a partnership between health, education, the legislature and law enforcement to meet the drug challenge. The Plan also called for the use of harm minimization (reduction).

The drug strategy for Australia has been updated several times since 1985. *The National Drug Strategy 2010–2015* outlines current national priorities (Ministerial Council on Drug Strategy 2011). There are three 'pillars' to this strategy. The first is demand reduction to prevent illicit drug use altogether or at least to delay its onset through drug treatment and the reintegration of people in recovery back into the general community. The second pillar is supply reduction. The police and criminal justice system will be used 'to reduce the production and supply of illicit drugs and to control ... the availability of legal drugs'. The third pillar is harm reduction. This is 'to reduce the adverse health, social and economic consequences of the use of alcohol, tobacco and other drugs' (Australia Ministerial Council on Drug Strategy 2004, p. ii).

There are regional plans as well which take slightly different approaches to dealing with the drugs problem among Aboriginal people, as in Tasmania (Tasmania Department of Community Health Services 1996). There are about half a million Aboriginal and Torres Strait peoples primarily in the vast north of Australia; they represent about 2.4 per cent of the Australian population. Up to 50 per cent of them report drinking heavily enough to cause short-term harm and another 20 per cent to risk long-term harm (Berends 2004). Being arrested and spending time in jail stops the immediate harm but does not address the underlying motives of Aboriginal heavy drinking and drug use. The local plans call for more frequent use of alternatives to jail, such as treatment and even job training. But there are problems with this. Aboriginal clients are far less likely to finish drug treatment than non-Aboriginals, and those who do have high relapse rates (Joudo 2008). Interventions into Aboriginal heavy drinking and drug taking must be community-based if the interventions are going to have any chance of succeeding (Berends 2004).

Harm reduction in Australia

There are several specific interventions implemented in Australia that reflect their harm-reduction approach (Kutin and Alberti 2004). First, diversion into treatment programmes is very popular and used for non-violent and first-time offenders. Second, drug courts are also extensively used as a response to drug-related crimes. Offenders are sentenced to do restitution, go into treatment, receive restrictive probations and show that they are searching for work. They generally have to report progress on fulfilling their sentencing regularly to the courts. Third, there are needle exchanges that work to reduce rates of HIV infection among injection drug users.

There is also an intervention unique to Australia that puts supply reduction (policing) closer to harm reduction. This is a cannabis cautioning programme (NCPIC 2013). Possession of drugs is still illegal in Australia; but now, in New South Wales, Victoria, Tasmania and Western Australia, anyone caught with less than 100 grams of cannabis or 20 grams of hashish will not be arrested. They will receive a written warning from the police that drug possession is illegal and allowed to go. Police action will be taken only after several warnings. The assumption is that one or two warnings will be sufficient for most users, especially new ones, to stop, reduce or at least not go out in public carrying drugs. The strong insistence from many in the public to address the drug problem through 'a war on drugs' limits the extent to which harm reduction can be implemented.

Public policy and drug abuse in Canada

The Canadian Parliament passed the 1908 Opium Act outlawing the sales, possession and use of opium except for medical purposes. This was done as an outcome of earlier efforts to ban the smoking of opium among Chinese immigrants

(Green 1979). This initial prohibition stance against illicit drugs stayed firmly in place until well after World War II. Canada then adopted a policy of encouraging skilled immigration to increase their population for economic development. During the 1960s, the country experienced a rapid increase in drug use.

After a decade of study and following public policies from the US and the UK, Canada produced its own drug strategy in 1987 (Collin 2006). This initial policy was intent on balancing efforts to reduce supply (trafficking and sales) and reduce demand (use and abuse). By 1992, the national drug strategy's second phase called for 60 per cent of the national effort (and budget) to be devoted to demand reduction (education and treatment) and 40 per cent to supply reduction (police) (ibid.). By 2003, the revised plan called for prevention, treatment, harm reduction and enforcement. These same priorities are in place today.

Harm reduction in Canada

The harm-reduction measures taken by the Canadian government are community-based outreach, needle exchange, methadone maintenance, medically managed and supervised prescription of heroin, and medically supervised injection sites (ibid.). These measures have been implemented in Canada's largest cities (Toronto, Montreal and Vancouver). Heroin injectors can also be found in Canada's smallest and most remote provincial capitals, such as St John in Newfoundland where the cost of implementing needle exchange and treatment programmes is prohibitive (Gustafson et al. 2008).

It turns out that young aboriginal people precondition their drug use with binge drinking and inject heroin at a higher frequency than other Canadians (Pearce 2006). In large cities there has been some success in reducing injection drug use through medical prescriptions, though these users tend to be white, have legal incomes, are non-injectors, have physical health problems and use private physician services (Fischer et al. 2008). Poorer, younger, Native Indian and aboriginal users are more likely not to use medical prescriptions and to use street drugs along with prescribed drugs.

Public policy and drug abuse in Switzerland

Illicit drug use and abuse became apparent in Switzerland in the late 1960s. Initial responses came from individual cantons (the 26 states within the Swiss federation). They attempted to reduce the supply of drugs by repressing use and trafficking. Abstinence-based treatment programmes were started as well. These early prohibition policies and efforts did not work (Collin 2002). By 1980, drug abuse had increased and the most obvious sign of this was its open public use in the cities of Bern and Zurich. This led to Zurich's infamous 'Needle Park' (Platzspitz park) where addicts were allowed to congregate, deal drugs and inject drugs openly (Somaini and Grob 2012). They were permitted to do so with the understanding that they would not pose the same public nuisance elsewhere in each city. As in other countries, the AIDS epidemic turned from being a public nuisance and a police problem into a crisis which had to be effectively dealt with.

In 1991, the government implemented a national drug strategy which included harm reduction (Collin 2002). The Swiss Federal Office of Public Health (SFOPH) initiated and financially supported more than 300 projects and programmes entitled 'ProMeDro' to devise evidenced-based ways to reduce the harm associated with drug use and abuse. As a result, progress has been made on several fronts. Heroin use is now stable; injection drug use is down; users seeking treatment is up; drug deaths and hepatitis C rates are down; and homeless drug use is in decline. 'Needle Park' in Zurich was shut down in 1995 and addicts ejected from the park were offered alternative treatment and social services. By 1998, a host of prevention, treatment and harm-reduction measures were put in place. Educational efforts aimed at prevention were enhanced and implemented down to the commune level (subdivisions of cantons).

Harm reduction in Switzerland

The harm-reduction interventions put in place after 1998 consisted of: needle exchanges for drug addicts and prison inmates; 'safe' injection sites; addicts in treatment and under care being offered employment and housing; special attention being given to women who prostitute themselves to buy drugs; and counselling services being set up for the children of drug-addicted parents (Collin 2002). Sixteen national treatment centres were set up for hard-core heroin addicts that could treat up to 1,650 clients. Approximately 50 per cent of all opium addicts in Switzerland were treated with medically prescribed methadone (ibid.). They also had access to abstinence-based treatment, specialized withdrawal centres and out-patient consultation services.

Drug dependent persons have access to all of these programmes without having to meet any prerequisites, and these interventions have been put in place at the canton and commune levels throughout the public health service. Even private institutions may provide these services. The SFOPH provides funding, technical support and advice to all of these programmes (ibid.).

What has been the outcome of all these services and interventions? For the canton of Zurich there are records of 7,256 patients between 1991 and 2005; 76 per cent were treated (Nordt and Stahler 2006). It was estimated that heroin incidence rates in the canton started at about 80 persons in 1975 and rose steadily to 850 persons by 1990. But incidence declined steadily over the next decade to about 505 persons in 2002. Two-thirds of those who left treatment re-entered within ten years. This tells us that the numbers of new heroin addicts (incidence) has declined, though the cessation rate (those who did not need to return to treatment and related services within ten years) is very low. In effect, the vast system put in place has contained the problem of heroin dependency in Zurich.

Public policy and drug abuse in the Netherlands

After World War II and the rebuilding of the Netherlands, the Dutch were strongly inclined to reject law enforcement as the primary drug abuse strategy. There is a popular consensus carried over into government policy that a certain amount of illicit drug use in modern society is inevitable. The Dutch consensus is that addicts should not be pushed out of society and stigmatized: this creates more harm than good. They should be able to pursue as normal a life course as possible. To do this requires pragmatic and non-moralistic approaches to drug use.

Harm reduction in the Netherlands

The public policy foundations of this approach was fully expressed in their revised Opium Act of 1976 which was clearly intended to separate the market for illicit drugs from the social context of users (Leuw 1991). Their goal was to remove as much as possible the profits from illicit drug dealing. In this policy, law enforcement efforts were concentrated on major traffickers and dealers: addiction to hard drugs was now to be considered a public health and social welfare problem. Assistance programmes added addicts as clients; methadone maintenance was started in 1968; treatment was expanded; and eventually needle exchanges were instigated to stop the injection-driven HIV/AIDS epidemic. The retail trade of cannabis was tolerated and permitted at a number of coffee shops (MacCoun 2011). The full set of harm-reduction strategies that evolved from these policies are outlined at the beginning of this chapter.

The Dutch government paid very close attention to the effectiveness of their efforts. They were not always successful (Kooyman 1984). Methadone maintenance did not end heroin addiction as anticipated: the number of addicts continued to increase into the 1980s, as did drug-related crime. Public pressure mounted to address the problem effectively. The outcome was to provide heroin to addicts via prescription, not primarily for treatment but as a means of social control. It turns out that a much larger problem in the Netherlands is binge drinking among young people (van de Luitgaarden et al. 2008). This problem has been addressed primarily through education, though there has been very little effort to apply harm reduction to it.

Some comparative points

What have been the comparative successes and challenges in international drug policies? An apparent success is that the Chinese government has come to recognize that supply reduction prohibition policies will not reduce drug abuse. Their challenge now is to explore harm reduction and to deploy interventions on a large enough scale. The USA is the most heavily committed to illicit drug prohibition and has demonstrated to the world community that these policies, in fact, contribute a certain amount of harmfulness themselves (Reuter et al. 2009). The recently formed national consensus that these policies are ineffective is a first step toward change. The medical and public health communities are ready to expand existing harm reduction based upon successful overseas experiences, though for the foreseeable future political opposition is still too strong for more than token efforts.

The British government has also come to realize that prohibition is not driving down drug use and abuse, though they are still ambivalent about fully adopting Dutch harm-reduction measures. Moralistic sentiment against 'going soft on drugs' is strong in the UK and is reflected in the most recent government's renewed emphasis in treatment before harm reduction. The medical community has successfully defined drug addiction for over 40 years by focusing on middle-class abusers and by advocating treatment as the solution (Berridge 2012). As a result, it is estimated that in the UK there are enough treatment facilities to accommodate close to 58 per cent of heroin and cocaine abusers. The main challenge is to address the poverty and social-class basis of drug use and abuse – users and those dependent are disproportionate among the poor and marginalized in British society.

Likewise, prohibition was Australia's initial reaction to drug abuse, and they too have been reluctant to adopt harm reduction. Needle exchanges have been permitted as an exception in order to reduce HIV infection rates. However, the Australians have defined their own approach by emphasizing diversionary pathways into treatment, drug courts and cannabis cautioning. The challenge is to determine the scope of the drug problem and to deploy sufficient interventions in sufficient numbers to cut drug abuse incidence and prevalence rates.

After years of parallel efforts at prohibition with their US neighbour, Canada has adapted harm reduction. What facilitated Canada's transition to harm reduction, as in the UK and Australia, was the establishment of a universal health plan where all Canadian citizens are covered, and which is funded through federal taxes (Benoit 2004). With the plan, prescription maintenance and treatment have been made available to all who need them as part of regular medical services. The challenge to Canadians is the same as it is to Australians – to determine the scope of their drug problem and to deploy enough prevention and treatment to address the problem.

In contrast, Switzerland has assessed the scope of their problem and, in the case of their Zurich canton, met approximately 70 per cent of the need for treatment and drug maintenance (Nebehay 2010). Harm reduction, especially medical prescription maintenance based on a universal health plan, has been the key to their success. Switzerland is the only country reviewed to come closest to addressing its drug problem fully and effectively. Their challenge now is to close in on the final 30 per cent of drug users and abusers not in the system.

Finally, the Netherlands has pioneered and fully deployed harm reduction. They have shown that it is possible to get the vast majority of those who abuse illicit drugs into the medical system and to minimize the personal and societal harm drug users can cause. Like Switzerland, they have come very close to addressing their drug problem fully and effectively. But their challenge is a unique one, and one that we might see if other countries reach the same point. Once addicts are fully in the system, it does not follow that all or most will reach abstinence and be able to live drug-free thereafter. Success in the Netherlands also means maintaining many people on opiate or other substitute therapies indefinitely.

A potential counter to harm reduction is abstinence from drug use – which will be covered in the next two chapters that focuses on prevention and treatment.

Review questions

■ What is harm reduction?
■ Can you briefly describe any harm-reduction interventions and their rationales?
■ How is public policy regarding drug abuse different in China as opposed to the USA?
■ Are there differences between harm-reduction measures in the UK and Switzerland?
■ What is the significance of the Netherlands in harm reduction?
■ Are there any preconditions to the effectiveness of harm reduction in the Netherlands and Switzerland that do not exist in China and the USA?

Further reading

Bloss, W. P. (2005) 'Comparative European and American drug control policy: an examination of efficacy and contributing factors', *ERCES Online Quarterly Review*, 2(2).

Hilton, B., Thompson, R., Moore-Dempsey, L. and Janzen, R. (2001) ' Harm reduction theories and strategies for control of human immunodeficiency virus: a review of the literature', *Journal of Advanced Nursing*, 33(3), 357–70.

Inciardi, J. A. (2008) *The War on Drugs IV: The Continuing Saga of the Mysteries and Miseries of Intoxication, Addiction, Crime, and Public Policy*, Boston, MA: Pearson/Allyn & Bacon.

Prevention

11

Chapter Overview

■ Who carries out prevention?
■ Levels of prevention
■ Level 1: knowledge
■ Level 2: affective learning
■ Level 3: prevention through normative change
■ How effective are normative interventions?

The single most effective and cost-efficient way to minimize drug abuse and its short and long-term harm is through prevention (Gerstein and Green 1993). The classic public health definition divides prevention into three stages (DHHS 1999):

■ *Primary prevention*: a disease is prevented from happening before it can strike.
■ *Secondary prevention*: recurrences or worsening of an existing disease are minimized.
■ *Tertiary prevention*: this is when one works to minimize the harm, damage and disabilities caused by a disease.

These classic distinctions are very important in describing all the ways that a disorder such as drug abuse must be addressed to keep it from becoming a pandemic – completely out of control. Prevention is our first and, as you will see, most effective line of defence.

There is now a second and more specific definition of drug abuse prevention. This second definition addresses the specific features of drug abuse and is derived from past research on prevention efforts (Institute of Medicine 1994). There are *risk factors* that make it more likely that one will abuse drugs when compared to someone without the same factors present. A risk variable or factor is present before the onset of dependency; and there are others present when drug use transforms to drug abuse. Next, there are *protective factors* that counter dependency. They protect an individual from initiating drug use or, once drug use has begun, they protect an individual from going to the next stage of abusing drugs. The objective of any prevention effort is *risk reduction*: that is, not only to reduce risks of becoming drug dependent but to improve protection against it as well. Another way to look at the object of prevention is to enhance protective factors, also described as fostering *resilience*.

Who carries out prevention?

Because of the scale and complexity of modern societies, the prevention of diseases and of drug abuse has become a primary function of government. It is the only social institution with the mission, resources and authority to work effectively toward improving the collective good of its citizens. Within government, the prevention of drug abuse as well as the treatment of those who abuse drugs within the medical community is the job of public health departments, services and agencies. These government entities in turn maximize their impact by working through and alongside a host of non-government organizations (NGOs), many of which are community-based organizations (CBOs).

Public health services

Public health departments, services and agencies along with their NGO and CBO networks are also heavily reliant on science, medicine and education. There are ten essential public health services performed by virtually all governments (APHA 2013):

1   monitor the status of community health;
2   diagnose and investigate health problems and hazards;
3   inform, educate and empower people about health issues;
4   mobilize community partnerships to identify and solve health problems;
5   develop policies and plans;
6   enforce laws and regulations that protect health and ensure safety;
7   link people to services that are needed and ensure access where they are unavailable;
8   provide assurance of a competent public health and personal healthcare workforce;
9   evaluate effectiveness, accessibility and quality of services;
10 research for new insights and innovative solutions to health problems.

The benefits of such an approach are that targeted and effective prevention are based upon accurate aetiological or causal knowledge. Science gets translated into accurate prevention messages and workable intervention for specific risk groups. In the outbreak of a deadly disease, public health officials are designated to take effective measures to stop the epidemic because of their expertise and experience. It is essential to know whether or not the incidence (new cases) and prevalence (accumulation of cases) of a disease and disorder are increasing or decreasing. The cost of primary prevention is only a fraction of the costs of treatment, and the cost of secondary prevention is only a fraction of the collateral costs of addiction in crime, criminal justice, imprisonment and lost economic productivity (Rand Corporation 1999).

There are also drawbacks that make work in public health challenging. If you fail, the results will be very self-evident (i.e. more people will be ill or dependent on specific drugs). If you succeed, there is no direct evidence that your efforts are responsible for the lack of disease (Reiss 2009). Public health agencies as government entities must run as bureaucratic organizations. The more bureaucratic an agency, the longer it takes to respond and the less effective it becomes. Public health is dependent upon political entities for funding. Funding controls what and how much a public health agency can do. And public health can seem expensive: it is not until the public's health is obviously threatened before the cost of public health becomes clearly justified. Finally, effective prevention interventions are inevitably going to conflict with some group's moral and/or religious values and beliefs.

Levels of prevention

Besides prevention across the disease/disorder spectrum (primary, secondary and tertiary) and specific to drug abuse (risk and protective factors, risk reduction and resilience), there are three approaches to prevention (Ellickson 1995): information, affective influence and social influence. We will add that each approach is more effective than the last and is a precondition of the next; there is, in fact, an effectiveness hierarchy. Knowledge is at level 1 and affective learning based upon knowledge is at level 2. A phase of level 2 with potential for greater effectiveness is aversion therapy. The most effective level is for prevention knowledge and affective learning to lead to a social norm. Each level is explained in what follows.

Level 1: knowledge

Knowledge of the personal and social effects of drug dependency, the risk one takes in using drugs and the ways that one can avoid using them are essential knowledge and basic to the prevention of drug dependency (UNODC 2004; Soole et al. 2005). Fortunately, no one starts without any knowledge whatsoever. Part of what drug dealers and many users do is to provide explanations and rationales for selling and using a drug. Invariably, one hears at the beginning of any drug marketing that the new drug is not addictive, is better than an already established drug, has health and life-style benefits, and is even legal. This is certainly now the case for new drugs being discussed on the Internet and on the streets, commonly referred to as 'street knowledge' (Davey et al. 2010). Older street knowledge claimed incorrectly that: marijuana enhances intelligence; one can drink a particular alcoholic beverage and never get drunk; heroin enhances creativity and is non-addictive; cocaine and crack are safer to use and enhance one's sex life. People who developed serious addictions to these drugs found out otherwise.

Prevention specialists have to learn what street knowledge is claiming with regard to specific drugs and then have to devise accurate counter-statements. In effect, expert knowledge has to counter street knowledge and become more salient. For some people, published reports and broadcast statements from experts and authorities are sufficient to replace street knowledge. For many others, and especially those most at risk of initiating, using and becoming dependent on drugs, the views of authorities and experts may not be salient, may be resisted or simply not be believed. The larger public and those most at risk have to be approached in other ways to get prevention messages across. The most cost effective way to get one's message heard in mass societies is through electronic media.

Prevention through media

The dream of prevention specialists is to be able to devise accurate and attractive drug education messages, present them in print, on television, radio, videos, via the Internet or on billboards, and secure vast public incorporation of the messages (Roy et al. 2007). That is: based upon one's message, there would be measurable and permanent change in public behaviours, beliefs and attitudes regarding some drug risk. This would be the most cost-efficient and effective way to do prevention. The problem is that there has been little empirical research on the impact of media-based approaches on rates of illicit drug use (Werb et al. 2011). A long history of media study evaluations suggests that for media campaigns to be effective: they have to be ongoing; they have to target specific audiences; the message has to be short and simple (easy to remember); the more times the message can be repeated the better; and the message has to be creative and unique to catch and hold risk takers' attention and to be remembered (Morgan 2002).

The most effective advertisements are, in effect, 'show-stoppers'. These are the ones that are in some way sensational, talked about and remembered long after the advertisement has gone. But even campaigns that do all of this and have been evaluated are still fairly limited in the extent to which they impact on risky behaviour and the attitudes and beliefs of potential drug takers (Yzer et al. 2011). Media campaigns appear to be more effective with adults and parents but much less so with youth (Soole et al. 2005). Specific messages and campaigns have to be devised to target youth and, even more specifically, youth who are at high risk. More often, these are young men and members of racial and ethnic groups isolated from the general public.

An example of an effective drug prevention media campaign was conducted in the San Francisco Bay Area in the late 1980s during the height of the crack cocaine epidemic. There was street knowledge that crack was cheap and harmless. To counter this message, a billboard appeared on all forms of public transportation of the inside of a frying pan with two eggs frying. The message was: 'This is your brain on cocaine'. In one simple message the notion that cocaine is harmless was refuted and a counter-message was dramatically conveyed: it is not only harmful, it can cause permanent and irreversible damage to one's brain. Lots of people who believed otherwise were given pause for thought.

Prevention through education

The majority of potential drug users cannot be effectively reached through media alone. They have to be approached directly. The only place where virtually all young people can be directly accessed repeatedly and over time is in school. As a result, the most common drug abuse prevention programmes worldwide are school-based (UNODC 2004). The largest and longest running school-based drug abuse prevention effort that has been evaluated is the Drug Abuse Resistance Education (DARE) programme started in the USA in 1983 (Kanof 2003). This consisted of uniformed police officers teaching elementary and high school students about the dangers of drug use. A national curriculum was developed making DARE interventions popular and standardized. By 1994, DARE programmes existed in 80 per cent of all school districts in the USA and there were sites overseas.

DARE was evaluated (ibid.). A representative sample of youngsters (randomly selected) who received the DARE training was immediately interviewed after completing the programme. A control group of young people (also randomly selected) who did not receive DARE training was also interviewed at the same time. The results showed that immediately after training significantly fewer DARE students had initiated drug use than those in the control group. DARE students who were already using drugs (mainly alcohol or marijuana) used less. This suggested that the programme worked. But there was a problem. Six months after the training, there was no significant difference in drug use between the DARE students and the control group. In effect, the programme effect was short-lived. Despite this repeated finding of limited and temporary effectiveness, police and politicians in the USA continued to support and fund the same DARE programme.

An in-depth analysis of DARE suggests that it was limited in effectiveness because the primary mode of education was police officers lecturing to students (ibid.). The students were passive learners. A relatively small percentage of them were cognitive learners and completely learned the message. An even smaller percentage could on their own figure out the behavioural implications of the message for themselves and then align their behaviour. But for most students, the message was not sufficient to make a lasting change even if they understood and agreed with the message. Regardless of how much or how little of the prevention message the students absorbed, none learned through the DARE curriculum how to apply the knowledge or to make the information personal. This leads to the second level of prevention.

Level 2: affective learning

Have you ever been warned about some danger and gone ahead and taken the risk anyway? This is a common experience. Knowing something is one thing, but abiding by that knowledge is another matter. To align behaviour with knowledge requires a lot more than cognitive skills and information. One way to make behaviour more consistent with knowledge is for that behaviour to accompany affective learning (Hofmann et al. 2010; Um et al. 2012). That is: one is *emotionally* disposed toward accepting or rejecting a particular behaviour. So, to know that something is not good for you does not in itself motivate compliance; but to *feel* that it is bad or good for you is motivating. So the trick is to get drug use associated with whatever one strongly feels is revolting, disgusting, unattractive and not fashionable. Affective learning is an additional requirement and goal of prevention education where programme outcomes can then become more deeply internalized and, therefore, become more long lasting. There are examples of attempts at affective learning in drug abuse prevention.

The UK's 'Blueprint'

Perhaps the most comprehensive drug abuse prevention education effort has recently been completed in the UK (Baker 2006). The 'Blueprint' was conducted in 29 schools in Cheshire, Derby City, Derbyshire and Lancashire in the spring of 2004 and 2005. Twenty-three schools received the intervention and students in six others served as control groups. Two hundred regular teachers were trained over six days to deliver the lessons. Each lesson was intended to be interactive and enjoyable; students were engaged in participatory learning to build their knowledge and skills about drugs. Teachers' manuals, student work books, classroom posters and cards were given to students informing them of local counselling and treatment services. Initial findings in 2009 suggest that the programme was well received by students and parents (Keane 2010). What is unique about this programme is that there are four other components, which will be discussed in the next section.

Enhanced DARE

After years of conflict between DARE proponents and researchers over its effectiveness or lack of it, an attempt was made to understand why schools wanted to maintain the programme despite its questionable effectiveness (Center for Court Innovation 2009). Through interviews, investigators found that local officials believed that researchers were in error when they focused exclusively on preventing drug use as the only and most important student outcome. In their mind, there were other outcomes that made the programme worthwhile: (1) students came to understand their communities better; (2) an important rapport was established between young people and the police; and

(3) DARE built working relations and collaborations between the schools and police. As can happen with interventions, they start out with one intended goal but end up fulfilling others. This is why follow-up evaluations are so important. It is essential to know if the original goal was met and, if not, why not, and what was the programme's actual impact.

Based on these findings, researchers met with school and DARE officials. The result was a rethinking and enhancement of DARE to make it more effective. The new DARE programme now has a curriculum that emphasizes affective learning and incorporates many of the lessons learned from the efforts and evaluations of the earlier programme (CCI 2009). The enhanced DARE emphasizes participatory and active learning, replaces the police as the direct instructors with regular teachers, builds the DARE curriculum into schools' health education programmes and attempts to reinforce the training wherever and as often as it can.

Elementary and high school students who receive the new DARE training report maintaining their programme effects for more than six months. Fewer students initiated drug use, and those who did used less than students who did not receive DARE. There have been periodic follow-ups to the initial training. If the programme is repeated, the positive effects can last through to the end of high school (Botvin 2000). But, there are troubling issues in the evaluation research itself. We know whether or not students have initiated drug use or have reduced it only from self-reports. That is: programme outcomes are entirely dependent upon students giving accurate information about their drug use. They know that when they are asked questions about drug use the second time that they and the programme are being evaluated. It is quite possible that some under-report drug use to please their teachers and the programme while others may over-report in defiance against some teachers or the school.

Aversion therapy

A higher level of effectiveness in affective learning can be achieved through aversion therapy. This approach internalizes affective learning much more deeply. Imagine some food or rich dessert that you simply will not and cannot avoid. You make or buy it often, eat most of it at one sitting, and crave it when you do not have it. Aversion therapy involves the strong attachment to eating this food and craving for it with something that is revolting or disgusting and which will make the very thought of this food immediately unattractive and inedible. The most effective way to develop an aversion to something, even the thought of it, is to make it not only psychologically but also physically revolting (Howard and Jenson 1990; Howard 2001). One becomes nauseous or sick in the stomach at the sight of a drug or at the thought of using it. This outcome can be achieved by fixing the aversion to the craving for a drug. Aversion therapy bridges prevention and treatment and is a direct application of social learning, operative conditioning and learning theory, as reviewed in Chapter 7 (Brush 1971).

The difficulty in getting an aversive effect through cognitive learning has led to more pharmaceutically based aversion efforts. There is the promise of using specific medicines to develop and maintain aversions to illegal drugs. US government research is committed to the promise of such pharmaceutical aversions. Drug abuse deterrent medicines are in development (Katz 2008). Because of ethical concerns, much of this research is initially conducted on animals. Ritanserin is one such antagonist that has been in human clinical trials as an aversion treatment for alcohol and cocaine dependency (Janssen 1994).

Critique of aversion therapy

Aversion therapy as it is now explored cannot effectively stop the initiation of drug use or the development of drug habits in a cost effective way. Medical aversion therapy as a form of behaviour modification requires one-on-one attention by a trainer-counsellor who has to find what the patient is averse to, develop a way to link the aversion to the drug use, and then to conduct the training. This makes aversion therapy much more of an adjunct to drug treatment.

Pharmaceutical aversions pose additional challenges. Drugs that work well with animals in a laboratory setting do not necessarily work as well with humans (Howard and Jenson 1990). There are a number of drugs that are successful at generating aversive effects, though they are general and not specific. So instead of blocking the craving for a specific drug such as alcohol or cocaine they block the effects of all medicines. This is specifically problematic when many food substances are also inadvertently blocked (Scalera 2002).

Targeted prevention

Even if school-based prevention is more effective and aversion therapy could be conducted on a large-scale, there are still major drawbacks to these approaches. The most critical problem is that the teens who are at greatest risk of using drugs and of becoming dependent on them are marginal to school or may not attend at all. They may be 'out of school' or on the streets. Furthermore, many young adults do not begin drug use until they finish school and are in their twenties. This means that large pools of drug users are not reached through school efforts such as DARE and the Blueprint. The basic demographics of drug use suggest that attention and limited resources must be aimed, not at all adults or at all school-age youth as with DARE, but as targeted prevention which works directly with those at highest risk of using drugs (O'Connell et al. 2009).

But there is an even more specific challenge to targeted interventions. Drug users in prohibition countries are engaged in an illegal and stigmatized activity: they hide from the authorities and are hard to reach. They are also inaccessible by general media campaigns. Those communicating the message might as well speak an unknown foreign language or be in another country. This means that if prevention efforts are going to work, an absolute precondition is to reach and engage specific drug users and high risk groups. They must be engaged when and where they are available and in a language that they understand – at 'their time and place' (Bowser et al. 2001). Wherever a drug abuse prevention technique is used, there are common principles for how one can successfully reach or target hidden, hard-to-reach and marginal groups. Since the early 1990s, these principles had to be refined and advanced to intervene in the drug-related HIV/AIDS epidemic (Regional Office of South-Asia 2007).

Critique of targeted prevention

Targeted interventions are almost never conducted at the scale needed to reach more than a small percentage of drug users and risk takers in any one community. So, their effectiveness is demonstrated but never fully applied. In the USA, targeted interventions are generally funded for five years by the federal government and, if proven to be effective, are supposed to continue under local funding. They rarely are. But then, even if they are continued, targeted interventions do not address the fundamental stigma, isolation, discrimination and inequalities that perpetuate illicit drug using in the community as a whole.

Level 3: prevention through normative social change

But there is still another level of prevention that if reached can be more effective than information alone, affective training or targeted interventions. If the basic social norms of a community can be shifted away from supporting use of any specific drug, the impact would be far more extensive than individual successes and even success among high risk groups (Rivis and Sheeran 2003; Latkin et al. 2003). Then, much larger numbers of people would not initiate drug use and, if they were already using, would find it hard to continue.

The non-use of a drug would be a social script that one would follow much like stopping at red lights and going on green lights – it would be conditioned and virtually automatic. In fact, if non-use of a drug became socially normative, there would be no need for a law against its use or to regulate its presence in society.

College and community-wide prevention

Changing social norms is extremely difficult where community boundaries are diffuse and there are lots of external influences. If drug use declines, how do we know that it was due to the intervention and not to some other influence on people in the community? One way to address this problem is to find largely self-contained communities where one can test interventions and evaluation strategies. For this reason college campuses are popular places to do drug prevention studies focused on alcohol. Binge-drinking poses a challenge to college students, administrations and researchers alike (Werch et al. 2000). So how can this be reduced, along with its accompanying harm to drinkers and non-drinkers alike? Of particular interest is the possibility of changing social norms among students with regard to binge-drinking.

In studies of student drinking it is necessary to determine what students perceive as norms regarding drinking. In study after study investigators have found that students generally over estimate the extent to which their friends and other students drink (Perkins et al. 2005) and use marijuana (Kilmer et al. 2006). So, instead of feeling that their drinking is normative, they feel that they are outsiders in an environment where heavier drinking is the norm. Furthermore, they feel the same way about resistance to drinking. They underestimate the extent to which other students resist heavy drinking as well (Benton et al. 2008). It turns out that what motivates frequent and occasional binge-drinking is a minority of students who personally favour this behaviour. This is particularly the case in student residences not directly under the university's control, such as social fraternities and sororities. Furthermore, these heavy drinkers influence other students to join in binge-drinking, making their 'drink till drunk' norms much stronger than alternative societal and college community-centred norms that prohibit such behaviour. Social norm interventions aimed at reducing binge-drinking will in some way have to make college community norms more salient and weaken student-centred drinking norms (Cho 2006).

Research on the social norms of college binge-drinking is an attempt to understand better what needs to be done to implement social normative interventions successfully as a way to bring about more long-lasting preventive behaviours. Several major efforts were made in the USA to reduce drug abuse in entire communities. A description of one of the most ambitious projects follows.

Kansas City project

Fifteen communities in the Kansas City metropolitan area were sites of a comprehensive community-based drug abuse prevention effort dating back to 1984 (Pentz et al. 1989). The objective of the project was to use community norms to reduce and prevent cigarette smoking, alcohol consumption and marijuana use among adolescents. The project included a mass media campaign, a school-based educational programme, parental education and outreach by community organizations. This was all introduced sequentially into the target communities over a six-year period. Systematic interviews of students at 42 area schools were conducted at the beginning of the project to determine the prevalence of drug use in the month prior to the interviews and then again two years later after the interventions had started. Among ninth and tenth graders, self-reports revealed that cigarette smoking was down from 24 to 17 per cent of respondents; those who used alcohol declined from 16 to 11 per cent; and marijuana use went down from 10 to 7 per cent of respondents (ibid.).

Several area schools delayed their prevention education efforts so that their students could serve as a control group. Students in the intervention schools and communities were compared with students in the control schools and communities. Their prevalence of cigarette, alcohol and marijuana use was half that of the control group. This finding was evidence that the campaign, especially its school-based component, was responsible for the declining drug-use prevalence where both adolescents at high and low risks could benefit (Johnson et al. 1990).

There has been a major effort underway by the National Institute on Drug Abuse (2003) to identify these 'evidence-based' interventions. The hope is that these programmes will serve as models of effective drug abuse prevention practices for anyone planning to start a new programme or who wishes to improve an existing one (August et al. 2004).

How effective are normative interventions?

Normative preventions are the most difficult to achieve, but they also hold the most promise. Anyone who has attempted to do such an intervention quickly comes to appreciate how difficult it is to affect community norms. It is much easier to convince a few people, even an entire social network, to change their behaviours than it is to change the social norms of an entire community. But when normative change does occur it results in widespread behavioural change. A second difficulty is in getting prevention norms internalized into the community culture and become self-perpetuating. No one has yet been able to claim an unmitigated success here.

In addition to the complexity of norm change and internalization of these changes as a goal, the single most critical point about normative interventions is that they are almost never done on a scale sufficient to stop specific drug use and abuse. Nor are they implemented long enough to become accepted as part of the very fibre of a community. An intervention may require at least a generation (25 years) to become normative. This is not simply a problem of insufficient political will to fund such efforts long enough and at the scale appropriate to the problem. There may be real theoretical and pragmatic limits to how much and how deeply one can intentionally and rationally intervene into community norms, even if one had the resources and time.

Abstinence as prevention

Some might wonder why more has not been said about abstinence as a form of prevention, and where it fits into the hierarchy of prevention. Abstinence in prevention is defined as 'reframing from using an illicit drug' or ideally as 'never initiating illicit drug use'. Alcoholics Anonymous is the best example of this approach (Lee et al. 2011). What seems straightforward is not the case when one considers all the different ways drugs and drug use can be defined.

Abstinence advocates pose that it is ethically and morally preferred over harm reduction, which appears more like facilitating drug abuse (Leshner 2008). The problem with abstinence versus harm reduction is that the two sides are not an either–or. Harm reduction in the Netherlands has never been presented as an alternative to abstinence. No such public policy exists. Harm reduction is intended for the vast majority of drug abusers who are unable or unwilling to abstain from harmful drug use (Marlatt and Witkiewitz 2010).

Some drug abusers reach a point where they are ready to go into treatment or to become 'clean and sober' without treatment. Harm reduction is not intended for drug users who reach this point. There is evidence that advocating abstinence from drug use and having it as an option in counselling might delay the initiation of drug use among adolescent non-drug users (Harper et al. 2010). But how such advocacy and counselling fit into the universe of all protective factors has yet to be determined (Maffina et al. 2013). Abstinence advocacy is certainly a form of prevention knowledge and could develop into affective training and normative change. But this would require greater precision and would tell us who the intervention will work for and how it will work amidst all the other factors that could affect the outcome.

Anyone engaged in drug abuse prevention would prefer abstinence as the preferred outcome; it is clearly the best outcome for former drug abusers (Best et al. 2013). But most drug abusers are not ready to give up their drug use. The scientific problem here is that we have not figured out the conditions and timing for when drug dependent persons become ready to abstain (Marlatt and Witkiewitz 2010). Outreach workers report that many people, on occasion, reach 'ready', but that it is a very narrow window. They have to be rushed into treatment on-demand. The real difference between abstinence and harm reduction is that abstinence advocacy has no effective interventions for the vast majority of drug abusers who are unwilling and unable to abstain. Harm reduction is designed specifically for these people.

Review questions

- What is the unique role that public health services play in preventing drug abuse?
- Are all prevention interventions equally effective or is there a hierarchy of effectiveness? What are the differences in effectiveness?
- What are the advantages and disadvantages of media and educational preventions?
- How does the initial DARE differ from enhanced DARE?
- What are the advantages of affective preventions over knowledge preventions?
- What are the difficulties of attempting normative change interventions?

Further reading

Campo, S., Cameron, K., Brossard, D. and Frazer, S. (2004) 'Social norms and expectancy violation theories: assessing the effectiveness of health communication campaigns', *Communication Monographs*, 71(4), 448–70.

Cuijpers, P. (2003) 'Three decades of drug prevention research', *Drugs: Education, Prevention & Policy*, 10(1), 7–20.

Janowiak, J. (2009) 'Lessons from the street: an introduction to drug education', *American Journal of Health Education*, 40(6), 378–81.

Lubman, D., Yucel, M. and Hall, W. (2007) 'Substance use and the adolescent brain: a toxic combination?', *Journal of Psychopharmacology*, 21(8), 792–4.

Rimal, R. and Real, K. (2005) 'How behaviors are influenced by perceived norms', *Communication Research*, 32(3), 389–414.

Wright, L.S. (2007) 'A norm changing approach to drug prevention', *Journal of Drug Education*, 37(2), 191–215.

Treatment

12

Chapter overview

- Psychotherapy
- Object relations
- Cognitive behavioural therapy
- The social model
- Residential treatment
- Family therapy
- Natural recovery

Substance use disorder treatment has grown from a religious-based approach to a variety of forms – from psychodynamic psychotherapy to social models to residential treatment – and from an emphasis on personal transformation to reducing the harm of drug abuse. As with medical treatments, concerns centre on the issue of 'which treatment works best?'. As we shall see, the answer is an approximation, from which many new questions are raised.

In many countries during the 19th century, there was recognition that drugs exerted powerful influences, leading some to premature death, while others were led to financial ruin along with the destruction of their marriages and families. Many wounded US Civil War soldiers (1860–65) were treated with morphine for their pain and developed addictions to the drug (Dean 1991). Religious perspectives dominated the public understanding of addictions in the 19th century. That approach saw drug use as a *moral failure*, amenable only by religious restoration following confession and punishment.

Psychotherapy

At the time in Europe, it was thought that hypnosis might be a way to provide treatment for a range of behavioural complaints. However, as Sigmund Freud found, hypnosis proved to be an unreliable treatment (Westen 1999). Using a model based on metaphors from the Industrial Revolution and biology, early psychodynamic thinkers linked urges to use drugs to biologically based instincts and faulty parenting practices (Cervone and Pervin 2008). Left unattended, these fault lines would make a person more likely to seek drugs or alcohol to dull the psychological pain. Since the origins of the problem are unknown, the individual cannot control his or her use of drugs or alcohol.

Treatment, according to this tradition, requires clients to perform 'free association', i.e. say whatever comes to mind (Westen and Arkowitz-Westen 1998). The therapist, using his or her knowledge of the client's unconscious processes, interprets the meaning of those thoughts. A good therapist uses the discussion to move the client to greater insight into his or her unconscious processes. A 'cure' is established when clients are aware of the unconscious origins of their emotions and thoughts. When they understand why they are using drugs to cope with an unconscious problem, they develop control over the process and can discontinue drug abuse.

Critique

Treatment, according to this model, requires uncovering the unhealthy displacements via talk therapy. Such treatments may be lengthy, and outcomes are rarely predictable. Highly skilled therapists are required to provide quality treatment. While some individuals reported benefits from such treatment, no reliable methods were developed by these early practitioners to determine whether an individual had been 'cured' (Mitchell 1995). Indeed, only a skilled therapist can determine whether the client is even making progress. Since there is no standardized measurement technique, like blood pressure or temperature reading, there is no way of knowing whether different therapists are treating the same thing, or seeing the same changes in unconscious processes (Smit et al. 2012). If the therapist says the client is better, is this sufficient?

Object relations

Following Freud's discoveries over the next half century, many others developed their own models. By 1950, newer methods of psychotherapy began to emerge. In England, in the 1940s, Melanie Klein and others devised another way of looking at mental suffering called 'object relations' (Mitchell 1983). Like attachment theory, it is based upon the development of positive relations with early caregivers to develop healthy adult states of mind. If these early relations are troubled or one's needs are not met, a healthy psychology does not develop (Cervone and Pervin 2008). Addiction to alcohol and drugs has been connected to poor early object relations (Ball and Legow 1996).

In this therapy the client is helped to develop a healthy sense of trust, called a 'therapeutic alliance' (Corso et al. 2012; Tsai et al. 2012). Clients learn to trust that the therapist cares about them, will maintain confidentiality and, despite calling up painful memories, is working to resolve their problems. The very fact that the therapist is actively listening shows the client that he or she is not like the person (usually a parent) who did not care for them in the past.

Hence clients can begin to develop healthy adult relationships, and in doing so shake off their reliance on drugs or alcohol.

Evidence

Researchers have systematically investigated psychotherapy. Woody summarizes this literature and concludes there is ample evidence for the effectiveness of traditional psychotherapy for the treatment of substance abuse disorders (Woody 2003).

Critique

Using object relations as their approach, practitioners have developed treatments that seek to mend unhealthy thought and behavioural habits. Talk therapy is still the treatment, which requires highly skilled therapists. The treatment is lengthy, and no reliable methods have been devised to determine if a person is 'cured', though many individuals reported relief from suffering. It is clear that this type of therapy works for some people, but there is no definitive evidence to show for whom it works or how well.

Cognitive behavioural therapy

By the 1960s psychology had moved away from psychodynamic approaches altogether. Newer theories emphasized an individual's capacity to grow and develop new ways of handling emotions without lengthy talk interventions. Among these has been the cognitive model (Cervone and Pervin 2008). This approach assumes a person develops habits of thought and perception that may be maladaptive. Working with a skilled therapist can identify these habits and replace them with healthier ones (Watkins et al. 2011). Cognitive therapy is based on the assumption that emotions and behaviour are caused by thoughts and perceptions. Thus, while one may not be able to change one's parents, or one's situations in life, one can change how one thinks about and perceives them.

In addiction treatment, cognitive therapists work with clients to identify the thoughts and emotions they had before and after they used drugs or alcohol. The technique, called 'functional analysis', can give the client some insight into why they use drugs (Wolpe 1993). Another technique, called 'skills training', focuses on teaching the client to unlearn old habits, change perceptions and develop better coping skills.

Evidence and promise

In one large-scale study of cocaine abuse treatment, clients who received six months of treatment along with group counselling showed the greatest improvement (Crits-Christoph et al. 1999). Results have shown cognitive behavioural treatments are as effective as other individual therapies, though they take less time, many being completed in 16 weeks of weekly sessions. The treatments have been linked to moderate reductions in drug use. Any relapses can be attributed to returning to negative thoughts and perceptions (Hides et al. 2010).

Critique

Again, it is not clear for whom cognitive treatments work best, or for how long. Such treatment requires a highly skilled therapist. Given that many individuals drop out of treatment before completion, it is very difficult to determine whether they dropped out because they achieved remission or because they were dissatisfied with their care. Different kinds of people may opt for short-term cognitive therapy rather than long-term psychodynamic therapy, making comparisons especially difficult. For all forms of therapy relapse is common. In a ten-year study of clients who achieved remission for six months, one-third relapsed in the first year, and the rest suffered a relapse within the ten-year period (Xie et al. 2005).

The social model

The medical approach to the treatment of alcoholics is inaccessible to most who need it. In time, it was realized that those in recovery could provide effective treatment for themselves through peer counselling and community-based groups. Addiction is also much more than an individual psychological or physiological problem. It is also a problem of community morale and spirit where the community and everyone around the addict needs some form of healing (Borkman et al. 1999).

The central treatment in the social model consists of group meetings where: participants' excuses for their drug use are critiqued; values and past behaviours are reviewed; new values are encouraged; help can be sought from those more advanced in recovery; and referrals can be made to medical care, job training, legal assistance, etc. (Kaskutas 1998). Frequent group attendance becomes the treatment and provides an alternative to self-medication.

Several beliefs are central to the social model and all of its variations. First, recovery is experiential: everyone is unique and has to find their way to sobriety. Second, recovery is life-long: no one is ever 'cured' and can risk returning to drugs and the behaviours and life-style associated with their addiction. Third, recovery is peer-based: it is essential to rely on others in recovery and to assist others when one is able (Borkman et al. 1999).

In treatment

There is a point in drug abuse where the addict 'hits bottom'. That is: they realize that they have to stop using or they will eventually die and/or get killed. This realization may last for only a few hours. During this time they might voluntarily go to a treatment programme on their own or through a community health outreach worker. After going through medical detoxification from the drugs they are addicted to, the first line of treatment they will enter is the group. This is where the social model comes into play. In addition, with the help of a therapist-counsellor leader and others who are also in recovery, they begin the slow process of realizing their excuses and rationales. They engage in introspection they may have avoided and are challenged to confront traumas and personal demons from the past. One hallmark of effective drug treatment groups is that others in treatment are the very best people to challenge you. They have used the same excuses, rationalized their past behaviour in the same way, and did what you did. It is virtually impossible to lie to them or to yourself in their presence.

Virtually all social model programmes have extensive educational components in addition to group sessions. An essential requirement of recovery is to understand fully the physiology of drug craving and addiction. The social model may also include many varieties of community engagement as a part of the treatment. There are programmes that have job training as an essential part of their treatment and which then provide initial work experience to enable clients to transit into living-wage employment and personal independence. Others require treatment clients to work as group leaders and community outreach workers to solidify their recovery identity and learn to work with and assist others in need of treatment. Still other programmes may require clients to seek out and acknowledge to others the suffering and hurt they may have caused them in the course of their addiction. In effect, the social model as a treatment modality is about rebuilding the person and reintegrating him or her into the community as a healthy and productive member.

After-care

After a person completes treatment he or she participates in after-care, which consists of group meetings of people in recovery. The purpose of these groups is to provide emotional, social and informational support for attendees. The emphasis is on taking responsibility for one's recovery, helping others, sharing one's experiences and accepting the role of God in one's life (Galanter 2008). Typically, no medical or psychological treatments are provided. Millions with alcohol problems have joined self-help groups to provide social support for each other. The most widely practised after-care social model is the Twelve-Step approach offered by Alcoholics Anonymous (AA), founded in 1935 in the USA. Twelve steps to sobriety are taught, and members are expected to learn these steps and utilize them daily. The goal is *total abstinence*.

Other features of Twelve-Step programmes include maintaining a close relationship with another member, called a sponsor. When one feels the urge to return to drinking, one is encouraged to contact one's sponsor for help. The emphasis is on overcoming addiction through social support and reliance on a 'higher power', that is God. Relapse is accepted as regrettable but all too common. Sessions are usually held in churches or other public buildings. Meetings open and close typically with a prayer. Members share their stories of dependence on alcohol; recount what they are doing to remain sober; give attention to one of the Twelve Steps to recovery; and hear from guest speakers. Meetings create a safe place for individuals to share their experiences; anonymity assures the confidentiality of their stories.

By 1990, AA reported over one million members (Room and Greenfield 1993). There are over 100,000 AA groups worldwide. Other self-help groups using similar approaches include Chemically Dependent Anonymous, Cocaine Anonymous, Narcotics Anonymous, and Crystal Meth Anonymous. Other Twelve-Step programmes provide support for spouses and families: Families Anonymous, Al-Anon/Alateen, Nar-Anon and Co-Anon. Some other groups prefer a non-religious emphasis. SMART recovery, for instance, is founded on the belief that addiction is a learned behaviour and can be unlearned using cognitive-behavioural principles (CSAT 2008). The Secular Organization for Sobriety emphasizes individual responsibility for overcoming addiction to alcohol or drugs, and stresses a cognitive approach to maintain lifelong abstinence (ibid.).

Promise

The attraction of social model treatments is that they are outpatient and cost a fraction of the cost of medical and residential treatments. The educational and training requirements for peer counsellors are much less formal than they are for psychiatric and psychological therapists. Community-based treatment is the most accessible and can target specific sub-populations of hard-to-reach, high-risk drug users, such as injection drug abusers, crack cocaine abusers, run away teens, sex traders and undocumented immigrants. The programme designs are flexible enough to accommodate racial, ethnic, gender, national and religious sub-cultural variations among people seeking treatment. Finally, psychotherapy and other forms of treatment can be combined within the social model. The best programmes are able to offer a variety of treatment modalities dependent on the needs of clients.

Evidence

Studies of participants in self-help groups have generally found they are effective for those who continue to attend (Kelly et al. 2006). A recent study found attendees who continue over a ten-year period show marked improvement (Pagano et al. 2012). The effectiveness of social model treatment programmes stand up well when compared with programmes using other modalities. There is strong evidence that outpatient treatment works for many people. Recent data collected by the federal agency in the USA that funds and studies drug treatment summarizes the outcomes of outpatient treatment (see Figure 12.1). As we can see, 42 per cent complete the treatment, while at least 29 per cent dropped out.

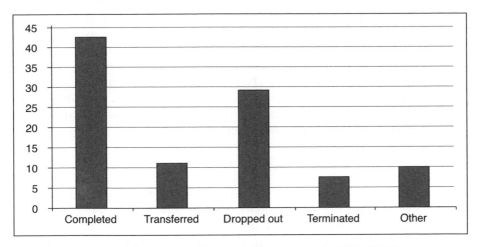

Figure 12.1 Reasons for discharge from outpatient treatment, 2001–11 (%)
Source: SAMHSA (2012).

Critique

If one were building cars or providing medical treatment, a 40 per cent completion would be a failure. Perhaps half or more of those who complete treatment here will relapse back to addictive drug use. Little is known about the fate of the 40–60 per cent who do not successfully complete treatment. We know some portion will try again in another programme. It is also important to note that not all individuals are comfortable with the religious emphasis of some groups, nor the belief that addiction is chronic or that complete abstinence is the primary goal. Many are reluctant to reveal their problems to strangers in a semi-public setting. It is impossible to know if those who attend self-help groups are the same kind of people who achieve remission on their own, have better social skills or find the religious emphasis consistent with their core beliefs.

Residential treatment

Another popular form of treatment that more closely follows a medical model is residential treatment (NIDA 2009). This is considered the most intensive form of treatment and is generally reserved for those who have failed with outpatient programmes by repeated relapse. Candidates for residential treatments are considered the most seriously dependent, with multiple causes for their addiction. Residential treatment consists of inpatient programmes that provide around-the-clock care in a live-in facility. These programmes offer multiple modalities of care simultaneously. Besides detoxification and medical maintenance (methadone), staff attempt to determine which specific treatments will benefit a patient, ranging from psychosocial groups to psychotherapy to cognitive behavioural therapy. Model programmes also attempt to reconstruct completely a client's social and personal life around a drug-free lifestyle by providing job training, career counselling and basic medical care (Secades-Villa et al. 2011). The objective is to be a total institution that reforms all aspects of a patient's life so that he or she can be drug free. In most countries, such residential treatment is voluntary. There are some cases, such as in China, where it is involuntary. Ideally, before completion, a patient is transitioned to AA, NA or some other continuing outpatient after-care.

Evidence

In the USA, the Substance Abuse and Mental Health Services Administration (SAMHSA) estimates that in 2010 more than 100,000 beds at residential treatment facilities were devoted to clients with substance abuse problems. More than one million persons received such treatment, of whom 38 per cent completed, 31per cent dropped out, 13 per cent transferred, 9 per cent had treatment terminated by the facility, and the remaining 9 per cent were listed as 'other' (SAMHSA 2005). Dropout rates are linked to relapse.

SAMHSA collected data from 45 states on the percentage of clients who completed various types of treatment. The results are summarized in Figure 12.2. As we can see, the majority completed treatment in all settings except medically assisted outpatient opioid therapy.

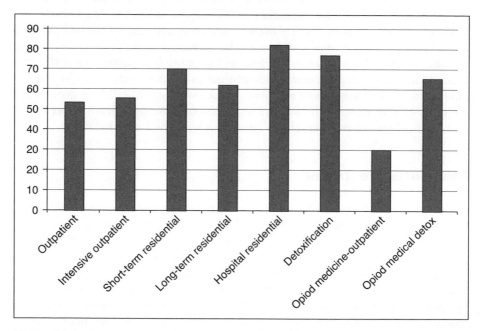

Figure 12.2 Percentage completing treatment, 2001–11

Source: SAMHSA (2012).

A review of residential treatment outcome studies found on average that clients stayed about one-third of the planned time. Only between 9 and 56 per cent completed their treatment. Relapse was common, and the best predictor of maintaining abstinence was programme completion (Sullivan et al. 2007; Malivert et al. 2012). In the UK, a five-year follow-up of clients treated at residential facilities revealed after four to five years substantial reduction in drug use (Gossop et al. 2003).

Critique

Comparisons are risky, because clients may have entered different treatments with different types of drug problems. Some may have come in to avoid prison. And there may be only one type of treatment available in many locations. Those with higher incomes have many more options, including long-term residential treatments that are not available to those without health insurance.

Given the great differences between types of treatments received at residential facilities, it is impossible to know which combination of treatments has the best outcomes. Some residential treatment centres use medicines to help users cope with the difficulties of detoxification, while others do not. Some combine medical treatments with individual or group therapies. Some focus primarily on alcohol abuse treatment, while others treat a variety of drug disorders. Further, it may be that those who can afford such treatments are not typical of those seeking care for substance use disorder.

Family therapy

In contrast to approaches that target the drug user as the primary focus of therapy, a newer approach has been developed since the 1970s – family therapy for addiction. This treatment process is based on the theoretical work of Salvador Minuchin (1974). Minuchin saw the family as the source of drug abuse problems, rather than the individual. The model assumes that every family is a 'homeostatic system' (one which seeks balance and stability among members) with powerful influences on all members, as outlined in Chapter 7.

In a series of studies of the families of heroin addicts, Minuchin's approach has been used to treat the addicted member of the family by addressing his or her unresolved problems. When the family problem is addressed, therapists report that the troubled family member's substance abuse usually ceases (Stanton 1979; Stanton and Shadish 1997). This approach has been particularly useful in treating adolescents. A family therapy intervention enrols the whole family to receive treatment together. It is expected that many families will be resistant to such treatment, and a series of techniques has been developed to get such families into care. The therapist asks questions to uncover how the family functions as a system. Then, the role of the drug user is explored, so as to discover how his or her drug use serves to obscure other problems in the family.

When the family comes to address its problems, the adolescent generally stops using drugs, having been freed from his or her need to do so.

Evidence

Studies of family treatments have found them to be effective in reducing adolescent drug abuse (Szapocznik et al. 2007; Szapocznik and Williams 2000; Henderson et al. 2010; Rowe 2012). In our own study of heroin addicts in Northern California, we found a striking pattern. Among heroin users, many reported a death in their family of origin before puberty (Bowser et al. 2003). Having experienced a death was not the important issue. Rather, in families where one or more members had developed a heroin habit, a sudden, often traumatic death was not mourned in the usual way. Often there was no funeral and no period for the family to come together for support while grieving. For a variety of reasons, they ignored the need to grieve, which does not make the loss go away. Instead, one or more members of the family unconsciously took on the role of the unmourned dead member (Coleman 1980).

Critique

Family therapy has not been shown to be superior to cognitive approaches (Hides et al. 2010). Getting families to come in for treatment is difficult. As with many innovative approaches, insufficient research has been conducted to determine which types of families are helped and what distinguishes these families from those that do not benefit. In addition, national survey data is lacking to support the proposition that it is families that are the genesis of drug abuse. Nor do we have data from societies that do not utilize the traditional family organization which is common in Europe and the USA. One wonders how family therapists' models might work in the Trobriand Islands, or rural Uganda, where family responsibilities for child-rearing are different (Levine 2007). Without that kind of data, we are left wondering if the families of those who come into treatment are the same as those where a member does not come in.

Natural recovery

No discussion of treatment for drug addiction is complete without exploring the elephant in the room – natural recovery. Despite impressive developments in individual and family treatments, residential treatment, harm-reduction strategies and Twelve Step programmes, most drug users who quit do so without any formal treatment. A study of 43,093 adults in the USA measured dependence on nicotine, alcohol, cannabis and cocaine. One half of those with cocaine dependence were in remission five years later (Lopez-Quintero et al. 2011). In Canada, the majority of individuals with alcohol or

---

Box 12.1   Principles of drug addiction treatment

Based upon research and practice since the 1970s, there are a number of important lessons that have been learned about drug treatment. They have been summarized as the following:

1   Addiction is a complex but treatable disease that affects brain function and behavior.
2   No single treatment is appropriate for everyone.
3   Treatment needs to be readily available.
4   Effective treatment attends to multiple needs of the individual, not just his or her drug abuse.
5   Remaining in treatment for an adequate period of time is critical.
6   Counseling – individual and/or group – and other behavioral therapies are the most commonly used forms of drug abuse treatment.
7   Medications are an important element of treatment for many patients, especially when combined with counseling and other behavioral therapies.
8   An individual's treatment and services plan must be assessed continually and modified as necessary to ensure that it meets his or her changing needs.
9   Many drug-addicted individuals also have other mental disorders.
10 Medically assisted detoxification is only the first stage of addiction treatment and by itself does little to change long-term drug abuse.
11 Treatment does not need to be voluntary to be effective.
12 Drug use during treatment must be monitored continuously, as lapses during treatment do occur.
13 Treatment programs should assess patients for the presence of HIV/AIDS, hepatitis B and C, tuberculosis, and other infectious diseases.

Source: National Institute on Drug Abuse (www.drugabuse.gov/sites/default/files/cadchart_2.pdf).

---

smoking habits stopped without receiving any formal treatment (Cunningham 1999).

Studies of drug users who have achieved remission without any formal treatment have found that natural recovery was influenced by support from family and friends. Support enabled individuals to make the decision to stop using. This support, termed 'social capital', has predicted who would remain abstinent and who would not (Granfield and Cloud 2001). Also commitment to remaining drug free is associated with having a life project and personal goals to focus one's sobriety (Perez Gomez and Sierra Acuna 2007).

Trajectories

One way of looking at how people come to stop using drugs is to examine the trajectories of abusers. Typically, drug use begins in adolescence and then becomes a habit in the mid-twenties. Some go on to a lifetime of drug use, while the majority does not. In a 20-year follow-up of heroin addicts admitted to treatment at the public health hospital in Lexington, Kentucky, 23 per cent died, 25 per cent were still using drugs, and between 35 and 42 per cent had achieved stable abstinence. Neither imprisonment nor voluntary treatment could explain how almost half reached abstinence (Vaillant 1974). In Sweden, a 25-year study of heroin addicts found of those in the general population who did not receive treatment that more than half had achieved sobriety over that period (Larm et al. 2010). In Australia, cannabis users tracked from age 18 to 24 found the majority of users at 18 were no longer using at 24 (Swift et al. 2008; Karlamangla et al. 2006).

Unfortunately it is difficult to determine precisely how many drug abusers are able to achieve remission or avoid relapse, because so many die along the way. It has been estimated that heroin users reduce their lifespan by 25 years or more (Scott et al. 2011; Hser et al. 2012).

Critique

What we know is that: many receive benefits from treatment; not all treatments work for all users; and relapse is all too common. This has led many treatment providers to recommend viewing drug use disorder as a chronic disease, like diabetes or congestive heart failure. No one expects medical treatment will 'cure' diabetes. Many with the condition struggle to minimize the harms associated with the disease and experience difficulties maintaining a healthy lifestyle that is considered essential to managing the disease. Similarly, some providers look to the overall benefits of drug treatment, rather than to frequent relapses. Treatments make life better for the user, his or her family and community, but they should be seen as an ongoing process rather than a permanent transformation (Reuter and Pollack 2006). While some critics insist that 'once an addict, always an addict', there is impressive evidence that some drug users stop without treatment, some stop following treatment, many die, and still others relapse. What is unclear is precisely who these people are. We do not know why some stop on their own after many years. What is quite clear is that treatment can work.

Review questions

■ How do people develop the capacity to stop using drugs, according to Freud's psychodynamic talk therapy?

■ Do most people with substance use disorders recover via treatment or natural recovery?

■ How do cognitive therapists treat people with drug use disorders?

■ What are the essential features of the social model?

■ Why are narcissists prone to develop substance use disorders, according to object relations treatment providers?

■ How do family therapists provide care for those with substance use disorders?

■ Discuss the evidence that one treatment technique works better for all persons with substance abuse disorders.

Further reading

Best, D.W., Gufran, S., Day, E., Ray, R. and Loaring, J. (2008) 'Breaking the habit: a retrospective analysis of desistence factors among formerly problematic heroin users', *Drug and Alcohol Review*, 27(6), 619–24.

EL-Guebaly, N. (2011) 'The meanings of recovery from addiction: evolution and promises', *Journal of Addictive Medicine*, 10, 1097.

Flores, P.J. (2013) *Group Psychotherapy with Addicted Populations: An Integration of Twelve Step and Psychodynamic Theory*, 3rd edn, London: Routledge.

Slutske, W.S. (2010) 'Why is natural recovery so common for addictive disorders?', *Addiction*, 105(9), 1520–1.

Further reading

IV

Conclusion

Recommendations and Afterthoughts

13

Chapter overview

- Recommendations
- Evidence of effective interventions
- A worldwide challenge
- Efforts to reduce the supplies of drugs
- Returning to the economics of drug trafficking and dealing
- Afterthoughts
- New frontiers
- Conclusion

Clearly, addressing alcohol and drug abuse is a work in progress that requires enlightened public policy and the very best of our social and behavioural sciences to guide those policies. The ways that public policy and the science behind treatment and prevention are coordinated and guide one another is initially done through expert panels and commissions. In some countries, major scientific contributors and respected public policy figures meet and review the most current research and progress reports. They call other experts and practitioners to testify, even do site visits and interview people in treatment. They bring to bear on the subject their wisdom, experience and creativity to make recommendations on what can be done to improve their national public policy in order to reduce drug use and abuse. These recommendations are hopefully turned into laws and practices by legislators and the executive branch of government. This is how law enforcement as well as new and improved prevention and treatment initiatives are funded. Hopefully, they will be funded at a sufficient level to have the anticipated outcomes which are monitored and adjusted by evidence-based evaluations. This, of course, is the ideal.

Experts and government officials from each country with scientific and public policy infrastructures then meet through international agencies such as the World Health Organization, the European Union and the United Nations to devise ways to coordinate national efforts. The carefully constructed reports of these world commissions generally reflect areas in which there are international consensuses among experts and government officials which in turn are eventually acted upon by each country's public policy community. What then are some of the current recommendations that we might look forward to seeing implemented in the future?

Recommendations

Global commission on drug policy

This special commission consists most notably of the former Presidents of Brazil, Colombia, Mexico and Switzerland; the Prime Minister of Greece; Kofi Annan, former Secretary General of the United Nations; Richard Branson, English billionaire; George Shultz, former US Secretary of the Treasury (1972–74) and US Secretary of State (1982–89); and Paul Volcker, former chairman of the US Federal Reserve (1979–87) and, most recently, chairman of the US Economic Recovery Advisory Board (2009–11). They along with other global advocacy organizations have called for an end to the war on drugs by acknowledging that it has failed to stem the tide of drug trafficking and abuse worldwide. In their petition to the United Nations they call for alternatives to incarceration for drug use, greater emphasis on public health, and decriminalization and experimentation with legal regulation, in particular, of marijuana. The following are their specific recommendations (Global Commission on Drug Policy 2012):

1   End the criminalization, marginalization and stigmatization of people who use drugs but who do no harm to others.
2   Encourage experimentation by governments with models of legal regulation of drugs (especially cannabis) to undermine the power of organized crime and safeguard the health and security of their citizens.
3   Ensure that a variety of treatment modalities are available – including not just methadone and buprenorphine treatment but also the heroin-assisted treatment programmes that have proven successful in many European countries and Canada.
4   Apply human rights and harm-reduction principles and policies both to people who use drugs as well as those involved in the lower ends of illegal drug markets such as farmers, couriers and petty salespersons.

This is the first series of high-level recommendations aimed at reducing the profits in drug trafficking by calling for governments to decriminalize and then regulate heroin, cocaine and other schedule A drugs. They also call for the use of the harm-reduction approach not only in prevention and treatment, but also in the production, trafficking and dealing of currently illicit drugs. These recommendations are clearly aimed at the current impasse in prohibition policies in the USA and to encourage the continued movement toward harm reduction in China and the UK.

The Commission on Narcotic Drugs (CND)

The CND is one of the longest-standing commissions based in the United Nations. It was established in 1946 as part of the Economic and Social Council and as a central drug policy forum for the world community. It has the authority to amend the international schedule of controlled substances currently enforced under the Single Convention on Narcotic Drugs. At the CND's 55th meeting in March 2012, it was noted that a clear imbalance has existed for some time in favour of supply-side solutions (use of criminal and military systems) over demand-side prevention and treatment (UNODC 2012a). Member states were urged to intensify prevention strategies as part of a more comprehensive response to drug demand, supply and trafficking.

While this recommendation is not like the bold steps suggested above by the Global Commission on Drug Policy, it is an accurate representation of consensus among world governments that current prohibition policies are not working and that greater emphasis is needed on prevention and treatment. A more balanced approach can have more positive outcomes.

United Kingdom Drug Policy Commission

This commission is a private charitable organization that brought together 'senior figures from policing, public policy and the media, along with leading experts from the medical and drug treatment fields'. The purpose of the commission is 'to encourage the formulation and adoption of evidence-based drug policies' in the UK. After a thorough review of the outcomes and effectiveness of policies and practices in the UK, they have made a series of recommendations. Their report is entitled *A Fresh Approach to Drugs* and the following are their first four and major recommendations (UKDPC 2012):

1   Tackle structural problems that increase risk of drug problems.
2   Develop and evaluate early interventions to help families and communities build resilience to drug problems alongside other problems.
3   Promote interventions which reduce the harms of drug use.
4   Involve local communities in law enforcement and assess its impact.

The evidence is weak for the efficacy of most traditional drug enforcement activity, especially that directed at major and middle-level drug dealers and criminal networks as well as border interdictions. But what there is supports interventions that take a problem-solving approach that involve local communities. The traditional indicators such as the numbers of arrests and amount of drugs seized do not necessarily reflect success in reducing the availability of drugs and the damage done to communities. All drug enforcement operations should be assessed to demonstrate their proven impact on communities and to allow for continuous improvements and better value for money.

There are nine additional recommendations that call for more evidence-based programmes, for a continued pursuit of those who produce and supply illicit drugs, and for improved research and policy analysis. Five of the thirteen recommendations call for attention to families and communities as vital to preventing drug abuse and moving toward more effective treatment. There are calls for critical reviews and changes of current policies.

US National Research Council (NRC)

The NRC is part of the US National Academy of Science, founded in 1916 to advance knowledge and to serve as the major scientific advisory board for the federal government and Congress. Issues that can be best understood and evaluated by science and are potential topics of legislation and federal policy are reviewed by expert panels called together by the NRC. At least one member of the panel, generally the chair, is a member of the National Academy of Science. The NRC has done a series of studies and made recommendations on ways to ameliorate drug abuse and to improve prevention and treatment in the USA. The most recent comprehensive report is entitled *Informing America's Policy on Illegal Drugs: What We Don't Know Keeps Hurting Us* (Institute of Medicine 2001). The focus of this panel was to explore ways to fill in gaps in current knowledge in order to improve future policy research. Three of the five recommendations are:

1 The committee recommends that work be started to develop methods for acquiring consumption data. Consumption information would permit better estimates of how much of each drug is consumed, what the scope of drug abuse is and how effective are interdiction efforts.
2 The committee recommends that work be started to develop methods for improving existing data and acquiring more reliable drug price data. One of the mysteries of drug abuse is actual pricing of illicit drugs in retail trade and changes in pricing. Police reports on pricing are not sufficiently comprehensive or accurate enough about actual pricing.
3 The committee recommends that the National Institute of Justice and the National Institute on Drug Abuse collaboratively undertake research on the declarative and deterrent effects, costs, and cost effectiveness of sanctions against the use of illegal drugs.

These recommendations do not call for any changes in policies as do the prior ones. But they would, if implemented, go a long way to providing more precise and focused data on the efficiency or effectiveness of current illicit drug interventions and policies. Knowledge of the specific outcomes of police-focused interdictions may reinforce and provide context for the overall sense that current prohibition policies are not working. Alternatively, measurement of specific outcomes might also provide surprises by uncovering unknown impacts and may reveal that other factors are at work and are more important than we currently realize. In which case, these recommendations could set the stage for more specific policy recommendations in the future.

Recommendations on treatment for drug dependence

A second NCR expert committee met in 2006 to focus specifically on injection drug users (Committee on the Prevention of HIV Infection 2009). It is believed by practitioners and policy-makers that there is room for improved practice and outcomes for injection drug users (IDUs) within current policy constraints, not just in the USA but worldwide. The initial recommendation from this panel report, entitled 'Preventing HIV Infection among Injecting Drug Users in High Risk Countries: An Assessment of the Evidence', highlights the current emphasis in the USA on pharmaco-therapies in the treatment of IDUs. Their key recommendations are:

1   Given the strong evidence of its effectiveness in treating opioid dependence, opioid agonist maintenance treatment should be made widely available where feasible.
2   Given the potential benefits and lack of harmful effects, multiple non-pharmaco-therapies should also be made available as part of a multi-component treatment system, and where feasible, a rigorous evaluation component should be included.

There are additional recommendations on sterile needle and syringe access, and on outreach and education. The major contribution of this report and recommendations is the integration of pharmaco-therapies into drug treatment. Initially, naltrexone and buprenorphine were aids in detoxification but are now also abstinence-based treatments.

Evidence of effective interventions

A team of researchers in the UK reviewed the intervention literature on both sides of the Atlantic. They pointed out that it is now possible for drug policies to be well informed by scientific evidence on the effectiveness of any proposed drug use or abuse intervention (Strang et al. 2012). There are selected key messages:

1   The effectiveness of most drug supply control policies is unknown because little assessment has been done, and very little evidence exists for the effectiveness of alternative development programmes in source countries.
2   Supply controls can result in higher drug prices, which can reduce drug initiation and use, but these changes can be difficult to maintain.
3   Wide-scale arrests and imprisonments have restricted prevention efforts, but drug testing of individuals under criminal justice supervision, accompa-

nied by specific, immediate and brief sentences (e.g. overnight), produce substantial reductions in drug use.
4   Prescription regimens minimize but do not eliminate non-medical use of psychoactive prescription drugs. Prescription monitoring systems can reduce inappropriate prescribing.

It will be interesting to see in coming years when and if any of these recommendations are adapted, and by whom. There is still a great deal of research, evaluation and creative thinking needed to constrain supplies of illicit drugs and to advance the effectiveness of prevention and treatment.

A worldwide challenge

We have seen that the abuse of illicit drugs has increased since 1960 in every country reviewed and that every government is struggling to stem the tide. While the incidence of alcohol and drug abuse has gone up in Western Europe, the USA, Australia and China, there is evidence that this trend may be levelling off due to changing demographics rather than to successful interventions (Reuter et al. 2009). Populations in these countries are getting older. As users get older, many grow out of using illicit drugs; for others, years of abuse have taken their toll on their health. The death rate for drug abusers is significantly higher than it is among their non-drug using peers in the general population.

The most troubling trend is that the abuse of illicit drugs is going up much faster in developing and transitional countries (Committee on the Prevention of HIV Infection 2009; Reuter et al. 2009). Historically countries that produced and transited heroin and cocaine, such as Afghanistan, Pakistan, Thailand, Cambodia, Vietnam, Colombia, Bolivia, Peru and Mexico, had relatively few users of these drugs. Producer and transit nations are rapidly developing illicit drug consumers of their own. The countries of Eastern Europe have become completely new markets and those who abuse drugs are rapidly increasing in numbers. We also see drug use taking root in West and South Africa as new markets for heroin and cocaine are emerging on the continent (Raguin et al. 2011).

If governments in Western Europe and the developed world are struggling to contain drug abuse, it is going to be all the more difficult for resource-poor countries to avoid even more serious harm. Countries like the Democratic Republic of Congo, Sierra Leone and Liberia in Africa have already fought bloody civil wars with drug-using and alcohol-fuelled rebel armies. The prevalence of addiction in these countries has not been estimated; prevention and treatment efforts have yet to be even conceptualized (Myers 2013). Throughout the world, the new landscape of drug abuse roughly follows urbanization and rural impoverishment (UNDCP 1995). The more urban a nation's population, the greater the potential there is for emerging illicit drug markets and for the increasing prevalence of drug abusers. The greater the rural poverty, the greater the potential for the production of illicit drugs.

Efforts to reduce the supplies of drugs

The greatest point of leverage on the trade of opiates, cocaine and marijuana is to choke its availability at production (Tam and Foo 2012). It takes time to grow these plants and the production regions are well known. Supply-side interdiction is still strategically the best point of leverage. But efforts to date have only resulted in traffickers moving their production locations to different regions and countries and dispersing production to smaller sites where it is more difficult to locate and to eradicate crops. The same flexibility and creativity have been exercised in the trafficking of illicit drugs into countries with aggressive efforts at interdiction.

The outcome of flexibility in production and trafficking is that heroin, cocaine, marijuana and any other drug designated as illegal are readily available in every country where there are potential users. There is no evidence that the best attempts to date to stop or control the global production of illicit drugs have worked (Reuter and Stevens 2007; Kilmer et al. 2012). A large part of the problem is that there are now few obvious traffickers such as big cartels who can be easily targeted. The market for illicit drugs is increasingly integrated horizontally where players only know their immediate supplier or dealer, and where there is intense competition. Anyone taken out of the business is immediately replaced by someone else aspiring for their role, market share and fortune.

The outcome of successful efforts by producers and traffickers to avoid interdiction is that illicit drugs are conveniently available in their primary markets. In the largest cities of Canada, people who were interviewed at random knew where to go if they wanted an illicit drug (Hadland et al. 2012). They did not have to go far to find them. We can infer that this is also the case in every other country we have studied. Perhaps in time, this will become a worldwide reality if it is not already. For many countries their greatest expenditure in addressing alcohol and drug abuse are police and military efforts to stop or reduce the flow of illicit drugs into their country. Yet no country has succeeded. At best, the country with the most aggressive effort, the USA, claims to stop no more than an estimated 1 to 10 per cent of the drugs flowing across its border (Staff 2011). There are consequences for this failure.

Marijuana normalization

Of growing importance for every developed country, except the Netherlands, is the normalization of marijuana despite its status as a schedule A illicit drug. By 21 years of age, virtually half of all youth in North America, Western Europe and Australia-New Zealand have used marijuana for recreational purposes at least once. Marijuana's use no longer carries a social stigma and the laws against it are now virtually unenforceable. The authorities and marijuana prohibition laws are on a collision course with public opinion. As suggested in Chapter 6, this has major implications for government claims that marijuana use is deviant, dangerous and justifiably prosecuted by law. When such a large proportion of the population has used the drug, it ceases to be deviant and viewed as a criminal offence.

Prescription drug abuse

The growing abuse of prescription drugs in the USA and Western Europe may be partly influenced by decades of the ready availability and commercialization of both non-prescription and prescription drugs along with illicit drugs (NIDA 2008). Use of illicit drugs has made it possible to medicate oneself for any reason without a doctor's counsel and prescription. Given their wide availability and convenience, it was only a matter of time before people would also turn to prescription drugs for self-medication (Institute of Medicine 2012). In the Western world there is now a general acceptance of drug therapies for virtually all physical and psychological problems.

The need for more prevention and treatment

A third consequence of the failure to stop illicit drugs is the need for ever-increasing prevention services and treatment modalities (Fischer et al. 2012). With the general failure of diplomatic, police and military efforts to stem production and international drug trafficking, the front-line for addressing drug abuse has become by default prevention and treatment. Since the availability of illicit and prescription drugs is a given, we now have to convince more and more people not to initiate illicit and prescription drug use. Or if they have already started, we have to convince them to use less if they will not quit altogether. Then, if they are dependent, we have to convince them to go into treatment.

Returning to the economics of drug trafficking and dealing

There is another way to look at the failure to constrict the supply of illicit heroin, cocaine and marijuana before it reaches the markets. This failure is fundamentally the inability of current interdiction to remove the extraordinary profits producers, traffickers and dealers make from illicit drugs worldwide (Storti and De Grauwe 2007). Small family farmers are being pushed into poverty worldwide by the massive production of farm goods by corporations and large farm cooperatives. The social and economic decline of rural and subsistent farm communities generates migrants to large regional cities. One outcome is that there are no legitimate agricultural products that can compete with the price return for producing coca, opium or marijuana. It is no coincidence that illicit drug producers are some of the poorest farmers on earth and what they receive in payment is well worth any risks they take to grow clandestinely these products. It is estimated that payment to farmers amounts to about 1 per cent of an illicit drug's retail cost (UNODC 2011a).

The level where the most profits are made is among illicit drug traffickers and high-level dealers. Drug trafficking generated about US$650 billion per year worldwide in the year 2000, which comes to about 1.5 per cent of global gross domestic product (ibid.). It is estimated that the combined efforts of all governments to interdict drugs and the money in this enterprise results in the interception of about 1 per cent of gross revenues (Reuter et al. 2009). The actual cost of drug traffickers and dealers to do business may come to another 7 per cent of their revenues. This means that profits are as high as 93 per cent. The production and trafficking of illicit drugs are wildly profitable. This is a huge incentive for engagement, especially when one's chances of being caught are so low. This also means that supply-side effects to combat drug trafficking are nowhere near drying up profits and taking the incentive out of illicit drug trafficking.

In fact, the biggest problem producers and traffickers have is laundering their fortunes – converting unaccounted cash profits into legally accounted-for money. One consequence of having such a huge profit margin is that producers and traffickers can take enormous losses and still beat the profit margins of virtually any legitimate business. They can double, triple or increase their costs fourfold and still come out way ahead. Producers and traffickers can also substantially reduce their prices to expand their market and meet competitive challenges. This is precisely what has happened in the past two decades. The retail prices of heroin and cocaine have gone down. It has been suggested that this is due to increasing costs and greater competition (Storti and De Grauwe 2007).

The expansion of the market of heroin and cocaine into the developing world has also reduced profitability. Until these new markets are fully up and running, relative costs are likely to be much higher than in already established markets (Reuter et al. 2009). A decline in retail pricing might also suggest that the demand for illicit drugs and the number of users in the developed world may have peaked. It could also mean that the market has been over-supplied. In the past two decades there has been no indication that heroin, cocaine or marijuana have been hard to get. If anything their availability has increased. The only place to report a price increase in heroin, substantial enough to reduce purity and consumption, was Australia in 1998 (UNODC 2008).

Until ways can be found to eliminate the extraordinary profits from illicit drug production and trafficking, there will be a strong incentive for continuing the trade. The market will continue to expand and there will be people willing to take whatever risks there are to make what amounts to small fortunes. Improvement and expansion of prevention and treatment cannot substitute for the inability of government agencies to remove the profits from drug trafficking. Harm reduction might improve the effectiveness of prevention and treatment but it is no answer to the ready availability of cheap illicit drugs (Reuter and Stevens 2007; Kilmer et al. 2012). Bridging the huge gap between what is now being done and what needs to be done to address drug profits is an area where extensive research and experimentation are needed (Greenfielda and Paolib 2012).

Afterthoughts

Each country touched on in this text is engaged in a struggle to minimize effectively drug dependency and the harm associated with it. This struggle has been to strike the most effective balance between on the one hand necessary criminal sanctions against illicit drug trafficking and dealing and on the other hand public health driven treatment and prevention. The countries with the most success, such as Switzerland and the Netherlands, have de-emphasized criminal justice approaches and have successfully minimized drug dependency and its social costs in their countries through harm reduction. But a macro and comparative view puts these 'successes' in perspective. That is, it should be clear to any dispassionate viewer who looks across the international scene that emphasizing criminal penalties for illicit drug use does not reduce the prevalence of drug dependency.

The assumption that the more severe the penalties the less the incentive to use illicit drugs is behaviourally invalid. It is wrong because this assumption presumes that rationality trumps addiction. The criminal justice approach that supports this view is ironically not well established in its own discipline (Chapter 6), nor has it been shown to be effective public policy (Chapter 10). The assumption is a fundamental error about the very nature of compulsive drug dependency. The fact is that addiction trumps rationality – that is the very nature of compulsive behaviour. There is no threat that will stop drug addicted persons from pursuing their addictions. Addictions increased in Red China during the 1960s and 1970s, even in the face of summary executions by firing squads. Any approach is more effective that in any way prevents the initiation of drug use, ameliorates dependency once it starts and reduces the harm that addicts can cause society and themselves.

Prohibition versus harm reduction

The fact that harm reduction has become the alternative to criminal justice approaches and is associated with more successful outcomes does not mean that it has won the international debates of 'drug wars' versus harm reduction. This dichotomy is in fact false. Every country we have surveyed recognizes the need to pursue and arrest illicit drug traffickers and dealers, including the Netherlands and Switzerland. The essential question is: what else is each country doing to address the consequences of drug use and abuse, especially when it is so clear that drug prohibition does not work? Harm reduction must be pursued in addition to prohibition. What separates the USA and the Netherlands at the extreme ends of the continuum is emphasis. The Netherlands is emphasizing what works, while the USA is not.

This is not an argument for the USA and China to just de-emphasize prohibition and adopt harm reduction. It is our estimation that, if the USA dropped its criminal justice approach and fully adopted harm reduction, it would still have significant incidence and prevalence of illicit drug abuse. This estimate is based upon a closer look at the Netherlands and Switzerland – the countries with the most success with harm reduction. The Netherlands has lower incidences of drug users than the USA (Degenhardt et al. 2008). Even with harm reduction, these countries have found that many drug abusers in their system have to be indefinitely maintained. They cannot reduce their chemical dependency. Then, there are still others who not only persist in their dependency but who continue to maintain their addictions through the illegal market. These addicts will pay drug dealers for their drugs even when they can get them free through the public health system and without criminal sanctions (Collin 2002).

There appear to be limits to harm reduction's effectiveness as a barrier to incidence and prevalence. The British presumption that drug abuse is a permanent and intrinsic part of modern society may in fact be very accurate. There are clear limits to what harm reduction can do. First of all, harm-reduction interventions work only for drug abusers who consistently use the interventions. Most do not. Thus, the only real barrier between increasing or persistent incidence rates of new users is prevention, where social normative interventions have yet to be fully proven. Second, harm reduction is associated with overall success in holding down the incidence and prevalence of drug dependency in the Netherland and Switzerland. A more careful look suggests that this success may be due to other factors. In other words, there are preconditions that have to be in place for harm reduction to succeed.

The first precondition for harm reduction to work is having nationalized medical care in which services are accessible to all and there are no out-of-pocket charges to users. This means that health services cover everyone: no citizen is excluded due to lack of access or the inability to pay. A second precondition is that harm-reduction services for drug dependent persons are provided as one of many regular health services. This minimizes the extent to which treating addiction can be stigmatized, viewed as a separate budgetary commitment and as a political target. In effect, access to pharmacy-quality drug surrogates and harm-reduction services is free and can be made readily available to all dependent individuals. This undercuts illicit drug prices: dealers cannot compete with free drugs. This is why in countries which offer harm reduction through national health services, they are able to undercut the illegal drug market once a person becomes dependent. This suggests that any effort on the part of the USA or China to implement harm reduction fully will have very disappointing outcomes if they are not part of a national health service that completely integrates treatment and medical maintenance.

New frontiers

The international debate between criminal justice versus harm reduction has obscured the place where new thinking is needed and, perhaps, where greater progress can be made. We must remember that the illicit drug use and abuse phenomenon is a continuum that starts with supply (growth, harvest, processing, trafficking and then dealing) and then continues as demand (initiation, regular use, addiction, prevention and treatment). Harm reduction has been fully developed in response to the demand-side of the continuum. This is where the progress has been made via harm reduction from national health services that have eliminated the profits and economic incentive in drug dealing to dependent persons. But this is too late or happens too far along the drug use and abuse continuum.

As suggested at the end of Chapter 10, the equivalent of harm reduction is needed earlier in the process on the supply-side of the continuum, where we are having the least success. The equivalent of harm reduction is needed on the supply-side to drive up production and trafficking costs to the point that producers and traffickers have no financial incentive to stay in the business. Of course, this side of the continuum has been the exclusive domain of law-enforcement agencies. The following are some suggested approaches.

Subsidize farmers

A new frontier would be to seek out farmers in opium, coca and marijuana growing areas, find out what illicit drug producers offer them as a going rate and offer them higher returns to grow alternative crops. It does not matter whether there is a market for these alternative crops. The objective is to make it prohibitively expensive for illicit drug producers to grow psychoactive crops and to divert farmers to grow other produce. This paid diversion has to go on long enough in specific growing areas for the market in psychoactive crops to collapse. Some of the poorest farmers in the world would then become relatively well-paid.

The pay-to-divert intervention would have to be done as part of a regional economic development programme that also builds schools, clinics and alternative markets in drug producing areas. In this way, payment to farmers would have a way to circulate and improve their lives and to generate legal businesses and enterprise. This was successfully done at the beginning of the heroin epidemic to stop Turkish heroin in the 1960s French Connection (Krueger 1980). It was reluctantly attempted in the Andes in the early 1980s, but was abandoned by the Reagan administration as 'welfare' to foreign farmers – thereafter growers moved drug production to neighbouring countries where the subsidy was not offered (Menzel 1996).

A variation of this intervention is to have local government licensed growers of psychoactive drugs. Bolivia is experimenting with this approach today (Neuman 2012). Licensed plots are carefully monitored by satellite imagery and local growers' unions. The coca is used for traditional use in local markets and for government export for medical purposes. To the surprise of many, especially the US Drug Enforcement Agency which is not a partner in this intervention, there has been a significant drop in coca planting without military style raids and the violence associated with the drug war approach. The Bolivian government pursues criminal sanctions only against unlicensed growers, permits only certain plot sizes and regulates the number of licences to keep the coca supply low and prices high. One of the most important features of this approach is that growers have strong incentives to police themselves. The Bolivian government views their local approach as eradication without violating human rights. National leadership such as this could produce other creative solutions to control and minimize effectively psychoactive drug producing markets.

Drug buy-backs

Another harm-reduction tactic on the supply-side of the drug use and abuse continuum would be to buy up the existing supplies of heroin, cocaine, etc. No questions would be asked. Instead of undercover attempts to buy drugs in order to arrest traffickers and dealers, why not simply buy the drugs so as to remove them from the open market? In the USA there are gun buy-backs to remove weapons from the streets and communities to prevent shootings. The same could be done for drugs: buy illicit drugs to get them off the market and out of the hands of dealers. Of course, there would have to be a very reliable way to test quickly the drugs turned in to make certain they are real. This would then begin to drive up the cost of illicit drugs that remain on the market. The higher the cost the more difficult it would be for many to maintain their dependency and the greater the incentive to go into treatment.

Drug cafés and prescriptions

As we know, there are cafés in the Netherlands that make 'soft drugs' available to citizens who want them. The idea is to remove the stigma and the control that drug dealers have over their availability. If users can get marijuana or hashish legally in a normal commercial and retail setting, it is not necessary to engage in illegal transactions with drug dealers. Having a legal and safe alternative provides a disincentive to participate in the illegal drug market where one risks arrest, murder and rape, and where one can end up paying more for drugs, yet with no assurance of the quality of the product. The concept of the drug café should be extended to so-called 'hard drugs'. But as an alternative to public cafés, we would suggest that heroin and cocaine (hard drugs) should be made available as take-outs from medical facilities at discreet locations for registered clients. Like medical marijuana dispensaries, users would have identification cards and an electronic record showing the amount of the drug they have purchased and when it was provided. They would be exempt from arrest for the possession of the registered drugs.

The argument that making hard drugs available in such a fashion would be an incentive for anyone and everyone to begin using hard drugs ignores reality. The widespread availability of hard drugs is already the case. The problem is that illegal drug dealers and traffickers control access and profit from it. This hard drug reduction strategy holds that it is better for the government to control directly the availability and link it to prevention, treatment and other health and social services.

But, more importantly, via government controlled drug cafes and hard drug dispensaries the source of profits in drug dealing could be eliminated. To maintain clientele, drug traffickers and dealers would have virtually to give their drugs away. For example, in the USA, state government takeovers of gambling were done to eliminate illegal gambling. State lotteries and state regulated casinos made it impossible to earn money running an illegal numbers business – they are now virtually non-existent except on the Internet, where there is no state competition.

Decriminalization

The debate for or against decriminalization finally has a national experiment: Portugal has decriminalized drug use and possession (Hughes and Winstock 2012). Trafficking and dealing are still illegal and prosecuted; but the stigma has been removed from users, who are no longer driven underground and out of society where the harm that they cause themselves and society is maximized. Now they can be counselled, educated and treated, and if necessary provided with an alternative source of drugs under medical care. This would not solve the problem of trafficking and dealing, but it does minimize the harm and the extent to which the market could grow by removing dependent users as steady clients of drug dealers.

Conclusion

The above are only four ideas which apply harm reduction to the supply-side of the drug use and abuse continuum which to date has been the sole purview of criminal justice agencies. These and already existing interventions on the demand-side of the continuum might for the first time eliminate major sources of profit from illegal drug trafficking and dealing. They could weaken this multi-billion dollar market. Where will the money come from to implement subsidies, buy-backs, state-controlled distribution and to counsel and educate users? From the same source as existing funds. Existing harm-reduction measures save large sums of money in criminal justice, medical and other social services by eliminating the harm that otherwise uncontrolled addictions cause. We suspect that the same cost savings would occur as an outcome of supply-side harm-reduction measures. The effectiveness of these or any other intervention should be subject to rigorous evaluation in order to measure their effectiveness or lack of it. Supply-side harm-reduction interventions would be a new frontier in drug abuse prevention.

Finally, these measures would have to be done on a worldwide basis. Drug abuse is a worldwide problem that ultimately cannot be effectively addressed in the long run by single national governments. The longer that ineffective actions continue to be taken the larger and more powerful drug traffic and dealing organizations become. They are already large enough to threaten national states, as we are witnessing in Afghanistan, Mexico, Colombia and in parts of the Caribbean, Thailand and Cambodia. A problem on a world scale requires solutions and entities that are also world scale. This public policy enterprise and the science to help drive new interventions are only just beginning.

Review questions

- Who are these recommendations addressed to and what can they do to make prevention, treatment and police interdiction more effective?
- What is it about drug abuse that all countries have in common?
- For every effort to reduce the supply of illicit drugs there are consequences. Can you add some more to the list of consequences already provided?
- Harm reduction addresses which side of the illicit drug use and abuse continuum (the supply reduction side or the demand reduction side)?
- Does this chapter conclude that prohibition or harm reduction is the answer to the drug problem? What is the relationship of one to the other?

Further reading

Beckerleg, S. E. and Hundt, G. L. (2004) 'The characteristics and recent growth of heroin injecting in a Kenyan coastal town', *Addiction Research & Theory*, 12(1), 41–53.

Cole, S. M. (2006) *New Research on Street Drugs*, New York: Nova Science Publishers.

Hadland, S. E., Marshall, B. D. L., Kerr, T., Lai, C., Montaner, J. S. and Wood, E. (2012) 'Ready access to illicit drugs among youth and adult users', *American Journal on Addictions*, 21(5), 488–90.

Reuter, P. H., Trautmann, F., Pacula, R. L., Kilmer, B., Gageldonk, A. and Gouwe, D. v. d. (2009) *Assessing Changes in Global Drug Problems, 1998–2007, Main Report*, London: RAND Europe.

UNODC (2011) *Estimating Illicit Financial Flows Resulting from Drug Trafficking and Other Transnational Organized Crimes*, Vienna: United Nations Office on Drugs and Crime.

Valentine, K. (2009) 'Evidence, values and drug treatment policy', *Critical Social Policy*, 29, 443–64.

References

Aalbers, M. B. (2006) '"When the banks withdraw, slum landlords take over": the structuration of neighbourhood decline through redlining, drug dealing, speculation and immigrant exploitation', *Urban Studies*, 43(7), 1061–86.

Aceijas, C., Friedman, S. R., Cooper, H. L., Wiessing, L., Stimson, G. V. and Hickman, M. (2006) 'Estimates of injecting drug users at the national and local level in developing and transitional countries, and gender and age distribution', *Sexually transmitted infections*, 82, 10–17.

Adler, P. A. (1993) *Wheeling and Dealing: An Ethnography of an Upper-Level Drug Dealing and Smuggling Community*, New York: Columbia University Press.

Acker, C. J. (1999) *Hep-Cats, Narcs, and Pipe Dreams: A History of America's Romance with Illegal Drugs, Journal of Social Policy*, Baltimore, MD: Johns Hopkins University Press.

Agnew, R. (1992a) 'An empirical test of general strain theory', *Criminology*, 30(4), 475–99.

Agnew, R. (1992b) 'Foundations for a general strain theory', *Criminology*, 30(1), 47–87.

Ainsworth, M. B. J. (1991) 'An ethological approach to personality development', *American Psychologist*, 46, 333–41.

Aitken, C. K., Higgs, P. and Bowden, S. (2008) 'Differences in the social networks of ethnic vietnamese and non-vietnamese injecting drug users and their implications for blood-borne virus transmission', *Epidemiology & Infection*, 136(3), 410–16.

Akers, R. L. and Lee, G. (1999) 'Age, social learning, and social bonding in adolescent substance use', *Deviant Behavior*, 20(1), 1–25.

Aldridge, J., Measham, F. and Williams, L. (2011) *Illegal Leisure Revisited*, London: Routledge.

Alexander, S. (1988) *The Pizza Connection: Lawyers, Money, Drugs, Mafia*, New York: Weidenfeld & Nicolson.

American Psychiatric Association (2013a) *Diagnostic and Statistical Manual of Mental Disorders*, 5th edn, Washington, DC: American Psychiatric Publishing.

American Psychiatric Association (2013b) *Highlights of Changes from DSM-IV-TR to DSM-5*, Washington, DC: American Psychiatric Publishing.

American Psychiatric Association (2013c) 'Substance-related and addictive disorders', available: www.dsm5.org/documents/substance.

Anda, R., Croft, J., Felitti, V., Nordenberg, D., Giles, W., Williamson, D. and Giovino, G. (1999) 'Adverse childhood experiences and smoking during adolescence and adulthood', *Journal of the American Medical Association*, 282(17), 1652–8.

Anda, R., Brown, D., Felitti, V., Bremner, J., Dube, S. R. and Giles, W. H. (2007) 'Adverse childhood experiences and prescribed psychotropic medications in adults', *American Journal of Preventive Medicine*, 32(5), 389–94.

Anderson, P. (2006) 'Global use of alcohol, drugs and tobacco', *Drug and Alcohol Review*, 25(6), 489–502.

Angrosino, M. (2003) 'Rum and ganja: indenture, drug foods, labor motivation and the evolution of the modern sugar industry in Trinidad' in Jankowiak, W. and Bradburd, D., eds, *Drugs, Labor and Colonial Expansion*, Tucson, AZ: The University of Arizona Press, 101–16.

Anonymous (1995) 'Nigerian drugs: internal trade', *The Economist*, 336(7929), 36.

APA (American Psychiatric Association) (1994) *Diagnostic and Statistical Manual of Mental Disorders: DSM-IV*, Washington, DC: American Psychiatric Association.

APHA (American Public Health Association) (2013) '10 Essential Public Health Services', available: www.apha.org/programs/standards/performancestandardsprogram/resexxentialservices.htm.

Archive, T. N. S. (2011) *The Contras, Cocaine, and Covert Operations*, Washington, DC: George Washington University.

Arnfred, S., ed. (2005) *Re-thinking Sexualities in Africa*, Uppsala, Sweden: Almqvist.

August, G. J., Winters, K. C., Realmuto, G. M., Tarter, R., Perry, C. and Hektner, J. M. (2004) 'Moving evidence-based drug abuse prevention programs from basic science to practice: "bridging the efficacy-effectiveness interface"', *Substance Use and Misuse*, 39(10–12), 2017–53.

Auld, J., Dorn, N. and South, N. (1986) 'Irregular work, irregular pleasures: heroin in the 1980s' in Matthews, R. and Young, J., eds, *Confronting Crime*, London: Sage.

Australia Ministerial Council on Drug Strategy (2004) *The National Drug Strategy: Australia's Integrated Framework: 2004–2009*, Canberra: Ministerial Council on Drug Strategy.

Babor, T. (2010) *Drug Policy and the Public Good*, New York: Oxford University Press.

Baker, P. J. (2006) 'Developing a blueprint for evidence-based drug prevention in England', *Drugs: Education, Prevention and Policy*, 13(1), 17–32.

Ball, A. L. (2007) 'HIV, injecting drug use and harm reduction: a public health response', *Addiction*, 102(5), 684–90.

Ball, S. A. and Legow, N. E. (1996) 'Attachment theory as a working model for the therapist transitioning from early to later recovery substance abuse treatment', *American Journal of Drug and Alcohol Abuse* 22(4), 533–47.

Bandura, A. (1977) *Social Learning Theory*, New York: General Learning Press.

Bandura, A. (1983) 'Model of causality in social learning theory' in Sukemune, S., ed., *Advances in Social Learning*, Toyko: Kaneko Shobo, 25–44.

Bandura, A. (1999) 'A sociocognitive analysis of substance abuse: an agentic perspective', *Psychological Science*, 10(3), 214–18.

Barden, D. (2013) 'Analyzing volatile organic chemicals in food: emerging trends and recent examples', *American Laboratory*, 45(2), 12–16.

Barendregt, C., Van Der Poel, A. and Van De Mheen, D. (2006) 'The rise of the mobile phone in the hard drug scene of Rotterdam', *Journal of Psychoactive Drugs*, 38(1), 77–87.

Barnes, D. L. G. (2002) 'Drug trafficking in Haiti', unpublished thesis, Naval Postgraduate School.

Barton, A. (2003) *Illicit Drugs: Use and Control*, London: Routledge.

Basov, S., Jacobson, M. and Miron, J. (2001) 'Prohibition and the market for illegal drugs', *World Economics*, 2(4), 1–25.

Baumeister, S. and Tossmann, P. (2005) 'Association between early onset of cigarette, alcohol and cannabis use and later drug use patterns: an analysis of a survey in European metropolises', *European Addiction Research*, 11(2), 92–8.

Beck, A. T. (1991) 'Cognitive therapy: a 30-year retrospective', *American Psychologist*, 46(4), 368–75.

Becker, G. (1968) 'Crime and punishment: an economic approach', *Journal of Political Economy*, 76(2), 169–217.

Becker, G. and Murphy, K. (1988) 'A theory of rational addiction', *Journal of Political Economy*, 96(4), 675–700.

Becker, H. (1953) 'Becoming a marihuana user', *American Journal of Sociology*, 59(3), 235–42.

Becker, H. (1963) *Outsiders: Studies in the Sociology of Deviance*, New York: Free Press.

Beeching, J. (1975) *The Chinese Opium Wars*, New York: Harcourt Brace Jovanovich.

Bennett, T. and Holloway, K. (2007) *Drug-Crime Connections*, Cambridge: Cambridge University Press.

Bennett, T., Holloway, K. and Farrington, D. (2008) 'The statistical association between drug misuse and crime: A meta-analysis', *Aggression & Violent Behavior*, 13(2), 107–18.

Benoit, E. (2004) 'National health insurance and health-based drug policy: an examination of policy linkages in the USA and Canada', *Journal of Social Policy*, 33(1), 133–51.

Benson, B. and Rasmussen, D. (1991) 'Relationship between illicit drug enforcement policy and property crimes', *Contemporary Economic Policy*, 9, 106–15.

Benton, S. L., Downey, R. G., Glider, P. J. and Benton, S. A. (2008) 'College students' norm perception predicts reported use of protective behavioral strategies for alcohol consumption', *Journal of Studies on Alcohol and Drugs*, 69(6), 859–65.

Berends, L. (2004) 'Alcohol and Aboriginal society: heavy drinking and allied responses' in Hamilton, M., King, T. and Ritter, A., eds, *Drug Use in Australia: Preventing Harm*, South Melbourne: Oxford University Press, 89–101.

Berman, S., O'Neill, J., Fears, S., Bartzokis, G., and London, E. (2008) 'Abuse of amphetamines and structural abnormalities in the brain', *Annals of the New York Academy of Sciences*, 1141, 195–220.

Bernburg, J. G., Thorlindsson, T. and Sigfusdottir, I. D. (2009) 'Neighborhood effects of disrupted family processes on adolescent substance use', *Social Science & Medicine*, 69(1), 129–37.

Berridge, V. (1978a) 'Opium eating and the working class in the nineteenth century: the public and official reaction', *British Journal of Addiction*, 73(1), 107–12.

Berridge, V. (1978b) 'War conditions and narcotics control: the passing of defence of the Realm Act Regulation 40B', *Journal of Social Policy*, 7(3), 285–304.

Berridge, V. (1984) 'Drugs and social policy: the establishment of drug control in britain 1900–30', *British Journal of Addiction*, 79(4), 17–29.

Berridge, V. (2012) 'The art of medicine: the rise, fall, and revival of recovery in drug policy', *Lancet*, 379(9810), 22–3.

Berry, W. D. and Sanders, M. S. (2000) *Understanding Multivariate Research: A Primer for Beginning Social Scientists*, Boulder, CO: Westview Press.

Best, D., Savic, M., Beckwith, M., Honor, S., Karpusheff, J. and Lubman, D. I. (2013) 'The role of abstinence and activity in the quality of life of drug users engaged in Treatment', *Journal of Substance Abuse Treatment*, 45(3), 273–9.

Bewley-Taylor, D., Hallam, C. and Allen, R. (2009) *The Incarceration of Drug Offenders: An Overview*, Beckley Foundation Report 16, Oxford: Beckley Foundation.

Beyerstein, B. L. and Laing, R.R., eds (2003) *Hallucinogens: A Forensic Drug Handbook*, London: Academic Press.

Biddle, B. (1979) *Role Theory: Expectations, Identities, and Behaviors*, New York: Academic Press.

Bischof, G., Rumpf, H. J., Meyer, C., Hapke, U. and John, U. (2005) 'Influence of psychiatric comorbidity in alcohol-dependent subjects in a representative population survey on treatment utilization and natural recovery', *Addiction*, 100(3), 405–13.

Blau, P., ed. (1975) *Approaches to the Study of Social Structure*, New York: The Free Press.

Blum, K., Chen, A. L. C., Giordano, J., Borsten, J., Chen, T. J. H., Hauser, M., Simpatico, T., Femino, J., Braverman, E. R. and Barh, D. (2012) 'The addictive brain: all roads lead to dopamine', *Journal of Psychoactive Drugs*, 44(2), 134–43.

Blumenthal, K. and Colvin, J. (2011) *Bootleg: Murder, Moonshine, and the Lawless Years of Prohibition*, New York: Roaring Brook Press.

Blumer, H. (1969) 'Society as symbolic interaction' in Rose, A. M., ed. *Human Behavior and Social Process: An Interactionist Approach*, New York: Houghton-Mifflin.

Boivin, R. (2011) 'Drug trafficking networks in the world economy', available: www.erdr.org/textes/boivin.pdf.

Borkman, T., Kaskutas, L. A. and Barrows, D. (1999) 'The social model: a literature review and history' in Kaskutas, L. A., ed. *The Social Model Approach to Substance Abuse Recovery: A Program of Research and Evaluation*, Berkeley, CA: Alcohol Research Group, 3–22.

Boscarino, J. A. (2004) 'Posttraumatic stress disorder and physical illness: results from clinical and epidemiologic studies', *Annals of the New York Academy of Sciences*, 1032(1), 141–53.

Bottomore, T. B. and Ruben, M., eds (1964) *Karl Marx: Selected Writings in Sociology and Social Philosophy*, New York: McGraw-Hill.

Botvin, G. J. (2000) 'Preventing drug abuse in schools: social and competence enhancement approaches targeting individual-level etiologic factors', *Addictive behaviors*, 25(6).

Bourdieu, P. (1972) *Outline of a Theory of Practice*, Cambridge: Cambridge University Press.

Bowlby, J. (2008) *A Secure Base: Parent-Child Attachment and Healthy Human Development*, New York: Basic Books.

Bowser, B., Word, C. O., Lockett, G. and Dillard-Smith, C. (2001) 'How drug abusers organize their participation in HIV/AIDS studies: their time and their place', *Journal of Drug Issues*, 31(4), 941–56.

Bowser, B., Word, C., Stanton, M. D. and Coleman, S. B. (2003) 'Death in the family and HIV risk-taking among intravenous drug users', *Family Process*, 42(2), 291–304.

Bowser, B., Quimby, E. and Singer, M., eds (2007) *When Communities Assess their AIDS Epidemics: Results of Rapid Assessment of HIV/AIDS in Eleven U.S. Cities*, Lanham, MD: Lexington Books.

Bradburd, D. and Jankowiak, W. (2003) 'Drugs, desire and European economic expansion' in Jankowiak, W. and Bradburd, D., eds. *Drugs, Labor and Colonial Expansion*, Tucson, AZ: The University of Arizona Press, 3–30.

Brain, R., Abel. L., Dunlop, D., Hudson, D., Macdonald, A., Macklin, A., Scott, S., and Partridge, M. (1961) *Report of the Interdependental Committee on Drug Addiction*, London: Ministry of Health, Department of Health for Scotland.

Brener, L., Von Hippel, W. and Von Hippel, C. (2012) 'Exploring the relationship between implicit self-representation and drug use', *Addiction Research & Theory*, 20(2), 133–7.

Breslau, J. (2005) 'Lifetime risk and persistence of psychiatric disorders across ethnic groups in the United States', *Psychological Medicine*, 35, 317–27.

Brickman, B. (1988) 'Psychoanalysis and substance abuse: toward a more effective approach', *Journal of the American Academy of Psychoanalysis*, 16(3), 359–79.

Brochu, S., Duff, C., Asbridge, M. and Erickson, P. G. (2011) '"There's what's on paper and then there's what happens, out on the sidewalk": Cannabis users knowledge and opinions of Canadian drug laws', *Journal of Drug Issues*, 41(1), 95–115.

Brownstein, H. H. and Taylor, B. G. (2007) 'Measuring the stability of illicit drug markets: Why does it matter?', *Drug and Alcohol Dependence*, 90(Supp. 1), 52–60.

Brush, F. R., ed. (1971) *Aversive Conditioning and Learning*, New York: Academic Press.

Burns, D. L. (2002) 'Drug trafficking in Haiti', available: http://handle.dtic.mil/100.2/ADA404648.

Buxton, J. (2006) *The Political Economy of Narcotics: Production, Consumption and Global Markets*, Nova Scotia: Fernwood Publishing.

Campbell, R. A. (2008) 'Making sSober citizens: the legacy of indigenous alcohol regulation in Canada, 1777–1985', *Journal of Canadian Studies*, 42(1), 105–26.

Carlson, N. R. (2007) *Physiology of Behavior*, 9th edn, Boston, MA: Pearson.

Carlson, P. (2008) 'Uneasy About Alcohol', *American History*, 43, 32–9.

Carter, C., Albert, R. and Brent, C. (1905) *Report of the Committee Appointed by the Philippine Commission to Investigate the Use of Opium and the Traffic Therein*, Washington, DC: US Bureau of Insular Affairs, War Department.

Caspers, K. M., Yucuis, R., Troutman, B. and Spinks, R. (2006) 'Attachment as an organizer of behavior: implications for substance abuse problems and willingness to seek treatment', *Substance Abuse Treatment, Prevention and Policy*, 1, 32.

Caulkins, J. P., Reuter, P. and Taylor, L. J. (2006) 'Can supply restrictions lower price? Violence, drug dealing and positional advantage', *Contributions to Economic Analysis & Policy*, 5(1), 1–18.

CCI (Centre of Civic Initiatives) (2009) *Lessons from DARE: The Complicated Relationship between Research and Practice*, New York: Center for Court Innovation.

CDCP (U.S. Centers for Disease Control and Prevention) (2011) 'Vital signs: overdoses of prescription opioid pain relievers – United States, 1999–2008', *Morbidity and Mortality Weekly Report*, 60(43), 1487–92.

Center for Court Innovation (2009) *Lessons from the Battle over DARE: The Complicated Relationship between Research and Practice*, Washington, DC: Bureau of Justice Assistance, US Department of Justice.

Cervone, D. and Pervin, L. (2008) *Personality: Theory and Research*, New York: John Wiley.

Chalk, P. (1998) *Low Intensity Conflict in Southeast Asia: Piracy, Drug Trafficking and Political Terrorism*, Leamington Spa: Research Institute for the Study of Conflict and Terrorism.

Charles, M. and Britto, G. (2001) 'The socio-cultural context of drug use and implications for drug policy', *International Social Science Journal*, 53(3), 467–74.

Charney, D. S. and Nestler, E. J. (2009) *Neurobiology of Mental Illness*, Oxford, New York: Oxford University Press.

Chein, I., Ferard, D., Lee, R. and Rosenfeld, F. (1964) *The Road to H: Narcotics, Delinquency and Social Policy*, London: Tavistock.

Chen, Z. and Huang, K. (2007) 'Drug problems in China: recent trends, countermeasures, and challenges', *International Journal of Offender Therapy and Comparative Criminology*, 51(1), 98–109.

Chepesiuk, R. (1999) *Hard Target: The United States War against International Drug Trafficking, 1982–1997*, Jefferson, NC: McFarland.

Chepesiuk, R. (2003) *The Bullet or the Bribe: Taking Down Colombia's Cali Drug Cartel* Westport, CT: Praeger Publishers.

Chepesiuk, R. (2007) *Gangs of Harlem: The Gritty World of New York's Most Famous Neighborhood*, Fort Lee, NJ: Barricade Books.

Cheung, J. T., Mann, R. E., Ialomiteanu, A., Stoduto, G., Chan, V., Ala-Leppilampi, K. and Rehm, J. (2010) 'Anxiety and mood disorders and cannabis use', *American Journal of Drug and Alcohol Abuse*, 36(2), 118–22.

Chin, K.-l. (2009) *The Golden Triangle: Inside Southeast Asia's Drug Trade*, Ithaca, NY: Cornell University Press.

Cho, H. (2006) 'Influences of norm proximity and norm types on binge and non-binge drinkers: examining the under-examined aspects of social norms interventions on college campuses', *Journal of Substance Use*, 11(6), 417–29.

Cohen, A. (1957) *Delinquent Boys: Culture of the Gang*, New York: Free Press.

Cohen, M. M. (2006) 'Jim Crow's drug war: race, Coca Cola, and the Southern origins of drug prohibition', *Southern Cultures*, 12, 55–79.

Coleman, S. (1980) 'Incomplete mourning and addict/family transactions: a theory for understanding heroin abuse' in Lettieri, D., Sayers, M. and Pearson, H., eds, *Theories on Drug Abuse*, Rockville, MD: NIDA, 83–9.

Coleman, S. B. (1981) 'Incomplete mourning in substance abusing families: theory, research and practice' in Wolberg, L. and Aronson, M., eds, *Group and Family Therapy: An Overview*, New York: Brunner/Mazel, 269–83.

Collett, M. (1989) *The Cocaine Connection: Drug Trafficking and Inter-American Relations*, New York, NY: Foreign Policy Association.

Collin, C. (2002) 'Switzerland's drug policy', available: www.parl.gc.ca/Content/SEN/Committee/371/ille/library/collin1-e.htm.

Collin, C. (2006) 'Substance abuse issues and public policy in Canada', available: http://epe.lac-bac.gc.ca/100/200/301/library%5Fparliament/substance%5Fabuse-e/PRB0615-e.pdf.

Colón, H. M., Sahai, H., Robles, R. R. and Matos, T. D. (1995) 'Effects of a community outreach program in HIV risk behaviors among injection drug users in San Juan, Puerto Rico: an analysis of trends', *AIDS Education and Prevention*, 7(3), 195–209.

Committee on the Prevention of HIV Infection (2009) *Preventing HIV Infection among Injecting Drug Users in High Risk Countries: An Assessment of the Evidence*, Washington, DC: National Academies Press.

Copeland, J. and Swift, W. (2009) 'Cannabis use disorder: epidemiology and management', *International Review of Psychiatry*, 21(2), 96–103.

Corso, K. A., Bryan, C. J., Corso, M. L., Kanzler, K. E., Houghton, D. C., Ray-Sannerud, B. and Morrow, C. E. (2012) 'Therapeutic alliance and treatment outcome in the primary care behavioral health model', *Family, Systems and Health*, 30(2), 87–100.

Cortes, R. (2012) *A Secret History of Coffee, Coca and Cola*, New York: Akashic Books.

Cotto, J. H., Davis, E., Dowling, G. J., Elcano, J. C., Staton, A. B. and Weiss, S. R. (2010) 'Gender effects on drug use, abuse, and dependence: a special analysis of results from the National Survey on Drug Use and Health', *Gender Medicine*, 7(5), 402–13.

Coulson, C. and Caulkins, J. P. (2012) 'Scheduling of newly emerging drugs: a critical review of decisions over 40 years', *Addiction*, 107(4), 766–73.

Courtwright, D. (1982) *Dark Paradise: Opiate Addiction in America Before 1940*, Cambridge: Harvard University Press.

Cox, M. J. and Paley, B. (2003) 'Understanding families as systems', *Current Directions in Psychological Science*, 12(5), 193–6.

Crits-Christoph, P., Siqueland, L., Blaine, J., Frank, A., Luborsky, L., Onken, L. and Beck, A. (1999) 'Psychosocial treatments for cocaine dependence: National Institute on Drug Abuse Collaborative Cocaine Treatment Study', *Archive of General Psychiatry*, 56(6), 493–502.

CSAT (2008) *An Introduction to Mutual Support Groups for Alcohol and Drug Abuse. Substance Abuse in Brief, Fact Sheet 5*, Rockville, MD: Substance Abuse and Mental Health Services Administration.

Cunningham, J. (1999) 'Untreated remissions from drug use: the predominant pathway', *Addictive Behavior*, 24(2), 267–70.

Czarra, F. R. (2009) *Spices: A Global History*, London: Reaktion.

Dahrendorf, R. (1954) *Class and Class Conflict in Industrial Society*, Stanford, CA: Stanford University Press.

Dalby, A. (2003) 'Stimulants' in Katz, S. and Weaver, W., eds, *Encyclopedia of Food and Culture*, New York: Charles Scribner, 344–8.

Darke, S. and Kaye, S. (2012) 'Predisposed violent drug users versus drug users who commit violence: does the order of onset translate to differences in the severity of violent offending?', *Drug & Alcohol Review*, 31(4), 558–65.

Davenport-Hines and Treadwell, R. P. (2002) *The Pursuit of Oblivion: A Global History of Narcotics*, New York: W. W. Norton.

Davey, Z., Corazza, O., Schifano, F. and Deluca, P. (2010) 'Mass-information: mephedrone, myths, and the new generation of legal highs', *Drugs & Alcohol Today*, 10(3), 24–8.

de Haan, H. A., Joosten, E. A., Wijdeveld, A. G., Boswinkel, P. B., van der Palen, J. and De Jong, C. A. (2011) 'Cognitive behavioural treatment is as effective in high- as in low-scoring alexithymic patients with substance-related disorders', *Psychotherapy and Psychosomatics*, 80(4), 254–5.

de la Torre, L. V. (2008) 'Drug trafficking and police corruption: a comparison of Colombia and Mexico', unpublished thesis, Naval Postgraduate School.

Dean, E. (1991) '"We will all be lost and destroyed": post-traumatic stress disorder and the civil war', *Civil War History*, 37(2), 138–53.

Decarie, G. (1990) 'Dry diplomacy: the United States, Great Britain, and prohibition', *Canadian Review of American Studies*, 21(3), 398–401.

Decker, S. H. and Chapman, M. T. (2008) *Drug Smugglers on Drug Smuggling: Lessons from the Inside*, Philadelphia, PA: Temple University Press.

Degenhardt, L. and Topp, L. (2003) '"Crystal meth" use among polydrug users in Sydney's dance party subculture: characteristics, use patterns and associated harms', *International Journal of Drug Policy*, 14(1), 17–24.

Degenhardt, L., Chiu, W., Sampson, N., Kessler, R., Anthony, J. and (2008) 'Toward a global view of alcohol, tobacco, cannabis and cocaine use: findings from the WHO World Mental Health Surveys', *PLoS Medicine*, 5(7), 141.

Degenhardt, L., Dierker, L., Chiu, W. T., Medina-Mora, M. E., Neumark, Y., Sampson, N., Alonso, J., Angermeyer, M., Anthony, J. C., Bruffaerts, R., de Girolamo, G., et al. (2010) 'Evaluating the drug use "gateway" theory using cross-national data: consistency and associations of the order of initiation of drug use among participants in the WHO World Mental Health Surveys', *Drug Alcohol Depend*, 108(1–2), 84–97.

Degenhardt, L., Bucello, C., Mathers, B., Briegleb, C., Ali, H., Hickman, M. and McLaren, J. (2011) 'Mortality among regular or dependent users of heroin and other opioids: a systematic review and meta-analysis of cohort studies', *Addiction*, 106(1), 32–51.

Deitche, S. M. (2012) 'The mafia and drugs', *Netplaces*, available: www.netplaces.com/mafia/just-say-no/the-mafia-and-drugs.htm.

Derks, H. (2012) *History of the Opium Poblem: The Assault on the East, ca. 1600–1950*, Boston, MA: Brill.

Devaney, M., Reid, G. and Baldwin, S. (2007) 'Prevalence of illicit drug use in Asia and the Pacific', *Drug and Alcohol Review*, 26(1), 97–102.

DHHS (1999) *Mental Health: A Report of the Surgeon General – Chapter Two*, Rockville, MD: US Department of Health and Human Services, Substance Abuse and Mental Health Services Administration, Center for Mental Health Services, National Institutes of Health, National Institute of Mental Health.

Dolan, K., Kimber, J., Fry, C., Fitzgerald, J., McDonald, D. and Trautmann, F. (2000) 'Drug consumption facilities in Europe and the establishment of supervised injecting centres in Australia', *Drug and Alcohol Review*, 19, 337–46.

Dorn, M. L. (2000) '(In)temperate zones: Daniel Drake's medico-moral geographies of urban life in the Trans-Appalachian American West', *Journal of the History of Medicine and Allied Sciences*, 55(1), 256–91.

Drummond, D. C. (2001) 'Theories of drug craving, ancient and modern', *Addiction*, 96(1), 33–46.

Drummond, D. C., Litten, R. Z., Lowman, C. and Hunt, W. A. (2000) 'Craving research: future directions', *Addiction*, 95 (supp. 2), 247–55.

Durkheim, E. (1951) *Suicide: A Study in Sociology*, New York: The Free Press.

Durkheim, E. (1982) *The Rules of Sociological Methods*, New York: The Free Press.

Dye, T. (2012) *Understanding Public Policy*, Englewood Cliffs, NJ: Prentice-Hall.

Edelson, M. (1985) *Hypothesis and Evidence in Psychoanalysis*, Chicago, IL: University of Chicago Press.

Edlin, B., Irwin, K., Faruque, S., McCoy, C., Word, C. O., Serrano, Y., Inciardi, J., Bowser, B., Schilling, R. and Holmberg, S. (1994) 'Intersecting epidemics: crack cocaine use and HIV infection among inner-city young adults', *New England Journal of Medicine*, 331, 1422–7.

Egginton, R. and Parker, H. (2002) 'From one-off triers to regular users: measuring the regularity of drug taking in a cohort of English adolescents (1996–1999)', *Addiction Research & Theory*, 10(1), 97–114.

Egley, A. , Maxson, C., Miller, J. and Klein M., eds (2007) *The Modern Gang Reader*, New York: Oxford University Press.

Ehrenhalt, A. (2012) *The Great Inversion and the Future of the American City*, New York: Alfred Knopf.

Ehrman, R., Ternes, J., O'Brien, C. P. and McLellan, A. T. (1992) 'Conditioned tolerance in human opiate addicts', *Psychopharmacology*, 108(1–2), 218–24.

Ellickson, P. L. (1995) 'Schools' in Coombs, R. and Ziedonis, D., eds, *Handbook on Drug Prevention*, Boston, MA: Allyn & Bacon, 93–120.

Farabee, D., Shen, H. and Sanchez, S. (2002) 'Perceived coercion and treatment need among mentally ill parolees', *Criminal Justice and Behavior*, 29(1), 76–86.

Fenton, M. C., Keyes, K., Geier, T., Greenstein, E., Skodol, A., Krueger, B., Grant, B. F. and Hasin, D. S. (2012) 'Psychiatric comorbidity and the persistence of drug use disorders in the United States', *Addiction*, 107(3), 599–609.

Fergusson, D. M. and Horwood, L. J. (1997) 'Early onset cannabis use and psychosocial adjustment in young adults', *Addiction*, 92(3), 279–96.

Fergusson, D. M., Poulton, R., Smith, P. F. and Boden, J. M. (2006) 'Cannabis and psychosis', *British Medical Journal*, 332(7534), 172–5.

Fergusson, D. M., Boden, J. M. and Horwood, L. J. (2008) 'The developmental antecedents of illicit drug use: evidence from a 25-year longitudinal study', *Drug and Alcohol Dependence*, 96(1–2), 165–77.

Ferraiolo, K. (2007) 'From killer weed to popular medicine: the evolution of American drug control policy, 1937–2000', *Journal of Policy History*, 19, 147–79.

Ferriter, D. (1999) *A Nation of Extremes: The Pioneers in Twentieth-Century Ireland*, Portland, OR: Irish Academic Press.

Fields, R. D. (2010) *The Other Brain: From Dementia to Schizophrenia, How New Discoveries about the Brain are Revolutionizing Medicine and Science*, New York: Simon & Schuster.

Finestone, H. (1964) 'Cats, kicks and color' in Becker, H., ed. *The Other Side: Perspectives on Deviance*, New York: The Free Press.

Fischer, B., Patra, J., Firestone Cruz, M., Gittins, J. and Rehm, J. (2008) 'Comparing heroin users and prescription opioid users in a Canadian multi-site population of illicit opioid users', *Drug and alcohol Review*, 27(6), 625–32.

Fischer, C. (1995) 'The subcultural theory of urbanism: a twentieth year assessment', *American Journal of Sociology*, 101(3), 543–77.

Fischer, J. A., Clavarino, A. M. and Najman, J. M. (2012) 'Drug, sex and age differentials in the use of Australian publicly funded treatment services', *Subst Abuse*, 6, 13–21.

Fish, J. M., ed. (2006) *Drugs and Society: U.S. Public Policy*, Lanham, MD: Rowman & Littlefield Publishers.

Fishbein, D. and Tarter, R. (2009) 'Infusing neuroscience into the study and prevention of drug misuse and co-occurring aggressive behavior', *Subst Use Misuse*, 44(9–10), 1204–35.

Flynn, P. M. and Brown, B. S. (2011) 'Implementation research: issues and prospects', *Addictive Behavior*, 36(6), 566–9.

Fontelle, L., Oostermeijer, S., Harrison, B., Pantelis, C. and Yucel, M. (2011) 'Obsessive-compulsive disorder, impulse control disorder and drug addiction', *Drugs*, 71(7), 827–40.

Ford, J. A. (2009) 'Nonmedical prescription drug use among adolescents: the influence of bonds to family and school', *Youth & Society*, 40(3), 336–52.

Ford, J. A. and Schroeder, R. D. (2009) 'Academic strain and non-medical use of prescription stimulants among college students', *Deviant Behavior*, 30(1), 26–53.

Ford, J. A., Watkins, W. C. and Blumenstein, L. (2011) 'Correlates of salvia divinorum use in a national sample: findings from the 2009 National Survey on Drug Use and Health', *Addictive Behavior*, 36(11), 1032–7.

Fothergill, K., Ensminger, M., Green, K., Robertson, J. and Juon, H. (2009) 'Pathways to adult marijuana and cocaine use: a prospective study of African Americans from age 6 to 42', *Journal of Health and Social Behavior*, 50(1), 65–81.

Frampton, M., Lopez, I. and Simon, J., eds (2008) *After the War on Crime: Race, Democracy and a New Reconstruction*, New York: New York University Press.

Frank, B. (2000) 'An overview of heroin trends in New York City: past, present and future', *The Mount Sinai Journal of Medicine*, 67(5&6), 340–6.

Friesendorf, C. (2007) *US Foreign Policy and the War on Drugs: Displacing the Cocaine and Heroin Industry*, London: Routledge.

Frisher, M., Collins, J., Millson, D., Crome, I. and Croft, P. (2004) 'Prevalence of comorbid psychiatric illness and substance misuse in primary care in England and Wales', *Journal of Epidemiology and Community Health*, 58(12), 1036–41.

Galante, P. and Sapin, L. (1979) *The Marseilles Mafia: The Truth Behind the World of Drug Trafficking*, London: W. H. Allen.

Galanter, M. (2008) 'The concept of spirituality in relation to addiction recovery and general psychiatry', *Recent Developments in Alcoholism*, 18, 125–40.

Gallahue, P. (2011) *The Death Penalty for Drug Offences: Global Overview 2011*, London: Harm Reduction International.

Gallet, C. and List, J. (2003) 'Cigarette demand: a meta-analysis of elasticities', *Health Economics*, 12, 821–35.

Gardner, M. (1999) 'Working on white womanhood: white working class women in the anti-Chinese movement 1877–1890', *Journal of Social History*, 33(1), 73–95.

Garland, D. (2001a) *The Culture of Control: Crime and Social Order in Contemporary Society*, Oxford: Oxford University Press.

Garland, D. (2001b) *Mass Imprisonment: Social Causes and Consequences*, London: Sage.

Garrett, B. E., Dube, S. R., Trosclair, A., Caraballo, R. S. and Pechacek, T. F. (2011) 'Cigarette smoking: United States, 1965–2008', *MMWR Surveillance Summaries*, 60 (Suppl), 109–13.

GCDP (2011) 'War on Drugs: Report of the Global Commission on Drug Policy', available: www.globalcommissionondrugs.org/Report.

Gelder, K. (2005) *Subcultures: Cultural Histories and Social Practice*, New York: Routledge.

Gergen, K. J. (1994) *Toward Transformation in Social Knowledge*, 2nd edn, London: Sage.

Gergen, K. (1997) 'Who speaks and who replies in human science scholarship?', *History of the Human Sciences*, 10(3), 151–73.

Gergen, K. (1999) *An Invitation to Social Construction*, London: Sage Publications.

Gerstein, D. R. and Green, L. (1993) *Preventing Drug Abuse: What Do We Know?*, Washington, DC: National Academy Press.

Gevitz, N. (1990) 'Domestic medical guides and the drug trade in nineteenth-century America', *Pharmacy in History*, 32(2), 51–6.

Gezon, L. (2012) *Drugs Effects: Khat in Biocultural and Socioeconomic Perspective*, Walnut Creek, CA: Left Coast Press.

Gibson, R. M. (2011) *The Secret Army: Chiang Kai-shek and the Drug Warlords of the Golden Triangle*, Singapore: John Wiley & Son (Asia).

Global Commission on Drug Policy (2012) 'War on Drugs', available: www.global commissionondrugs.org/reports/.

Goffman, E. (1963) *Stigma: Notes on the Management of Spoiled Identity*, Englewood Cliffs, NJ: Prentice-Hall.

Goldstein, P. (1985) 'The drugs/violence nexus: a tripartite conceptual framework', *Journal of Drug Issues*, 39, 143–74.

Golub, A., Johnson, B. D. and Dunlap, E. (2005) 'Subcultural evolution and illicit drug use', *Addiction Research and Theory*, 13(3), 217–29.

Gootenberg, P. (2003) 'Between coca and cocaine: a century or more of US–Peruvian drug paradoxes, 1860–1980', *Hispanic American Historical Review*, 83, 119–50.

Gossop, M., Marsden, J., Stewart, D. and Kidd, T. (2003) 'The National Treatment Outcome Research Study (NTORS): 4–5 year follow-up results', *Addiction*, 98(3), 291–303.

Goulden, C. and Sondhi, A. (2001) *At the Margins: Drug Use by Vulnerable Young People in the 1998/99 Youth Lifestyles Survey*, London: Home Office Research, Development and Statistics Directorate.

Granfield, R. and Cloud, W. (2001) 'Social context and "natural recovery": the role of social capital in the resolution of drug-associated problems', *Subst Use Misuse*, 36(11), 1543–70.

Grant, B. F. (1995) 'Comorbidity between DSM-IV drug use disorders and major depression: results of a national survey of adults', *Journal of Substance Abuse*, 7(4), 481–97.

Green, D. P. and Winik, D. (2010) 'Using random judge assignments to estimate the effects of incarceration and probation on recidivism among drug offenders', *Criminology*, 48(2), 357–87.

Green, K. M. (2010) 'Low social integration in young adulthood linked to later onset of drug use', *DATA: The Brown University Digest of Addiction Theory & Application*, 29(8), 5–6.

Green, M. (1979) 'A history of Canadian narcotics Control: the formative years', *University of Toronto Faculty Law Review*, 42, 42–8.

Greenfielda, V. A. and Paolib, L. (2012) 'If supply-oriented drug policy is broken, can harm reduction help fix it? Melding disciplines and methods to advance international drug-control policy', *International Journal of Drug Policy*, 23, 6–15.

Greiff, P. D., ed. (1999) *Drugs and the Limits of Liberalism: Moral and Legal Issues*, Ithaca, NY: Cornell University Press.

Groff, R. (2008) *Revitalizing Causality: Realism about Causality in Philosophy and Social Science*, New York: Routledge.

Gupta, V., Levenburg, N., Moore, L., Motwani, J. and Schwarz, T. (2011) 'The spirit of family business: a comparative analysis of Anglo, Germanic and Nordic nations', *International Journal of Cross Cultural Management*, 11(2), 133–51.

Gureje, O., Vazquez-Barquero, J. L. and Janca, A. (1996) 'Comparisons of alcohol and other drugs: experience from the WHO Collaborative Cross-Cultural Applicability Research (CAR) Study', *Addiction*, 91(10), 1529–38.

Gureje, O., Mavreas, V., Vazquez-Barquero, J. L. and Janca, A. (1997) 'Problems related to alcohol use: a cross-cultural perspective', *Culture, Medicine and Psychiatry*, 21(2), 199–211.

Gustafson, D. L., Goodyear, L. and Keough, F. (2008) 'When the dragon's awake: a needs assessment of people injecting drugs in a small urban centre', *The International Journal on Drug Policy*, 19(3), 189–94.

Guydish, J., Bucardo, J., Clark, G. and Bernheim, S. (1998) 'Evaluating needle exchange: a description of client characteristics, health status, program utilization, and HIV risk behavior', *Subst Use Misuse*, 33(5), 1173–96.

Hadland, S. E., Marshall, B. D. L., Kerr, T., Lai, C., Montaner, J. S. and Wood, E. (2012) 'Ready access to illicit drugs among youth and adult users', *American Journal on Addictions*, 21(5), 488–90.

Haemmig, R. B. (1995) 'Harm reduction in Bern: from outreach to heroin maintenance', *Bulletin of the New York Academy of Medicine*, 72(2), 371–9.

Hakkarainen, P., Tigerstedt, C. and Tammi, T. (2007) 'Dual-track drug policy: normalization of the drug problem in Finland', *Drugs: Education, Prevention and Policy*, 14(6), 543–58.

Hale Jr, N. G. (1995) *The Rise and Crisis of Psychoanalysis in the United States: Freud and the Americans, 1917–1985*, New York: Oxford University Press.

Hall, D. H. and Queener, J. E. (2007) 'Self-medication hypothesis of substance use: testing Khantzian's updated theory', *Journal of Psychoactive Drugs*, 39(2), 151–8.

Hall, W. (2010) 'What are the policy lessons of National Alcohol Prohibition in the United States, 1920–1933?', *Addiction*, 105(7), 1164–73.

Hammett, T. M., Wu, Z., Duc, T. T., Stephens, D., Sullivan, S., Liu, W., Chen, Y., Ngu, D. and Des Jarlais, D. C. (2008) 'Social evils and harm reduction: the evolving policy environment for human immunodeficiency virus prevention among injection drug users in China and Vietnam', *Addiction*, 103(1), 137–45.

Harper, C. C., Henderson, J. T., Schalet, A., Becker, D., Stratton, L. and Raine, T. R. (2010) 'Abstinence and teenagers: prevention counseling practices of health care providers serving high-risk patients in the United States', *Perspectives on Sexual & Reproductive Health*, 42(2), 125–32.

Harrington, M., Robinson, J., Bolton, S. L., Sareen, J. and Bolton, J. (2011) 'A longitudinal study of risk factors for incident drug use in adults: findings from a representative sample of the US population', *Canadian Journal of Psychiatry*, 56(11), 686–95.

Hartney, C. (2006) *US Rates of Incarceration: A Global Perspective*, Oakland, CA: National Council on Crime and Delinquency.

Head, L. S. and Gross, A. M. (2009) 'Systematic desensitization' in O'Donohue, W. and Isher, J., eds, *General Principles and Empirically Supported Techniques of Cognitive Behavior Therapy*, Hoboken, NJ: John Wiley & Sons Inc.

Heap, C. C. (2009) *Slumming: Sexual and Racial Encounters in American Nightlife, 1885–1940*, Chicago, IL: University of Chicago Press.

Henderson, C., Dakof, G., Greenbaum, P. and Liddle, H. (2010) 'Effectiveness of multidimensional family therapy with higher severity substance-abusing adolescents: report from two randomized controlled trials', *Journal of Consulting and Clinical Psychology*, 78(6), 885–97.

Henrichson, C. and Delaney, R. (2012) *The Price of Prisons: What Incarceration Costs Taxpayers* New York: Vera Institute of Justice.

Hides, L., Samet, S. and Lubman, D. (2010) 'Cognitive behaviour therapy (CBT) for the treatment of co-occurring depression and substance use: current evidence and directions for future research', *Drug and Alcohol Review*, 29(5), 508–17.

Higgins, G. E., Mahoney, M. and Ricketts, M. L. (2009) 'Nonsocial reinforcement of the nonmedical use of prescription drugs: a partial test of social learning and self-control theories', *Journal of Drug Issues*, 39(4), 949–64.

Hirschi, T. (1969) *Causes of Delinquency*, 2nd edn, Berkeley, CA: University of California Press.

Ho, C. M. and Bello, W. F. (2007) *Down with Colonialism!*, New York: Verso.

Hofmann, W., Perugini, M., De Houwer, J., Baeyens, F. and Crombez, G. (2010) 'Evaluative conditioning in humans: a meta-analysis', *Psychological Bulletin*, 136(3), 390–421.

Holmes, J. and de Pineres, S. G. (2006) 'The illegal drug industry, Violence and the Colombian economy: a department level analysis', *Bulletin of Latin American Research*, 25(1), 104–18.

Homer, B. D., Solomon, T. M., Moeller, R. W., Mascia, A., DeRaleau, L. and Halkitis, P. N. (2008) 'Methamphetamine abuse and impairment of social functioning: a review of the underlying neurophysiological causes and behavioral implications', *Psychological Bulletin*, 134(2), 301–10.

Howard, M. O. (2001) 'Pharmacological aversion treatment of alcohol abuse', *American Journal of Drug and Alcohol Abuse*, 27(3), 561–85.

Howard, M. O. and Jenson, J. M. (1990) 'Chemical aversion treatment of alcohol dependence. I. Validity of current criticisms', *International Journal of the Addictions*, 25(10), 1227–62.

Hser, Y. I., Evans, E., Huang, D., Brecht, M. L. and Li, L. (2008) 'Comparing the dynamic course of heroin, cocaine, and methamphetamine use over 10 years', *Addictive Behaviors*, 33(12), 1581–9.

Hser, Y. I., Kagihara, J., Huang, D., Evans, E. and Messina, N. (2012) 'Mortality among substance-using mothers in California: a 10-year prospective study', *Addiction*, 107(1), 215–22.

Hu, X., Primack, B. A., Barnett, T. E. and Cook, R. L. (2011) 'College students and use of K2: an emerging drug of abuse in young persons', *Substance Abuse, Treatment, Prevention and Policy*, 6, 16.

Huang, S., Trapido, E., Fleming, L., Arheart, K., Crandall, L., French, M., Malcolm, S. and Prado, G. (2011) 'The long-term effects of childhood maltreatment experiences on subsequent illicit drug use and drug-related problems in young adulthood', *Addictive Behaviors*, 36(1–2), 95–102.

Hughes, B. and Winstock, A. R. (2012) 'Controlling new drugs under marketing regulations', *Addiction*, 107(11), 1894–9.

Hughes, C. and Stevens, A. (2010) 'What can we learn from the Portuguese decriminalisation of illicit drugs?', *British Journal of Criminology*, 50, 999–1022.

Hughes, C. E. and Stevens, A. (2012) 'A resounding success or a disastrous failure: re-examining the interpretation of evidence on the Portuguese decriminalisation of illicit drugs', *Drug and Alcohol Review*, 31(1), 101–13.

Hughes, R. A. (2001) 'The lives of drug injectors and English social policy', *Journal of Health & Social Policy*, 13(2), 75–91.

Hunt, G., Moloney, M. and Evans, K. (2010) *Youth, Drugs and Nightlife*, New York: Routledge.

Hyman, H. H. and Singer, E., eds (1968) *Readings in Reference Group Theory and Research*, New York: The Free Press.

Iguchi, M., Belding, M., Morral, A., Lamb, R. and Husband, S. (1997) 'Reinforcing operants other than abstinence in drug abuse treatment: an effective alternative for reducing drug use', *Journal of Consulting and Clinical Psychology*, 65, 421–8.

Inciardi, J. A., ed. (1981) *The Drugs-Crime Connection*, Beverly Hills, CA: Sage Publications.

Inciardi, J. (1990) 'The crack-violence connection within a population of hard-core adolescent offenders' in De La Rosa, M., Lambert, E. and Gropper, B., eds. *Drugs and Violence: Causes, Correlates, and Consequences*, NIDA Monograph 103, Washington, DC: NIDA.

Institute of Medicine (1991) *Research and Service Programs in the PHS: Challenges in Organization*, Washington, DC: National Academy Press.

Institute of Medicine (1994) *Reducing Risks for Mental Disorders: Frontiers for Preventive Intervention Research*, Washington, DC: National Academy Press.

Institute of Medicine (2001) *Informing America's Policy on Illicit Drugs: What We Don't Know Keeps Hurting Us*, Washington, DC: National Academy Press.

Institute of Medicine (2012) *Best Care at Lower Cost: The Path to Continuously Learning Health Care in America*, Washington, DC: National Academy of Science.

Jacobs, B. (1999) *Dealing Crack: The Social World of Streetcorner Selling*, Boston, MA: Northeastern University Press.

Janssen, P. A. (1994) 'Addiction and the potential for therapeutic drug development', *EXS*, 71, 361–70.

Jellinek, E. (1960) *The Disease Concept of Alcoholism*, New Haven, CT: Hillhouse.

Jewkes, R. K., Dunkle, K., Nduna, M., Jama, P. N. and Puren, A. (2010) 'Associations between childhood adversity and depression, substance abuse and HIV and HSV2 incident infections in rural South African youth', *Child Abuse Neglect*, 34(11), 833–41.

Johnson, C. A., Pentz, M. A., Weber, M. D., Dwyer, J. H., Baer, N., MacKinnon, D. P. and Hansen, W. B. (1990) 'Relative effectiveness of comprehensive community programming for drug abuse prevention with high-risk and low-risk adolescents', *Journal of Consulting and Clinical Psychology*, 58(4), 447–56.

Johnson, M. W., Richards W.A., and Griffiths, R.R. (2008) 'Human hallucinogen research: guidelines for safety', *Journal of Psychopharmacology*, 22(6), 603–20.

Jones, J. B., Jr. (1994) 'Selected aspects of drug abuse in nineteenth and early twentieth-century Tennessee history, 1830–1920', *West Tennessee Historical Society Papers*, 1–23.

Jordanova, L. (1995) 'The social construction of medical knowledge', *Social History of Medicine*, 8(3), 361–81.

Joudo, J. (2008) *Responding to Substance Abuse and Offending in Indigenous Communities : Review of Diversion Programs*, Canberra: Australian Institute of Criminology.

Kalaydjian, A., Swendsen, J., Chiu, W. T., Dierker, L., Degenhardt, L., Glantz, M., Merikangas, K. R., Sampson, N. and Kessler, R. (2009) 'Sociodemographic predictors of transitions across stages of alcohol use, disorders, and remission in the National Comorbidity Survey Replication', *ComparativePsychiatry*, 50(4), 299–306.

Kalra, S. P. and Kalra, P. S. (2004) 'Overlapping and interactive pathways regulating appetite and craving', *Journal of Addictive Diseases*, 23(3), 5–21.

Kandel, E. R., Schwartz, J. H., Jessell, T. M. (2000) *Principles of Neural Science*, 4th edn, New York: McGraw-Hill.

Kanof, M. E. (2003) 'Youth illicit drug use prevention DARE long-term evaluations and federal efforts to identify effective programs', available: http://purl.access.gpo.gov/GPO/LPS30362.

Kantak, K. M. (2003) 'Vaccines against drugs of abuse: a viable treatment option?', *Drugs*, 63, 341–52.

Karch, S. (2006) *A Brief History of Cocaine: From Inca Monarchs to Cali Cartels: 500 Years of Cocaine*, Boca Raton: CRC/Taylor & Francis.

Karlamangla, A., Zhou, K., Reuben, D., Greendale, G. and Moore, A. (2006) 'Longitudinal trajectories of heavy drinking in adults in the United States of America', *Addiction*, 101(1), 91–9.

Kaskutas, L.A., ed. (1998) *Journal of Substance Abuse Treatment*, 15(1).

Katz, N. (2008) 'Abuse-deterrent opioid formulations: are they a pipe dream?', *Current Rheumatology Reports*, 10(1), 11–18.

Keane, Martin (2010) 'Blueprint drugs education: findings from an evaluation', *Drugnet Ireland*, 32, 19.

Kelly, A. B., O'Flaherty, M., Connor, J. P., Homel, R., Toumbourou, J. W., Patton, G. C. and Williams, J. (2011) 'The influence of parents, siblings and peers on pre- and early-teen smoking: a multilevel model', *Drug and Alcohol Review*, 30(4), 381–7.

Kelly, J., Stout, R., Zywiak, W. and Schneider, R. (2006) 'A 3-year study of addiction mutual-help group participation following intensive outpatient treatment', *Alcoholism: Clinical and Experimental Research*, 30(8), 1381–92.

Kendler, K. and Prescott, C. (1998) 'Cannabis use, abuse and dependence in a population-based sample of female twins', *American Journal of Psychiatry*, 155(8), 1016–22.

Kerner, O. (1968) *Report of the National Advisory Commission on Civil Disorders*, New York: Bantam Books.

Kerr, T., Small, W. and Wood, E. (2005) 'The public health and social impacts of drug market enforcement: a review of the evidence', *International Journal of Drug Policy*, 16(4), 210–20.

Kerr, T., Marshall, B. D., Miller, C., Shannon, K., Zhang, R., Montaner, J. S. and Wood, E. (2009) 'Injection drug use among street-involved youth in a Canadian setting', *BMC Public Health*, 9, 171.

Kerr, T., Small, W., Buchner, C., Zhang, R., Li, K., Montaner, J. and Wood, E. (2010) 'Syringe sharing and HIV incidence among injection drug users and increased access to sterile syringes', *American Journal of Public Health*, 100(8), 1449–53.

Keys, D. (2008) 'Myth-making and opiate abuse: an early symbolic interactionist theory of addiction in the fieldwork of Alfred Lindesmith and its opposition', *Contemporary Justice Review*, 11(2), 177–86.

Khantzian, E. J. (1997) 'The self-medication hypothesis of substance use disorders: a reconsideration and recent applications', *Harvard Review of Psychiatry*, 4(5), 231–44.

Kilmer, B., Caulkins, J., Pacula, R., MacCoun, R. and Reuter, P. (2010) *Altered State? Assessing How Marijuana Legalization in California Could Influence Marijuana Consumption and Public Budgets*, Santa Monica, CA: RAND.

Kilmer, B., Jonathan P. Caulkins, Pacula, R. L. and Reuter, P. H. (2012) *The U.S. Drug Policy Landscape: Insights and Opportunities for Improving the View*, Santa Monica, CA: RAND Drug Policy Research Center.

Kilmer, J. R., Walker, D. D., Lee, C. M., Palmer, R. S., Mallett, K. A., Fabiano, P. and Larimer, M. E. (2006) 'Misperceptions of college student marijuana use: implications for prevention', *Journal of Studies on Alcohol*, 67(2), 277–81.

Kiple, K. F. and Ornelas, K.C., eds (2000) *The Cambridge World History of Food*, New York: Cambridge University Press.

Koch, J. W. (1995) *Social Reference Groups and Political Life*, Lanham, MD: University Press of America.

Konova, A. B., Moeller, S. J., Tomasi, D., Parvaz, M. A., Alia-Klein, N., Volkow, N. D. and Goldstein, R. Z. (2012) 'Structural and behavioral correlates of abnormal encoding of money value in the sensorimotor striatum in cocaine addiction', *European Journal of Neuroscience*, 36(7), 2979–88.

Kooyman, M. (1984) 'The drug problem in the Netherlands', *Journal of Substance Abuse Treatment*, 1(2), 125–30.

Kraly, S. (2009) *The Unwell Brain: Understanding the Psychobiology of Mental Health*, New York: W.W. Norton.

Krueger, H. (1980) *The Great Heroin Coup: Drugs, Intelligence and International Fascism*, Boston, MA: South End Press.

Kutin, J. and Alberti, S. (2004) 'Law enforcement and harm minimisation' in Hamilton, M., King, T. and Ritter, A., eds, *Drug Use in Australia: Preventing Harm*, South Melbourne: Oxford University Press, 144–58.

Kuusisto, K., Knuuttila, V. and Saarnio, P. (2011) 'Clients' self-efficacy and outcome expectations: impact on retention and effectiveness in outpatient substance abuse treatment', *Addictive Disorders & Their Treatment*, 10(4), 157–68.

LaBrie, J. W., Hummer, J. F. and Lac, A. (2011) 'Comparing injunctive marijuana use norms of salient reference groups among college student marijuana users and nonusers', *Addictive Behaviors*, 36(7), 717–20.

Lafrenière, G. (2001) 'National drug policy: United Kingdom', available: /www.parl.gc.ca/Content/SEN/Committee/371/ille/library/kingdom-e.htm.

Lamme, M. O. (2007) 'Alcoholic dogs and glory for all: the Anti-Saloon League and Public Relations, 1913 ', *Social History of Alcohol Review*, 21(2), 138–59.

Lampe, K. v. (2006) 'The interdisciplinary dimensions of the study of organized crime', *Trend in Organized Crime*, 9(3), 77–95.

Lang, K. (2007) *Poverty and Discrimination*, Princeton, NJ: Princeton University Press.

Larm, P., Hodgins, S., Tengstrom, A. and Larsson, A. (2010) 'Trajectories of resilience over 25 years of individuals who as adolescents consulted for substance misuse and a matched comparison group', *Addiction*, 105(7), 1216–25.

Latkin, C. (2010) 'Compass or blinders: the role of theory in studying health behaviors and addiction', *Addiction*, 105(11), 1893–4.

Latkin, C. A., Forman, V., Knowlton, A. and Sherman, S. (2003) 'Norms, social networks, and HIV-related risk behaviors among urban disadvantaged drug users', *Social Science & Medicine*, 56(3), 465–76.

Lau, J. T. F., Feng, T., Lin, X., Wang, Q. and Tsui, H. Y. (2005) 'Needle sharing and sex-related risk behaviours among drug users in Shenzhen, a city in Guangdong, southern China', *AIDS Care*, 17(2), 166–81.

Lay, S., ed. (1992) *The Invisible Empire in the West*, Urbana, IL: University of Illinois Press.

Lee, C., Mun, E. Y., White, H. R. and Simon, P. (2010) 'Substance use trajectories of black and white young men from adolescence to emerging adulthood: a two-part growth curve analysis', *Journal of Etnicity in Substance Abuse*, 9(4), 301–19.

Lee, H. S., Engstrom, M. and Petersen, S. R. (2011) 'Harm reduction and 12 Steps: complementary, oppositional, or something in-between?', *Substance Use and Misuse*, 46(9), 1151–61.

Lee, J. (1996) *Drugs and Drug Trafficking*, Ottawa: Library of Parliament, Research Branch.

Lemming (2012) 'Amsterdam coffee shop directory', available: www.coffeeshop. freeuk.com/.

Leri, F. (2003) 'Understanding polydrug use: review of heroin and cocaine co-use', *Addiction*, 98(1), 7–22.

Leshner, A. I. (2008) 'By now, "harm reduction" harms both science and the public health', *Clinical Pharmacology and Therapeutics*, 83(4), 513–14.

Leuw, E. (1991) 'Drugs and drug policy in the Netherlands', *Crime and Justice*, 14, 229–76.

Levine, H. G. and Reinarman, C. (1991) 'From Prohibition to regulation: lessons from alcohol policy for drug policy', *The Milbank Quarterly*, 69(3), 461–94

Levine, R. (2007) 'Ethnographic studies of childhood: a historical overview', *American Anthropologist*, 109(2), 247–60.

Lewis, M. (2008) 'Access to saloons, wet voter turnout, and statewide prohibition referenda, 1907–1919', *Social Science History*, 32, 373–404.

Li, J., Liu, H., Li, J., Luo, J., Koram, N. and Detels, R. (2011) 'Sexual transmissibility of HIV among opiate users with concurrent sexual partnerships: an egocentric network study in Yunnan, China', *Addiction*, 106(10), 1780–7.

Li, Q., Wang, Y., Zhang, Y., Li, W., Yang, W., Zhu, J., Wu, N., Chang, H., Zheng, Y., Qin, W., Zhao, L., Yuan, K., Liu, J., Wang, W. and Tian, J. (2012) 'Craving correlates with mesolimbic responses to heroin-related cues in short-term abstinence from heroin: an event-related FMRI study', *Brain Research*, 1469, 63–72.

Liddle, H. A., Rowe, C. L., Dakof, G. A., Henderson, C. E. and Greenbaum, P. E. (2009) 'Multidimensional family therapy for young adolescent substance abuse: twelve-month outcomes of a randomized controlled trial', *Journal of Consulting and Clinical Psychology*, 77(1), 12–25.

Lindesmith, A. (1938) 'A sociological theory of drug addiction', *American Journal of Sociology*, 43, 593–613.

Lindesmith, A. (1947) *Opiate Addiction*, Bloomington, IN: Principia Press.

Lloyd, M. (2000) 'Analysis on the move: deconstructing troublesome health questions and troubling epidemiology', *Qualitative Health Research*, 10(2), 149–63.

Lo, C. C. (2003) 'An application of social conflict theory to arrestees' use of cocaine and opiates', *Journal of Drug Issues*, 33(1), 237–66.

Lopez-Quintero, C., Hasin, D., de Los Cobos, J., Pines, A., Wang, S., Grant, B. and Blanco, C. (2011) 'Probability and predictors of remission from life-time nicotine, alcohol, cannabis or cocaine dependence: results from the National Epidemiologic Survey on Alcohol and Related Conditions', *Addiction*, 106(3), 657–69.

Lopez, F. I. (1987) 'A study on the dynamics of political behavior in a Latin American revolution: Cuban social classes, 1959–1977', unpublished thesis, Florida International University.

Luthar, S. S., ed. (2003) *Resilience and Vulnerability: Adaptation in the Context of Childhood Adversities*, New York: Cambridge University Press.

MacCoun, R. J. (2011) 'What can we learn from the Dutch cannabis coffeeshop system?', *Addiction*, 106(11), 1899–1910.

MacCoun, R. and Reuter, P. (2011) 'Assessing drug prohibition and its alternatives: a guide for agnostics', *Annual Review of Law and Social Science*, 7, 61–78.

MacGregor, S. and Thickett, A. (2011) 'Partnerships and communities in English drug policy: the challenge of deprivation', *International Journal of Drug Policy*, 22(6), 478–90.

Madruga, C., Laranjeira, R., Caetano, R., Ribeiro, W., Zaleski, M., Pinsky, I. and Ferri, C. (2011) 'Early life exposure to violence and substance misuse in adulthood: the first Brazilian national survey', *Addictive Behavior*, 36(3), 251–5.

Maffina, L., Deane, F. P., Lyons, G. C. B., Crowe, T. P. and Kelly, P. J. (2013) 'Relative importance of abstinence in clients' and clinicians' perspectives of recovery from drug and alcohol abuse', *Substance Use Misuse*, 48(9), 705–12.

Malivert, M., Fatseas, M., Denis, C., Langlois, E. and Auriacombe, M. (2012) 'Effectiveness of therapeutic communities: a systematic review', *European Addiction Research*, 18(1), 1–11.

Marlatt, G. A. and Witkiewitz, K. (2010) 'Update on harm-reduction policy and intervention research', *Annual Review of Clinical Psychology*, 6, 591–606.

Marlatt, G. A., Larimer, M. E. and Witkiewitz, K. (2011) *Harm Reduction: Pragmatic Strategies for Handling High Risk Behaviors*, New York: Guilford Press.

Martin, S. C. (2000) 'Violence, gender, and intemperance in early national Connecticut', *Journal of Social History*, 34(2), 309–25.

McArdle, P., Wiegersma, A., Gilvarry, E., Kolte, B., McCarthy, S., Fitzgerald, M., Brinkley, A., Blom, M., Stoeckel, I., Pierolini, A., Michels, I., Johnson, R. and Quensel, S. (2002) 'European adolescent substance use: the roles of family structure, function and gender', *Addiction*, 97(3), 329–36.

McBride, D. C., Terry-McElrath, Y., Harwood, H., Inciardi, J. A. and Leukefeld, C. (2009) 'Reflections on drug policy', *Journal of Drug Issues*, 39(1), 71.

McCaffrey, B. R. (1999) *The Destructive Impact of Drugs on the United States: How the Legalization of Drugs Would Jeopardize the Health and Safety of the American People and our Nation*, Washington, DC: The Office of National Drug Control Policy.

McCoy, A. W. (2003) *The Politics of Heroin: CIA Complicity in the Global Drug Trade, Afghanistan, Southeast Asia, Central America*, Chicago: Lawrence Hill.

McCoy, A. W. and Block, A. A., eds (1992) *War on Drugs: Studies in the Failure of US Narcotics Policy*, Boulder, CO: Westview Press.

McGowen, R. S. (2003) 'Central Asian drug trafficking dilemma', unpublished thesis, Naval Postgraduate School.

McGuinness, T. M. and Newell, D. (2012) 'Risky recreation: synthetic cannabinoids have dangerous effects', *Journal of Psychosocial Nursing and Mental Health Services*, 50(8), 16–18.

McHugh, R. K., Hearon, B. A. and Otto, M. W. (2010) 'Cognitive behavioral therapy for substance use disorders', *Psychiatric Clinics of North America*, 33(3), 511–25.

McKeganey, N. (2007) 'The challenge to UK drug policy', *Drugs: Education, Prevention and Policy*, 14(6), 559–71.

Mead, G. H. (1977) *George Herbert Mead on Social Psychology*, Chicago, IL: University of Chicago Press.

Menard, S. and Mihalic, S. (2001) 'The tripartite conceptual framework in adolescence and adulthood: evidence from a national sample', *Journal of Drug Issues*, 31, 905–38.

Menzel, S. H. (1996) *Fire in the Andes: US Foreign Policy and Cocaine Politics in Bolivia and Peru*, Lanham, MD: University Press of America.

Merton, R. K. (1938) 'Social structure and anomie', *American Sociological Review*, 3, 672–82.

Merton, R. K. and Kitt, A. (1950) 'Contributions to the theory of reference group behavior' in Merton, R. K. and Lazarsfeld, P.F., eds, *Continuities in Social Research*, New York: Free Press, 40–105.

Metrebian, N., Carnwath, Z., Mott, J., Carnwath, T., Stimson, G. and Sell, L. (2006) 'Patients receiving a prescription for diamorphine (heroin) in the United Kingdom', *Drug and Alcohol Review*, 25(2), 115–21.

Meyers, L. S., Gamst, G. and Guarino, A. J. (2006) *Applied Multivariate Research: Design and Interpretation*, Thousand Oaks, CA: Sage Publications.

Miczek, K. A., DeBold, J. F., Haney, M., Tidey, J., Vivian, J. and Weerts, E. M. (1994) 'Alcohol, drugs of abuse, aggression and violence' in Albert J. Reiss, J. and Roth, J., eds, *Understanding and Preventing Violence: Social Influences*, Washington, DC: National Academy Press.

Milby, J., Schumacher, J., Wallace, D., Frison, S., McNamara, C. and Usdan, S. (2003) 'Day treatment with contingency management for cocaine abuse in homeless persons: 12-month follow-up', *Journal of Consulting and Clinical Psychology*, 71, 619–21.

Miller, H. V., Jennings, W. G., Alvarez-Rivera, L. L. and Miller, J. M. (2008) 'Explaining substance use among Puerto Rican adolescents: a partial test of social learning theory', *Journal of Drug Issues*, 38(1), 261–83.

Ministerial Council on Drug Strategy (2011) *National Drug Strategy 2010–2015: A Framework for Action on Alcohol, Tobacco and Other Drugs*, Canberra: Ministerial Council on Drug Strategy.

Minuchin, S. (1974) *Families and Family Therapy*, Cambridge, MA: Harvard University Press.

Miron, J. (1999) 'Violence and the US prohibitions of drugs and alcohol', *American Law & Economics Review*, 1, 78–114.

Miron, J. (2003) 'The effect of drug prohibition on drug prices: evidence from the markets for cocaine and heroin', *Review of Economics & Statistics*, 85(3), 522–30.

Miron, J. and Zwiebel, J. (1991) 'Alcohol consumption during prohibition', *American Economic Review*, 81, 242–7.

Mitchell, S. A. (1983) *Object Relations in Psychoanalytic Theory*, Cambridge, MA: Harvard University Press.

Mitchell, S. (1995) *Freud and Beyond: A History of Modern Psychoanalytic Thought*, New York: Basic Books.

Mitchell, S. and Black, M. (1995) *Freud and Beyond: A History of Modern Psychoanalytic Thought*, New York: Basic books.

Moore, J. (2011) 'Behaviorism', *The Psychological Record*, 61(3), 449–64.

Moore, L. (1991) *Citizen Klansmen: The Ku Klux KLan in Indiana, 1921–1928*, Chapel Hill, NC: University of North Carolina Press.

Morgan, M., ed. (2002) *Against the Mainstream: The Selected Works of George Gerbner*, New York: Peter Lang.

Mott, J. (1975) 'The criminal histories of male non-medical opiate users in the United Kingdom', *Bulletin on Narcotics*, 4, 41–8.

Murphy, D. A., Shetty, V., Herbeck, D. M., Der-Martirosian, C., Urata, M. and Yamashita, D. D. (2010) 'Adolescent orofacial injury: association with psychological symptoms', *Psychology, Health and Medicine*, 15(5), 574–83.

Murray, J. B. (1986) 'Marijuana's effects on human cognitive functions, psychomotor functions, and personality', *Journal of General Psychology*, 113(1), 22–55.

Myers, B. (2013) 'Barriers to alcohol and other drug treatment use among black African and coloured South Africans', *BMC Health Services Review*, 13, 177.

Nakken, C. (1996) *The Addictive Personality: Understanding the Addictive Process and Compulsive Behavior*, Center City, MN: Hazelden.

Nash, D. L., Wilkinson, J., Paradis, B., Kelley, S., Naseem, A. and Grant, K. M. (2011) 'Trauma and substance use disorders in rural and urban veterans', *Journal of Rural Health*, 27(2), 151–8.

National Institute on Drug Abuse (2003) *Preventing Drug Abuse among Children and Adolescents: A Resesarch-Based Guide for Parents, Educators and Community Leaders*, 2nd edn, Bethesda, MD: US Department of Health and Human Services, National Institute of Health, National Institute on Drug Abuse.

Naylor, R. T. (2003) 'Towards a general theory of profit-driven crimes', *British Journal of Criminology*, 43, 81–101.

NCPIC (2013) 'Cannabis and the law: factsheet', available: www.ncpic.org.au.

Nebehay, S. (2010) 'Swiss drug policy should serve as model: experts', available: www.reuters.com/article/2010/10/25/us-swiss-drugs-idUSTRE6903VI20101025.

Nelson, J., ed. (2000) *Police Brutality: An Anthology*, New York: W.W. Norton & Co.

Neuman, W. (2012) 'Coca licensing is a weapon in bolivia drug war', *The New York Times*, 27 December 27, A1, A4.

Newman, R. (2007) 'Early British encounters with the Indian opium eater' in Mills, J. and Barton, P., eds, *Drugs and Empire: Essays in Modern Imperialism and Intoxication, 1500–1930*, Basingstoke: Palgrave Macmillan, 57–80.

NIDA (2008) *Prescription Drug Abuse: A Research Update*, Bethesda, MD: National Institute on Drug Abuse.

NIDA (2009) *NIDA InfoFacts: Treatment Approaches for Drug Addiction*, Rockville, MD: US Department of Health and Human Services.

Nomura, Y., Hurd, Y. L. and Pilowsky, D. J. (2012) 'Life-time risk for substance use among offspring of abusive family environment from the community', *Substance Use and Misuse*, 47(12), 1281–92.

Nordt, C. and Stahler, R. (2006) 'Incidence of heroin use in Zurich, Switzerland: a treatment case register analysis', *Lancet*, 367, 1830–4.

Nutt, D. J., King, L. A. and Phillips, L. D. (2010) 'Drug harms in the UK: a multicriteria decision analysis', *Lancet*, 376, 1558–65.

Nycander, S. (1998) 'Ivan Bratt: the man who saved Sweden from prohibition', *Addiction*, 93(1), 17–25.

O'Connell, M. E., Boat, T. and Warner, K. E., eds (2009) *Preventing Mental, Emotional, and Behavioral Disorders among Young People: Progress and Possibilities*, Washington, DC: The National Academies Press.

ONDCP (1997–2012) *High Intensity Drug Trafficking Area Annual Reports*, Washington, DC: Office of National Drug Control Policy.

ONDCP (2010) *ADAM II: 2009 Annual Report*, Washington, DC: Office of National Drug Control Policy.

ONDCP (2012) 'Obama Administration officials announce $22 million expansion of innovative health program aimed at detecting and intervening in drug addiction early', Press Release, 25 July.

Orson, F. M., Kinsey, B.M., Singh, R.A., Yan, W., Gardner, T. and Kosten, T. (2008) 'Substance abuse vaccines', *Annuals of the New York Academy of Science*, 1141, 257–69.

Ostergaard, J. (2009) 'Learning to become an alcohol user: adolescents taking risks and parents living with uncertainty', *Addiction Research &Theory*, 17(1), 30–53.

Pagán, E. O. (2003) *Murder at the Sleepy Lagoon: Zoot Suits, Race & Riots in Wartime L.A.*, Chapel Hill, NC: University of North Carolina Press

Pagano, M. E., White, W. L., Kelly, J. F., Stout, R. L., Carter, R. R. and Tonigan, J. S. (2012) 'The 10 Year Course of AA participation and long-term outcomes: a follow-up study of outpatient subjects in project MATCH', *Substance Abuse*, 34(1), 51–9.

Park, S. H. (2001) 'Three sheets to the wind: marine temperance in antebellum nineteenth America', *International Journal of Maritime History*, 13(1), 137–49.

Parker, H. and Newcombe, R. (1987) 'Heroin use and acquisitive crime in an English community', *British Journal of Sociology*, 38(3), 331–50.

Parker, H., Aldridge, J. and Measham, F. (1998) *Illegal Leisure: The Normalization of Adolescent Recreational Drug Use*, London: Routledge.

Parker, H., Williams, L. and Aldridge, J. (2002) 'The normalization of "sensible" recreational drug use: further evidence from the North West England longitudinal study', *Sociology*, 36, 941–64.

Parker, K. F. and Maggard, S. R. (2005) 'Structural theories and race-specific drug arrests: what structural factors account for the rise in race-specific drug arrests over time?', *Crime & Delinquency*, 51(4), 521–47.

Pearce, J. (1887) *The Life and Teachings of Joseph Livesey*, London: National Temperance Publication Depot.

Pearce, M. E. (2006) *Women at Greatest Risk: Reducing Injection Frequency among Young Aboriginal Drug Users in British Columbia*, Burnaby, BC: Simon Fraser University.

Pearson, G. (1987) 'Social deprivation, unemployment and patterns of heroin use' in Dorn, N. and South, N., eds, *A Land Fit for Heroin?*, London: Macmillan.

Peel, E. (2010) 'Pregnancy loss in lesbian and bisexual women: an online survey of experiences', *Human Reproduction*, 25(3), 721–7.

Pelchat, M. (2009) 'Food addictions in humans', *Journal of Nutrition*, 139(3), 620–2.

Pentz, M. A., Dwyer, J. H., MacKinnon, D. P., Flay, B. R., Hansen, W. B., Wang, E. Y. I. and Johnson, C. A. (1989) 'A multicommunity trial for primary prevention of adolescent drug abuse: effects on drug use prevalence', *Journal of the American Medical Association*, 261, 3259–66.

Perez Gomez, A. and Sierra Acuna, D. (2007) 'Natural recovery and treatment recovery from drug and alcohol abuse', *Adicciones*, 19(4), 409–21.

Perkins, H. W., Haines, M. P. and Rice, R. (2005) 'Misperceiving the college drinking norm and related problems: a nationwide study of exposure to prevention information, perceived norms and student alcohol misuse', *Journal of Studies on Alcohol and Drugs*, 66(4), 470–8.

Petry, N. (2012) *Contingency Management for Substance Abuse Treatment: A Guide to Implementing this Evidence-based Practice*, London: Routledge.

Phillips, W. (1980) '"Six o'clock swill": the introduction of early closing of hotel bars in Australia', *Historical Studies*, 19(75), 250–66.

Pollard, M. S., Tucker, J. S., Green, H. D., Kennedy, D. and Go, M. H. (2010) 'Friendship networks and trajectories of adolescent tobacco use', *Addictive Behaviors*, 35(7), 678–85.

Poroy, I. I. (1981) *An Economic Model of Opium Consumption in Iran and Turkey during the Nineteenth Century*, San Diego, CA: San Diego State University Center for Research in Economic Development.

Porter, R. (1996) 'The history of the "drugs problem"', *Criminal Justice Matters*, 24, 3–5.

Pratt, T., Cullen, F., Blevins, K., Daigle, L. and Madensen, T. (2006) 'The empirical status of deterrence theory: a meta-analysis' in Cullen, F., Wright, J. and Blevins, K., eds, *Taking Stock: The Status of Criminological Theory*, New Brunswick, NJ: Transaction.

Prendergast, M., Podus, D., Finney, J., Greenwell, L. and Roll, J. (2006) 'Contingency management for treatment of substance use disorders: a meta-analysis', *Addiction*, 101, 1546–60.

Preston, P., Jennings, W. G. and Gover, A. R. (2006) 'Marijuana use as a coping response to psychological strain: racial, ethnic, and gender differences among young adults', *Deviant Behavior*, 27(4), 397–421.

Price, D. H. (1989) *Atlas of World Cultures: A Geographical Guide to Ethnographic Literature*, Newbury Park, CA: Sage.

Price, R. K., Risk, N.K. and Spitznagel, E.L. (2001) 'Remission from drug abuse over a 25 year period: patterns of remission and treatment use', *American Journal of Public Health*, 91(7), 1107–13.

Raguin, G., Lepretre, A., Ba, I., Ndoye, I., Toufik, A., Brucker, G. and Girard, P. M. (2011) 'Drug Use and HIV in West Africa: A Neglected Epidemic', *Tropical Medicine & International Health*, 16(9), 1131–3.

Ramirez, A. (1993) 'Cheep beeps: across nation, electronic pagers proliferate', *New York Times*, 142(49397), A1.

Rand Corporation (1999) *The Benefits and Costs of Drug Use Prevention*, Santa Monica, CA: Rand Corporation.

Rassool, G. (2006) 'Policy and clinical effectiveness in service provision for substance abusers in the United Kingdom', *Journal of Addictions Nursing*, 17(1), 59–63.

Ratner, M. S. (1993) *Crack Pipe as Pimp : An Ethnographic Investigation of Sex-for-crack Exchanges*, New York: Lexington Books.

Regional Office of South-Asia (2007) *National AIDS Programs Management, Module 4: Targeted HIV Prevention and Case Management*, New Delhi: World Health Organization.

Reinarman, C. (2009) 'Cannabis policies and user practices: market separation, price, potency, and accessibility in Amsterdam and San Francisco', *International Journal of Drug Policy*, 20(1), 28–37.

Reiss, J. (2009) 'Causation in the social sciences: evidence, inference, and purpose', *Philosophy of the Social Sciences*, 39(1), 20–40.

Reith, M., ed. (1997) *Neurotransmitter Transporters: Structure, Function, and Regulation*, Totowa, NJ: Humana Press.

Reuter, P. (1995) 'The decline of the American mafia', *Public Interest*, 120, 89–99.

Reuter, P. and Pollack, H. (2006) 'How much can treatment reduce national drug problems?', *Addiction*, 101(3), 341–7.

Reuter, P. and Stevens, A. (2007) *A Monograph Prepared for the UK Drug Policy Commission*, London: UK Drug Policy Commission.

Reuter, P. and Stevens, A. (2008) 'Assessing UK drug policy from a crime control perspective', *Criminology & Criminal Justice*, 8(4), 461–82.

Reuter, P., Trautmann, F., Pacula, R., Kilmer, B., Gageldonk, A. and van der Gouwe, D. (2009) *Assessing Changes in Global Drug Problems, 1998–2007*, Santa Monica, CA: RAND.

Ridings, J. (2010) *Chicago to Springfield: Crime and Politics in the 1920s*, Charleston, SC: Arcadia Pub.

Ritter, A. and Cameron, J. (2006) 'A review of the efficacy and effectiveness of harm reduction strategies for alcohol, tobacco and illicit drugs', *Drug and Alcohol Review*, 25(6), 611–24.

Rivis, A. and Sheeran, P. (2003) 'Descriptive norms as an additional predictor in the theory of planned behaviour: a meta-analysis', *Current Psychology*, 22(3), 218–33.

Rivlin, G. (1995) *Drive-By*, London: Quartet Books.

Robins, L. N. and Slobodyan, S. (2003) 'Post-Vietnam heroin use and injection by returning US veterans: clues to preventing injection today', *Addiction*, 98(8), 1053–60.

Robinson, J., Sareen, J., Cox, B. J. and Bolton, J. M. (2011) 'Role of self-medication in the development of comorbid anxiety and substance use disorders: a longitudinal investigation', *Archives of General Psychiatry*, 68(8), 800–7.

Room, R. and Greenfield, T. (1993) 'Alcoholics Anonymous, other 12-step Movements and psychotherapy in the US population, 1990', *Addiction*, 88(4), 555–62.

Room, R. and Reuter, P. (2012) 'How well do international drug conventions protect public health?', *The Lancet*, 379, 84–91.

Room, R., Fischer, B., Hall, W., Lenton, S. and Reuter, P. (2010) *Cannabis Policy: Moving Beyond Stalemate*, New York: Oxford University Press.

Rose, J. E. (2008) 'Disrupting nicotine reinforcement from cigarette to brain', *Annuals of the New York Academy of Science*, 1141, 233–56.

Rosmarin, A. and Eastwood, N. (2012) *A Quiet Revolution: Drug Decriminalization Policies in Practice Across the Globe*, London: Release.

Ross, E. A. (1969) *Social Control: A Survey of the Foundations of Order*, Cleveland, OH: Press of Case Western Reserve University.

Rouse, S. M. and Arce, M. (2006) 'Drug-laden balloon: U.S. military assistance and coca production in the central Andes', *Social Science Quarterly*, 87(3), 540–57.

Rowe, C. (2012) 'Family therapy for drug abuse: review and updates 2003–2010', *Journal of Marital and Family Therapy*, 38(1), 59–81.

Roy, E., Denis, V., Gutierrez, N., Haley, N., Morissette, C. and Boudreau, J.-F. (2007) 'Evaluation of a media campaign aimed at preventing initiation into drug injection among street youth', *Drugs: Education, Prevention & Policy*, 14(5), 401–14.

Rudolph, A. E., Crawford, N. D., Latkin, C., Heimer, R., Benjamin, E. O., Jones, K. C. and Fuller, C. M. (2011) 'Subpopulations of illicit drug users reached by targeted street outreach and respondent-driven sampling strategies: implications for research and public health practice', *Annals of Epidemiology*, 21(4), 280–9.

Rumbarger, J. (1989) *Profits, Power, and Prohibition: Alcohol Reform and the Industrializing of America, 1830–1930*, Albany: State University of New York Press.

SAMHSA (2005) *Treatment Episode Data Set (TED) 2005*, available: wwwdasis.samhsa.gov/teds05/TEDSAd2k5Index.htm.

SAMHSA (2011) *Results From the 2010 National Survey on Drug Use and Health: Summary of National Findings*, NSDUH Series H-41, Rockville, MD: SAMHSA.

SAMHSA (2012) *Treatment Episode Data Set (TEDS): 2009. Discharges from Substance Abuse Treatment Services*, DASIS Series: S-60, HHS Publication No. (SMA) 12-4704, Rockville, MD: SAMSHA.

Saner, H., MacCoun, R. and Reuter, P. (1995) 'On the ubiquity of drug selling among youthful offenders in Washington, D.C., 1985–1991: age, period, or cohort effect?', *Journal of Quantitative Criminology*, 11, 337–62.

Sarang, A., Rhodes, T., Sheon, N. and Page, K. (2010) 'Policing drug users in Russia: risk, fear, and structural violence', *Substance Use & Misuse*, 45(6), 813–64.

Sariola, S. (1954) 'Prohibition in Finland, 1919–1932: its background and consequences', *Quarterly Journal of Studies in Alcohol*, 15(3), 477–90.

Sayers, J. (1993) *Mothers of Psychoanalysis: Helen Deutsch, Karen Horney, Anna Freud, and Melanie Klein*, New York: W.W. Norton & Company.

Scalera, G. (2002) 'Effects of conditioned food aversions on nutritional behavior in humans', *Nutritional Neuroscience*, 5(3), 159–88.

Scheier, L. M. (2010) *Handbook of Drug Use Etiology: Theory, Methods, and Empirical Findings*, Washington, DC: American Psychological Association.

Schindler, A., Thomasius, R., Petersen, K. and Sack, P. M. (2009) 'Heroin as an attachment substitute? Differences in attachment representations between opioid, ecstasy and cannabis abusers', *Attachment and Human Development*, 11(3), 307–30.

Schivelbusch, W. (1992) *Tastes of Paradise: A Social History of Spices, Stimulants and Intoxicants*, New York: Pantheon Books.

Schlinger, H. D., Jr. (2011) 'Skinner as missionary and prophet: a review of Burrhus F. Skinner: Shaper of Behaviour', *Journal of Applied Behavior Analysis*, 44(1), 217–25.

Schlosser, E. (1998) 'The prison-industrial complex', available: www.theatlantic.com/magazine/archive/1998/12/the-prison-industrial-complex/4669/.

Schmidt, M. M., Sharma, A., Schifano, F. and Feinmann, C. (2011) '"Legal highs" on the net-evaluation of UK-based websites, products and product information', *Forensic Science International*, 206(1–3), 92–7.

Schrad, M. L. (2007) 'Constitutional blemishes: American alcohol prohibition and repeal as policy punctuation', *Policy Studies Journal* 35(3), 437–63.

Schwartz, G. (1972) *Youth Culture: An Anthropological Approach*, Reading, MA: Addison-Wesley.

Scott, C. K., Dennis, M., Laudet, A., Funk, R. and Simeone, R. (2011) 'Surviving drug addiction: the effect of treatment and abstinence on mortality', *American Journal of Public Health*, 101(4), 737–44.

Scott, J. (1991) *Social Network Analysis: A Handbook*, Newbury Park, CA: Sage Publications.

Secades-Villa, R., García-Rodríguez, O., García-Fernández, G., Sánchez-Hervás, E., Fernandez-Hermida, J. R. and Higgins, S. T. (2011) 'Community reinforcement approach plus vouchers among cocaine-dependent outpatients: twelve-month outcomes', *Psychology of Addictive Behaviors*, 25(1), 174–9.

Seddon, T. (2000) 'Explaining the drug-crime link: theoretical, policy and research issues', *Journal of Social Policy*, 29(1), 29(1) 95–107.

Seddon, T. (2006) 'Drugs, crime and social exclusion: social context and social theory in British drugs-crime research', *British Journal of Criminology*, 46, 680–703.

Seddon, T. (2010) 'Regulating markets in vice', *Criminal Justice Matters*, 80, 6–7.

Seddon, T., Williams, L. and Ralphs, R. (2012) *Tough Choices: Risk, Security and the Criminalization of Drug Policy*, Clarendon Studies in Criminology, Oxford: Oxford University Press.

Seelke, C. R., Wyler, L. S., Beittel, J. S. and Sullivan, M. P. (2011) *Latin America and the Caribbean: Illicit Drug Trafficking and U.S. Counterdrug Programs*, Washington, DC: Congressional Research Service.

Sharp, C. W. (1984) *Mechanisms of Tolerance and Dependence*, Washington, DC: NIDA, US Government Printing Office.

Shepard, E. and Blackley, P. (2005) 'Drug enforcement and crime: recent evidence from New York State', *Social Science Quarterly*, 86, 323–42.

Sherif, M. (1964) *Reference Groups: Exploration into Conformity and Deviation of Adolescents*, New York: Harper & Row.

Sherman, D. W., Haber, J., Hoskins, C. N., Budin, W. C., Maislin, G., Shukla, S., Cartwright-Alcarese, F., McSherry, C. B., Feurbach, R., Kowalski, M. O., Rosedale, M. and Roth, A. (2012) 'The effects of psychoeducation and telephone counseling on the adjustment of women with early-stage breast cancer', *Applied Nursing Review*, 25(1), 3–16.

Shiner, M. and Newburn, T. (1997) 'Definitely, maybe not? The normalisation of recreational drug use amongst young people', *Sociology*, 31(3), 511–29.

Shiner, M. and Newburn, T. (1999) 'Taking tea with Noel: the place and meaning of drug use in everyday life' in South, N., ed. *Drugs: Cultures, Controls and Everyday Life*, London: Sage.

Singer, M. (2008) *Drugging the Poor: Legal and Illegal Drugs and Social Inequality*, Long Grove, IL: Waveland Press.

Sivolap Iu, P. (2010) 'Subject and basic definitions of the addictive medicine: the notion of addictive disorders', *Zh Nevrol Psikhiatr Im S S Korsakova*, 110(5 Pt 2), 3–10.

Sklar, H. (2013) 'Your hormones', *Health*, 27(4), 81.

Skocpol, T. (1980) *States and Social Revolutions: A Comparative Analysis of France, Russia and China*, New York: Cambridge University Press.

Smart, R. G. (1974) 'The effect of licencing restrictions during 1914–1918 on drunkenness and liver cirrhosis deaths in Britain', *British Journal of Addiction to Alcohol & Other Drugs*, 69(2), 109–21.

Smelser, N. (1988) 'Social structure' in Smelser, N., ed., *The Handbook of Sociology*, London: Sage Publications.

Smit, Y., Huibers, M. J. H., Ioannidis, J. P. A., van Dyck, R., van Tilburg, W. and Arntz, A. (2012) 'The effectiveness of long-term psychoanalytic psychotherapy: a meta-analysis of randomized controlled trials', *Clinical Psychology Review*, 32(2), 81–92.

Smith, J. P. (1990) 'Research, public policy and drug abuse: current approaches and new directions', *The International Journal of the Addictions*, 25(2A), 1990–1.

Snelders, S., Kaplan, C. and Pieters, T. (2006) 'On cannabis, chloral hydrate, and career cycles of psychotrophic drugs in medicine', *Bulletin of the History of Medicine*, 80(1), 95–114.

Somaini, B. and Grob, P. (2012) 'How and why AIDS changed drug policy in Switzerland', *Journal of Public Health Policy*, 33(3), 317–24.

Soole, D., Mazerolle, L. and Rombouts, S. (2005) *School Based Drug Prevention: A Systematic Review of the Effectiveness on Illicit Drug Use*, Drug Policy Modelling Project Monograph 07, Fitzroy, Vic: Turning Point Alcohol and Drug Centre.

South, N., ed. (1999) *Drugs: Culture, Controls and Everyday Life*, London: Sage.

Souza, G. B. (2007) 'Developing habits: opium and tobacco in the Indonesian archipelago, 1619–1794' in Mills, J. and Barton, P., eds, *Drugs and Empire: Essays in Modern Imperialism and Intoxication, 1500–1930*, Basingstoke: Palgrave Macmillan, 39–56.

Speaker, S. L. (2001) '"Struggle of mankind against its deadliest foe": Themes of Counter-subversion in Anti-Narcotic Campaigns, 1920–1940', *Journal of Social History*, 34, 591–610.

Spear, H. B. (1969) 'The growth of heroin addiction in the United Kingdom', *British Journal of Addiction*, 64(2), 245–55.

Staff (2009) *Blueprints Drug Education: The Response of Pupils and Parents to the Programme*, London: British Home Office.

Staff (2010) 'Adverse childhood experiences reported by adults: five states, 2009', *Morbidity and Mortality Weekly Report*, 59(49), 1609–13.

Staff (2011) 'ONDCP stresses importance of treatment, not incarceration ... Office of National Drug Control Policy', *Alcoholism & Drug Abuse Weekly*, 23(46), 4–5.

Stanley, J. M. and Lo, C. C. (2009) 'School-related factors affecting high school seniors' Methamphetamine Use', *Journal of Drug Education*, 39(4), 401–18.

Stanton, M. (1979) 'Drugs and the family: a review of the recent literature', *Marriage and Family Review*, 2, 1–10.

Stanton, M. and Shadish, W. (1997) 'Outcome, attrition, and family-couples treatment for drug abuse: a meta-analysis and review of the controlled, comparative studies', *Psychological Bulletin*, 122(2), 170–91.

Stanton, M. D. and Todd, T. C., eds (1982) *The Family Therapy of Drug Abuse and Addiction*, New York: Guilford.

Stephan, J. J. (2004) *State Prison Expenditures, 2001*, Washington, DC: Bureau of Justice Statistics, US Department of Justice.

Stephens, R. C. (1991) *The Street Addict Role: A Theory of Heroin Addiction*, Albany, NY: State University of New York Press.

Stepick, A. (1992) *Miami Now! Immigration, Ethnicity, and Social Change*, Gainesville, FL: University Press of Florida.

Stevens, A. (2011) *Drugs, Crime and Public Health: The Political Economy of Drug Policy*, London: Routledge.

Storti, C. C. and De Grauwe, P. (2007) 'Globalization and the price decline of illicit drugs', available: http://hdl.handle.net/10419/26035.

Strang, J., Babor, T., Caulkins, J., Fischer, B., Foxcroft, D. and Humphreys, K. (2012) 'Drug policy and the public good: evidence for effective interventions', *Lancet*, 379(9810), 71–83.

Strike, C., Watson, T. M., Lavigne, P., Hopkins, S., Shore, R., Young, D., Leonard, L. and Millson, P. (2011) 'Guidelines for better harm reduction: evaluating implementation of best practice recommendations for needle and syringe programs (NSPs)', *International Journal of Drug Policy*, 22(1), 34–40.

Sudbury, J., ed. (2005) *Global Lockdown: Race, Gender, and the Prison-Industrial Complex*, New York: Routledge.

Sullivan, C., McKendrick, K., Sacks, S. and Banks, S. (2007) 'Modified therapeutic community treatment for offenders with MICA disorders: substance use outcomes', *American Journal of Drug and Alcohol Abuse*, 33(6), 823–32.

Sweet, R. W. and Harris, E. A. (1993) 'Review essay: just and unjust wars – the war on the War on Drugs: some moral and constitutional dimensions of the War on Drugs', *Northwestern University Law Review*, 87(4), 1302–73.

Swift, W., Coffey, C., Carlin, J., Degenhardt, L. and Patton, G. (2008) 'Adolescent cannabis users at 24 years: trajectories to regular weekly use and dependence in young adulthood', *Addiction*, 103(8), 1361–70.

Szapocznik, J. and Williams, R. (2000) 'Brief strategic family therapy: twenty-five years of interplay among theory, research and practice in adolescent behavior problems and drug abuse', *Clinical Child and Family Psychology*, 3(2), 117–34.

Szapocznik, J., Prado, G., Burlew, A., Williams, R. and Santisteban, D. (2007) 'Drug abuse in African American and Hispanic adolescents: culture, development, and behavior', *Annual Review of Clinical Psychology*, 3, 77–105.

Tam, C.-L. and Foo, Y.-C. (2012) 'Contributory factors of drug abuse and the accessibility of drugs', *International Journal of Collaborative Research on Internal Medicine & Public Health*, 4(9), 1621–5.

Tasmania Department of Community Health Services (1996) *Tasmanian Drug Strategic Plan, 1996–2000*, Hobart: Ministers for Community and Health Services, Police and Public Safety, Education and Vocational Training.

Taylor, B., ed. (2002) *I-ADAM in Eight Countries: Approaches and Challenges*, Washington, DC: Department of Justice.

Teesson, M., Hall, W., Slade, T., Mills, K., Grove, R., Mewton, L., Baillie, A. and Haber, P. (2010) 'Prevalence and correlates of DSM-IV alcohol abuse and dependence in Australia: findings of the 2007 National Survey of Mental Health and Wellbeing', *Addiction*, 105(12), 2085–94.

Thrasher, L. (1933) *The Gang*, Chicago, IL: University of Chicago Press.

Timko, C. and Moos, R. H. (2002) 'Symptom severity, amount of treatment, and 1-year outcomes among dual diagnosis patients', *Administration and Policy in Mental Health*, 30(1), 35–54.

Torrey, E. F. (1994) *Schizophrenia and Manic-depressive Disorder: The Biological Roots of Mental Illness as Revealed by the Landmark Study of Identical Twins*, New York: Basic Books.

Tsai, J., Lapidos, A., Rosenheck, R. A. and Harpaz-Rotem, I. (2012) 'Longitudinal association of therapeutic alliance and clinical outcomes in supported housing for chronically homeless adults', *Community Mental Health Journal*, 49(4), 438–43.

UKDPC (2012) *A Fresh Approach to Drugs: The Final Report of the UK Drug Policy Commission*, available: www.ukdpc.org.uk/.

Um, E., Plass, J. L., Hayward, E. O. and Homer, B. D. (2012) 'Emotional design in multimedia learning', *Journal of Educational Psychology*, 104(2), 485–98.

UNDCP (1995) *The Social Impact of Drug Abuse*, Vienna: United Nations Office on Drugs and Crime.

UNODC (2004) *Schools: School-Based Education for Drug Abuse Prevention*, Vienna: Global Youth Network, United Nations Office on Drugs and Crime.

UNODC (2008) *Drug Policy and Results in Australia*, Vienna: United Nations Office on Drugs and Crime.

UNODC (2010) *World Drug Report 2010*, Geneva: United Nations Office on Drug Control.

UNODC (2011a) *Estimating Illicit Financial Flows Resulting from Drug Trafficking and Other Transnational Organized Crimes: Research Report*, Vienna: United Nations Office on Drugs and Crime.

UNODC (2011b) *World Drug Report 2011*, Vienna: United Nations.

UNODC (2012a) '55th Annual Meeting', available: www.unodc.org/unodc/commissions/CND/.

UNODC (2012b) *World Drug Report 2012*, Vienna: United Nations Office on Drugs and Crime.

Urada, D., Evans, E., Yang, J., Conner, B., Campos, M., Brecht, L., Anglin, M., Fan, J., Hunter, J., Rutkowski, B., et al. (2009) *Evaluation of Proposition 36: The Substance Abuse and Crime Prevention Act of 2000. 2009 Report*, Los Angeles, CA: UCLA Integrated Substance Abuse Programs.

US CDC (2010) 'Condom distribution as a structural level intervention', available: www.cdc.gov/hiv/resources/factsheets/PDF/condom_distribution.pdf.

Vaillant, G. (1974) 'Outcome research in narcotic addiction: problems and perspectives', *American Journal of Drug and Alcohol Abuse*, 1(1), 25–36.

Valencia-Martin, J. L., Galan, I. and Rodriguez-Artalejo, F. (2009) 'Alcohol and self-rated health in a Mediterranean country: the role of average volume, drinking pattern, and alcohol dependence', *Alcoholism: Clinical and Experimental Research*, 33(2), 240–6.

van de Luitgaarden, J., Thush, C., Wiers, R. and Knibbe, R. (2008) 'Prevention of alcohol problems in Dutch youth', *Evaluation & the Health Professions*, 31(2), 167–81.

Van Gundy, K. and Rebellon, C. J. (2010) 'A life-course perspective on the "gateway hypothesis"', *Journal of Health and Social Behavior*, 51(3), 244–59.

van Leeuwen, A. P., Verhulst, F. C., Reijneveld, S. A., Vollebergh, W. A., Ormel, J. and Huizink, A. C. (2011) 'Can the gateway hypothesis, the common liability model and/or, the route of administration model predict initiation of cannabis use during adolescence? A survival analysis: the TRAILS study', *Journal of Adolescent Health*, 48(1), 73–8.

VanderWaal, C. J., Chriqui, J. F., Bishop, R. M., McBride, D. C. and Longshore, D. Y. (2006) '2006 State drug policy reform movement: the use of ballot initiatives and legislation to promote diversion to drug treatment', *Journal of Drug Issues*, 36(3), 619–48.

Veillette, C. (2006) *Andean Counterdrug Initiative (ACI) and Related Funding Programs FY2006 Assistance*, CRS report for Congress, RL33253, Washington, DC: Congressional Research Service, Library of Congress.

von Sydow, K., Lieb, R., Pfister, H., Höfler, M. and Wittchen, H. (2002) 'What predicts incident use of cannabis and progression to abuse and dependence? A 4-year prospective examination of risk factors in a community sample of adolescents and young adults', *Drug & Alcohol Dependence*, 68(1), 49.

Vuchinich, R. and Heather, N., eds (2003) *Choice, Behavioural Economics and Addiction*, Oxford: Pergamon Press.

Wadsworth, M. E., Santiago, C. D., Einhorn, L., Etter, E. M., Rienks, S. and Markman, H. (2011) 'Preliminary efficacy of an intervention to reduce psychosocial stress and improve coping in low-income families', *American Journal of Community Psychology*, 48(3–4), 257–71.

Wagenaar, A., Salois, M. and Komro, K. (2009) 'Effects of beverage alcohol price and tax levels on drinking: a meta-analysis of 1003 estimates from 112 studies', *Addiction*, 104, 179–90.

Waldorf, D. and Biernacki, P. (1979) 'Natural recovery from heroin addiction: a review of the incidence literature', available: www.druglibrary.eu/library/articles/narehead.htm.

Walker, S. (2011) *Sense and Nonsense about Crime, Drugs, and Communities*, Belmont, CA: Wadsworth.

Walters, G. D. (1994) *Escaping the Journey to Nowhere: The Psychology of Alcohol and other Drug Abuse*, Washington, DC: Taylor & Francis.

Wang, Z., Du, J., Sun, H., Wu, H., Xiao, Z. and Zhao, M. (2010) 'Patterns of childhood trauma and psychological distress among injecting heroin users in China', *PLoS One*, 5(12), e15882.

Washio, Y., Higgins, S. T., Heil, S. H., McKerchar, T. L., Badger, G. J., Skelly, J. M. and Dantona, R. L. (2011) 'Delay discounting is associated with treatment response among cocaine-dependent outpatients', *Experimental and Clinical Psychopharmacology*, 19(3), 243–8.

Wasserman, S. and Galaskiewicz, J. (1994) *Advances in Social Network Analysis: Research in the Social and Behavioral Sciences*, Thousand Oaks: Sage Publications.

Watkins, K., Hunter, S., Hepner, K., Paddock, S., de la Cruz, E., Zhou, A. and Gilmore, J. (2011) 'An effectiveness trial of group cognitive behavioral therapy for patients with persistent depressive symptoms in substance abuse treatment', *Archives of General Psychiatry*, 68(6), 577–84.

Webb, G. (1998) *Dark Alliance: The CIA, the Contras, and the Crack Cocaine Explosion*, New York: Seven Stories Press.

Weitzer, R. J. (2011) *Legalizing Prostitution: from Illicit Vice to Lawful Business*, New York: New York University Press.

Werb, D., Mills, E. J., DeBeck, K., Kerr, T., Montaner, J. and Wood, E. (2011) 'The effectiveness of anti-illicit-drug public-service announcements: a systematic review and meta-analysis', *Journal of Epidemiology & Community Health*, 65, 834–40.

Werb, D., Kerr, T., Nosyk, B., Strathdee, S., Montaner, J. and Wood, E. (2013) 'The temporal relationship between drug supply indicators: an audit of international government surveillance systems', *BMJ Open*, 3(9).

Werch, C. E., Pappas, D. M., Carlson, J. M., DiClemente, C. C., Chally, P. S. and Sinder, J. A. (2000) 'Results of a social norm intervention to prevent binge drinking among first-year residential college students', *Journal of American College Health*, 49(2), 85–92.

Westen, D. (1999) 'The scientific status of unconscious processes: is Freud really dead?', *Journal of the American Psychoanalytic Association*, 47(4), 1061–106.

Westen, D. and Arkowitz-Westen, L. (1998) 'Limitations of Axis II in Diagnosing Personality pathology in clinical practice', *American Journal of Psychiatry*, 155(12), 1767–71.

WHO (World Health Organization) (2010) *International Statistical Classification of Diseases and Related Health Problems*, available: www.who.int/classifications/icd/en/.

Wickizer, T. M. (2013) 'State-level estimates of the economic costs of alcohol and drug abuse', *Journal of Health Care Finance*, 39(3), 71–84.

Wiebel, W. W., Jimenez, A., Johnson, W., Ouellet, L., Jovanovic, B., Lampinen, T., Murray, J. and O'Brien, M. U. (1996) 'Risk behavior and HIV seroincidence among out-of-treatment injection drug users: a four-year prospective study', *Journal of Acquired Immune Deficiency Syndromes and Human Retrovirology*, 12(3), 282–9.

Winfree, L. T., Giever, D., Maupin, J. and Mays, G. L. (2007) 'Drunk driving and the prediction of analogous behavior: a longitudinal test of social learning and self-control theories', *Victims & Offenders*, 2(4), 327349.

Winstock, A., Mitcheson, L., Ramsey, J., Davies, S., Puchnarewicz, M. and Marsden, J. (2011) 'Mephedrone: use, subjective effects and health risks', *Addiction*, 106(11), 1991–6.

Wodak, A. (1997) 'Injecting nation: achieving control of hepatitis C in Australia', *Drug and Alcohol Review*, 16(3), 275284.

Wolpe, J. (1973) 'The current status of systematic desensitization', *The American Journal of Psychiatry*, 130(9), 961–5.

Wolpe, J. (1993) 'Commentary: the cognitivist oversell and comments on symposium contributions', *Journal of Behavior Therapy and Experimental Psychiatry*, 24(2), 141–7.

Woody, G. (2003) 'Research findings on psychotherapy of addictive disorders', *American Journal on Addictions*, 12(Suppl 2), S19–26.

World Bank (1997) *Confronting AIDS: Public Priorities in a Global Epidemic*, New York: Oxford University Press.

Worrall, J. E. (2004) 'Impact of the Ku Klux Klan and prohibition on Denver's Little Italy', *Journal of the West*, 43(4), 32–40.

Worrall, J. L. and Kovandzic, T. V. (2010) 'Police levels and crime rates: an instrumental variables approach', *Social Science Research*, 39(3), 506–16.

Wright, H. (1909) 'The Opium Conference at Shanghai', *Proceedings of the American Society of International Law at Its Annual Meeting (1907–1917)*, 3, 89–95.

Wright, Q. (1924) 'The Opium Question', *American Journal of International Law*, 18(2), 281–5.

Wu, L. T. and Blazer, D. G. (2011) 'Illicit and nonmedical drug use among older adults: a review', *Journal of Aging and Health*, 23(3), 481–504.

Xie, H., McHugo, G., Fox, M. and Drake, R. (2005) 'Substance abuse relapse in a ten-year prospective follow-up of clients with mental and substance use disorders', *Psychiatric Services*, 56(10), 1282–7.

Yates, R. (2002) 'A brief history of British drug policy, 1950–2001', *Drugs: Education, Prevention and Policy*, 9(2), 113–25.

Young, J. H. (1961) *The Toadstool Millionaires: A Social History of Patent Medicines in America before Federal Regulation*, Princeton, NJ: Princeton University Press.

Young, J. (1971) *The Drugtakers: The Social Meaning of Drug Use*, London: MacGibbon & Kee.

Yzer, M. C., Vohs, K. D., Luciana, M., Cuthbert, B. N. and MacDonald, A. W. (2011) 'Affective antecedents of the perceived effectiveness of antidrug advertisements: an analysis of adolescents' momentary and retrospective evaluations', *Prevention Science*, 12(3), 278–88.

Zentner, J. L. (1974) 'Opiate use in America during the 18th and 19th centuries: the origin of a modern scourge', *Studies in History and Society*, 5(2), 40–54.

Zhang, J., Ou, J. X. and Bai, C. X. (2011) 'Tobacco smoking in China: prevalence, disease burden, challenges and future strategies', *Respirology*, 16(8), 1165–72.

Zickler, P. (1999) 'Twin studies help define the role of genes in vulnerability to drug abuse', *NIDA Notes*, 14(4), 1–8.

Zinbarg, R. E. and Griffith, J. W. (2008) 'Behavior therapy' in Lebow, J., ed., *21st Century Psychotherapies*, Hoboken, NJ: John Wiley & Sons Inc., 8–42.

Zobel, F. and Gotz, W. (2011) 'Drug use in Europe: specific national characteristics or shared models?' in Hunt, G., Milhet, M. and Bergeron, H., eds, *Drugs and Culture: Knowledge, Consumption and Policy*, Farnham: Ashgate.

Index

Printed and bound by CPI Group (UK) Ltd, Croydon, CR0 4YY